)

I7

I7

,7

5

D1428879

THE TUDOR COMMONWEALTH
1529-1559

The Tudor Commonwealth 1529–1559

A study of the impact of the social and economic developments of mid-Tudor England upon contemporary concepts of the nature and duties of the commonwealth

WHITNEY R. D. JONES

UNIVERSITY OF LONDON
THE ATHLONE PRESS
1970

Published by
THE ATHLONE PRESS
UNIVERSITY OF LONDON
at 2 Gower Street, London W C I
Distributed by Tiptree Book Services Ltd
Tiptree, Essex

Australia and New Zealand
Melbourne University Press

U.S.A.
Oxford University Inc.
New York

© *Whitney R. D. Jones*, 1970

485 11108 X

Printed in Great Britain by
WESTERN PRINTING SERVICES LTD
BRISTOL

E.E.J., M.P.J.,
and in memory of
H.W.J.

Preface

A WORD of explanation is needed in regard to one or two points of presentation. Quotations have been rendered into modern English, but their original punctuation retained; any interpolations of my own, as distinct from those present in the source cited, are in square brackets. Consideration of the format of the word or phrases which lie at the heart of this book has posed intractable problems, for I have found no uniformity of treatment elsewhere. The following working rule has been adopted: *commonwealth* is used when a straightforward reference to the realm or body politic is made, *Commonwealth* when a specific type of attitude is implied, as in *Commonwealth ideals* or *Commonwealth thought*; '*Commonwealth Party*' and '*Commonwealth Men*' are rendered without inverted commas after the first reference. Exigencies of space, and the frequency of quotation, have enforced the adoption of a summary form of footnotes, and of a number of short-titles, but a full and detailed bibliography is appended.

I wish to acknowledge the help of the staffs of the British Museum, the Bodleian, Cardiff University College, Cardiff Central, and Monmouthshire County Libraries. I am indebted to the staff of the Athlone Press for their assistance in preparing the book for the printer. Thanks are due to Mr Lionel H. Williams for his supervision of the thesis from which the book evolved and for his reading of an early draft, and to Dr Christopher E. Challis for his comments and suggestions regarding Chapter 8. I am most grateful to Professor S. T. Bindoff for all his help, and for stimulating and constructive criticism at a vital stage. Professor A. G. Dickens has exemplified his own allusion (in his preface to *The English Reformation*) to 'the unselfishness with which scholars still give their hard-won knowledge and precious time to improving the work of others'. Without his generous encouragement and

vii

assistance, from start to finish, a dream would never have become reality. To my wife, for her patient and tolerant help through the years, and to my parents for their love and sacrifice, I owe more than I can express in a note of dedication.

W. R. D. J.

Contents

SHORT-TITLES AND ABBREVIATIONS

Anon., *Policies*   *Policies to reduce this realme of England vnto a prosperus wealthe and estate* (1549), printed in *T.E.D.*, iii

Armstrong, C., *Treatise*   *A treatise concerninge the Staple and the commodities of this realme* (*c.* 1519–35), printed in *T.E.D.*, iii

—, *Reforme*   *Howe to reforme the Realme in settyng them to werke and to restore Tillage* (*c.* 1535–6), printed in *T.E.D.*, iii

Bull. Inst. H.R.   *Bulletin of the Institute of Historical Research*

Christopherson, J., *An exhortation* *An exhortation to all menne to take hede and beware of rebellion* (1554)

Crowley, R., *Philargyrie*   *The Fable of Philargyrie The Great Gigant* (1551), ed. W. A. Marsden (London, 1931)

—, *Works*   *The Select Works of Robert Crowley*, ed. J. M. Cowper, E.E.T.S. (London, 1872)

Discourse   Anon. (J. Hales or Sir T. Smith?), *A Discourse of the Common Weal of this Realm of England* (1549), ed. E. Lamond (Cambridge, 1893)

Econ. H.R.   *Economic History Review*

E.E.D.S.   Early English Drama Society

E.E.T.S.   Early English Text Society

E.H.R.   *English Historical Review*

Forrest, W., *Princelie Practise* *Pleasaunt Poesye of Princelie Practise* (1548), printed in *England in the reign of King Henry the Eighth*, Part I, *Starkey's Life and Letters*, ed. S. J. Herrtage, E.E.T.S. (London, 1878)

Frith, J., *Works*   Works of Frith printed in Vol. iii of *The Works of William Tyndale and John Frith*, ed. T. Russell (London, 1831)

Hales, J., 'Charges'   'The charges of Mr. John Hales . . . for the execution of the commission for redress of enclosures', including 'Instructions . . . to . . . commissioners', printed in Vol. ii (Part II) of Strype

—, 'Defence'   'The defence of John Hales ayenst certeyn

xi

	sclaundres and false reaportes made of hym' (1549), printed in *Discourse*
Heywood, J., *Spider and Flie*	*The Spider and the Flie* (1556), ed. J. S. Farmer, E.E.D.S. (London, 1908)
L. and P. Henry VIII	*Letters and Papers, Foreign and Domestic, of the Reign of Henry VIII*, ed. J. S. Brewer, J. Gairdner and R. H. Brodie (London, 1862–1932)
Morison, Sir R., *Lamentation*	*A Lamentation in whiche is shewed what Ruyne and destruction cometh of seditious rebellyon* (1536)
—, *Remedy*	*A Remedy for Sedition* (1536)
Ponet, J., *Politike power*	*A Shorte Treatise of politike power, and of the true Obedience which subiects owe to kynges and other ciuile Gouernours* (1556)
Proclamations	*Tudor Royal Proclamations*, i, *The Early Tudors (1485–1553)*, ed. P. L. Hughes and J. F. Larkin (Yale, 1964)
Starkey, T., *An Exhortation*	*An Exhortation to the people, instructynge theym to Unitie and Obedience* (1536)
—, *Dialogue*	*A Dialogue between Cardinal Pole and Thomas Lupset* (1538), printed in *England in the Reign of King Henry the Eighth*, Part II, *The Dialogue*, ed. J. M. Cowper, E.E.T.S. (London, 1871)
Strype	J. Strype, *Ecclesiastical Memorials*, 3 vols. (Oxford, 1822)
T.E.D.	R. H. Tawney and E. Power, *Tudor Economic Documents*, 3 vols. (London, 1953 edn.)
Trans. R.H.S.	*Transactions of the Royal Historical Society*
Tyndale, W., *Works*	*The Works of William Tyndale and John Frith*, ed. T. Russell, 3 vols. (London, 1831)
Tytler	P. F. Tytler, *England under the Reigns of Edward VI and Mary*, 2 vols. (London, 1839)

CHAPTER ONE

Introductory: the Commonwealth and its Inheritance

T HE term 'commonwealth' has a continuous history from
the Middle Ages to the present day.[1] At first it was usually
a synonym for 'body politic' or 'realm'. Between 1649 and
1660 it served to describe the experiment of government without a
king in England. In our own century it has been accepted as
more appropriate than 'Empire' to describe the association of
free peoples which make up the British Commonwealth, while
some will remember it as the title of a short-lived political party.
Clearly, the precise implications of the word have shifted with
changing circumstances. But the present position of the Crown
as head of the Commonwealth is itself indicative of the fact that
the concept has never necessarily been anti-monarchical—even
after the events of the mid-seventeenth century. Indeed, one
might urge that the present ideal of the Commonwealth as
representing a genuine community of interests transcending
diversity of membership suggests a common constant of meaning
which has endured throughout the centuries.

At certain times of crisis the concept of the commonwealth has
been the subject of eager debate. Historically the best-known use
of the term is that made during and after the Civil Wars of the
seventeenth century, but it was also at the centre of the discussion
of the social and economic, as well as religious and political,
problems of society which came to a climax in the disturbed
middle decades of the sixteenth. In this context it served not only
as an alternative to realm or body politic but also, and far more
significantly, to describe the welfare of the members of that body

[1] W. K. Hancock, 'A Veray and True Comyn Wele', in *Politics in Pitcairn*,
94–109.

and to imply the duty of government to further that welfare. It is perhaps sweeping, but hardly inapposite, to describe the ideal of the Commonwealth as held by some radical Protestant reformers as the mid-Tudor equivalent of the Welfare State.

This book will attempt to trace the impact made by social and economic developments in mid-sixteenth-century England upon contemporary ideas of the nature and significance of the commonwealth. The period 1529–59 may be described as a crisis period for Tudor England in an economic and social, as well as a religious and constitutional, context. While the lines of demarcation at either end are not intended to be sharp, the dates are chosen as embracing the thirty-year period between the first meeting of the Reformation Parliament and the establishment by Elizabeth I of a new *via media* in the sphere of religion.

The importance of religious changes during these decades needs no elaboration. More recent is the assertion that they also witnessed revolutionary constitutional developments, that 1529 is a more significant date than 1485, and that the events of the next ten years were in many ways more truly revolutionary in their implications than those of the mid- and late seventeenth century.[1] But if the period between 1529 and 1540 was of crucial importance in the evolution both of relationships between Church and State and of the means by which royal policy was implemented, that between 1547 and 1558 is generally accepted as the testing time of the Tudor monarchy, though Professor Elton's reference to the 'failure of Tudor government between 1540 and 1558'[2] suggests as the turning-point the death of Cromwell rather than that of Henry VIII. During the period 1529 to 1559 the trend of religious policy was reversed more than once, and government and dynasty were threatened by several rebellions. Indeed, events during the reigns of a minor and a woman seemed amply to justify Henry VIII's fears as to the succession.

There are equally valid grounds for stressing the critical nature of concurrent economic and social developments. For the problems to which these gave rise were often exacerbated by religious, constitutional and political developments, and in turn confronted government with another danger. The growth of individual

[1] G. R. Elton, *The Tudor Revolution in Government*, 3 and 19.
[2] Ibid., 417.

freedom (and contingent loss of communal security) in economic relationships, the enclosure movement, the decline of the gilds, and the apparently growing inadequacy of the remedies for poverty, were all long-term problems. To these were now added the successive debasements of the coinage, the dissolution of the monasteries, and the boom in woollen exports. These in conjunction led to the crisis of 1549–51. Against this background, and that of the change in Church-State relationships after 1529, one might expect to find much evidence of discussion of the economic standards and problems of society and of the function of Church and State in this sphere.

Most of the material which will form the basis of our study is drawn from mid-Tudor social, religious and economic literature of various types. It may be urged that a study of contemporary opinion about economic and social developments is sometimes a better guide to what people believed to be happening than it is to what was actually taking place. Yet many commentators of the mid-Tudor period showed far more percipience and accuracy than are often allowed them. To an increasing degree, specific contentions of contemporary observers are being validated by the conclusions of detailed research. Thus the spate of protest literature in the 1540s and 1550s has puzzled certain modern critics, but statistical investigations confirm that these decades were characterized by extreme, and frightening, variations in food prices and that the fear of depressed living standards had a very real basis.[1] It has been suggested also that there is a monotonous sameness in the literature of social complaint in all eras. In so far as endemic frailties of human nature are concerned, this is true; but the nature of the accepted code of behaviour which moralizers defend is surely subject to change. The justification for a study of the economic and social literature of this period lies in the fact that the convergence of several currents of change gave rise to an expansion of the social and economic duties and functions of the State—an expansion of which contemporaries were well aware and which they frequently discussed.

Discussion of the nature and purpose of the political and social order was, of course, in the medieval tradition. But from the fourteenth and fifteenth centuries onwards a significant change

[1] Below, 115–16.

in emphasis, associated with such terms as *respublica* or *publica utilitas*, has been traced. Concern for the body politic or commonwealth did not displace reverence for the monarchy; rather were there attempts to synthesize the interests of king and community into one harmonious concept. Indeed, the accomplishment of this identification has been suggested as a major criterion of the emergence of the modern State.[1] The evolution of such ideas in the sixteenth century must be seen in relation to economic, social and religious, as well as political developments, since it was very largely in these terms that the responsibilities of the government of the commonwealth were discussed.

We may suggest several reasons for increasing concern with the economic and social aspects of governance during the mid-Tudor period. First, with the increased complexity of economic life and the extension of the market purely local regulation of economic relationships inevitably became more and more inadequate. The gilds had attempted to ensure fair treatment for producer and consumer and to prevent exploitation both in production and in marketing, whose relatively small-scale and localized characteristics made possible successful regulation. But the growth of a national market destroyed the assumptions upon which such local regulation and protection were based, while increasing the need for such protection, which was felt more and more to be the ultimate duty of national authority.

The implied duty of the Crown to intervene in economic affairs on the ground of equity points to a second factor. Traditionally, moral precepts in economic and social relationships were enunciated by the Church. But now, while changes in society were making both definition and enforcement of such precepts increasingly difficult, the Church in England became subordinated to the Crown. This increased the latter's prestige—but also made it the inheritor of the duty of defending and implementing the social and economic teaching of the Church. The evolution of poor relief exemplifies this expansion of the duties of government; the Crown's gradual acceptance of responsibility, exercised through an ecclesiastical unit, the parish, is symbolic.

---

[1] Although the term 'State' itself was rarely used in its modern sense in mid-Tudor England, below, 19, 120 and 184, for instances of its use by Starkey and Vives.

Thirdly, there is the undoubted fact that social and economic problems were thrown into particularly sharp relief at the time of this changed relationship between Church and State. It is suggested that the 'redistribution of [Church] land . . . and the changes in social structure, personnel, methods, and outlook which accompanied it, amounted to a revolution which had no parallel since the Norman Conquest', so that 'in economic and social affairs the fifteen-thirties, more than any other time, mark the close of medieval England'.[1] Thus 'our mid-Tudor period . . . saw Englishmen exposed to politico-social and economic pressures of exceptional strength'.[2] This was particularly true of the period 1547–58; 'in English economic and social history these years were a "dangerous corner" '.[3] Under Edward VI 'society itself seemed in danger of imminent dissolution. Religious anarchy and extremism, administrative corruption, financial collapse, currency and exchange chaos, agrarian unrest, extravagant and fruitless military enterprises, political control by a group of most unscrupulous and irresponsible careerists, all combined with the most violent fluctuations in the main export trade to produce a situation of acute crisis.'[4]

To this analysis one might add the outbreak of several serious rebellions in which social and economic discontent played an often critical part, and the persistent threat and fear of more. This suggests a fourth consideration of crucial importance: that of security. Internal disorder would menace both the power of the Crown and the stability of society, while weakening the realm in face of its enemies. Further, the correlation between economic prosperity and social harmony, and potential military strength, was clearly grasped.

Events in England take on an added significance within their European context, for an increasingly secular approach to the problems of social theory, political thought and government can be dated at latest from the work of Marsilius of Padua in the fourteenth century. A suggested unity of the period between the fourteenth and seventeenth centuries is that intellectual and literary

[1] A. R. Myers, *England in the Late Middle Ages (1307–1536)*, 216–17.
[2] A. G. Dickens, *Lollards and Protestants in the Diocese of York, 1509–1558*, 205.
[3] S. T. Bindoff, *Tudor England*, 146.
[4] L. Stone, 'State Control in Sixteenth Century England', 116.

discussion was characterized by a fundamentally lay, yet still Christian, attitude. Indeed, one provocative study has gone so far as to distinguish as the 'major Reformation' that movement towards 'humanistic religion' as expressed in philosophical and ethical terms and in the conduct of everyday life, in contradistinction to the debate on theological dogma and the means of salvation of an alleged 'minor Reformation'.[1]

Certainly a basic characteristic of Renaissance Humanism was an increased awareness of the problems of effective government and of the contribution which the educated man might make to their solution. Erasmus (to whose influence in England we shall return)[2] emphasized the duty of the Christian ruler to his subjects, and his responsibility for the common good.[3] Developments in England must be related to this 'perspective of a pan-European movement of humanist reform'.[4] Meanwhile the economic and social policy of government became an increasingly important aspect of statecraft in response to the changing and more complex economic and social environment of the later Middle Ages.[5]

These were trends of general significance in Western Europe. In defining the range of responsibility of secular government as one of the component functions of the 'social corpus of Christendom' Luther described it as 'spiritual in status, although it discharges a secular duty. It should operate, freely and unhindered, upon all members of the entire corpus . . .'[6] The extension of the powers and duties of the State or civil government in Tudor England was not unique. Henry VIII was not the only monarch effectively to limit the power of the Church as a competing *imperium in imperio*, while the problem of organization of poor relief by largely secular bodies, as distinct from individual almsgiving and sporadic charity by the Church, was common to several countries.[7]

---

[1] H. A. Enno van Gelder, *The Two Reformations in the Sixteenth Century.*

[2] Below, 18, 25, 29, 31.

[3] W. M. Southgate, 'Erasmus: Christian humanism and political theory', 249–52; J. K. McConica, *English Humanists and Reformation Politics*, 29–31; also below, 18.

[4] McConica, op. cit., 12.

[5] E. Miller, in *Cambridge Economic History of Europe*, iii, ed. M. M. Postan, E. E. Rich and E. Miller, 282–9 and 338–40.

[6] M. Luther, *An Appeal to the Ruling Class of German Nationality*, in Woolf, i, 117.

[7] Below, Chapter 7.

Through all debate on the nature and duties of the common-wealth we shall find a recurrent appeal for the enforcement of certain traditional social and economic standards. What was the nature of this code which the Commonwealth idealists of the mid-Tudor era inherited? In brief, it was the interpretation by the Catholic Church of the basic economic and social facts of the Middle Ages. In an essentially agrarian and feudal society econo-mic relationships were more personal and immediate, in the sense of time, of distance and of consequence, and therefore also more essentially social relationships, than those of the market-geared economy of a later period. The broad picture, despite the qualifications of recent research, remains that of an economy in which the typical units were the manor and the gild, in which there was still a marked tendency towards local self-sufficiency, and in which status and custom were more important than contract.

Against this background the Church evolved its social philo-sophy, and strove towards the relative approximation of actual social institutions and economic relationships to its ideals. Its teleological interpretation of society at once comprehended and transcended the facts; potentially diverse interests were harmon-ized and integrated in the pursuit of an essentially spiritual aim. Differences of function and of status were explained by the analogy between human society and the human body. The Church's teachings on economic issues must be seen as but part of the broader subject of general social ethics. In contrast with the modern approach to economic phenomena, that of medieval writers was primarily moralistic; they were more interested in evaluating the economic system than in analysing how it worked.

The values and the conduct sanctioned by the traditionalist approach of the Church were those normally deriving from the material circumstances of the time. The land and power of the lord of the manor were delegated in trust. His rights and duties were essentially complementary, and he was largely responsible for the protection and the temporal welfare of his peasants. These in turn had a no less clearly implied code of social conduct, dictated by traditional usage, by the economic environment which shaped in broad outline the working of the land, and by the teachings of the Church. The rules of the gilds reveal the same

7

emphasis upon the need for security based upon co-operation between all members of the body; their social and religious consciousness was of a relatively high order. The Church's attitude towards commerce was strongly coloured by the suspicion that the trader did not really produce but exploited or even created a need of the community to his personal advantage. Like the financier, he seemed to be a parasite upon rather than a member of the social organism; the combination of temptation and opportunity made his calling inevitably dangerous in a moral sense. But as long as he took only such profit as would reasonably enable him to live at an appropriate standard, and served society by the transport and exchange of necessary goods, then he might be accepted.

The medieval concepts of property, status, and charity were closely related. Private holding of property did not imply a right of selfish disposal. The correct use of possessions was ordered by the concept of *liberalitas*, avoiding the extremes of avarice and of prodigality. A virtuous moderation in consumption would leave something over for the needs of the less fortunate, whose poverty was a reproach neither to themselves nor to society as a whole. Poverty was a challenge and a blessing: a test of Christian humility among those on whom it was imposed, a test of love among the rich, endowed with possessions in order to relieve it. The poor man fulfilled a function in society, as the rich man's way to heaven.

This is an idealized sketch. Critics have observed that too much of reality was glossed over, that the Church failed to practise what it preached, and that even in that preaching it made too many concessions to mammon. Perception of the alleged contrast between this tendency to compromise with the world, and the genuinely Christian way of life derived from the radical law of the Scriptures, led to the appearance of heretical, sometimes communistic sects. In England this strain of criticism found expression in Langland's attack on Church wealth: 'Then take their land from them, you nobles, and let them live on their tithes! For surely, if property is a deadly poison that corrupts them, it would be good for Holy Church's sake to relieve them of it.'[1] It continued in such Wycliffite tracts as *Of the Leaven of Pharisees*

[1] W. Langland, *Piers the Ploughman*, in J. F. Goodridge's version, 233.

8

and *The Clergy may not hold Property*,[1] and even in parliamentary proposals for disendowment.[2]

But any shortcomings of the Church's teachings on the grounds of inadequacy or non-observance were now aggravated by changes in the economic and social substructure. One may, perhaps, justifiably suggest that, in a narrow sense at least, the medieval Christian order nurtured the seeds of its own downfall: the establishment of Christian values extended peace and order and therefore made possible more complex economic developments, but within this wider framework the economic teachings of the Church—essentially local and personal in nature—seem to have become more difficult to apply.

The time and speed of economic change varied throughout Europe, but we may distinguish its general characteristics. The *type* of the early medieval manor was essentially localized and self-subsistent; its economic relationships were also personal relationships based upon custom and a sense of social obligation. It could not survive unchanged the growth of trade, of specialization, and of the notion that economic transactions were essentially impersonal. By the fourteenth century clear signs appeared that the customary framework of rural society was crumbling. Meanwhile, expansion of trade, widening markets, and changes in technique or organization involving production on a larger scale or a more flexible and competitive approach, all appear to cut straight across the basic assumptions of the gilds.[3]

Economic change, in particular the increased importance of trade and finance, posed a problem for the Church. We may suggest that its teachings were supremely well-fitted to the realities of early medieval society because its economic relationships were also overwhelmingly personal relationships with an implied moral character. Could this code of behaviour be reconciled with the increasing complexity and impersonality of economic transactions? Or were the new developments to be either rejected or accepted as necessary evils outside Church jurisdiction? Recent studies of the touchstone concepts of the just price and of

---

[1] *The English Works of Wyclif*, 1–27 and 359–404.
[2] M. E. Aston, 'Lollardy and Sedition 1381–1431', 16–19. Below, 75–6, for the continuation of this line of thought in the sixteenth century.
[3] Below, Chapter 9, for a fuller treatment of these points.

9

usury[1] agree that medieval economic teaching showed much more elasticity in response to environment than was at one time supposed. While it remained essentially and primarily moralistic, it also tried to reconcile fundamental Christian values, and the legal and theological inheritance from the past, with current economic realities.[2]

But the issue was now complicated, first by the changes in Church–State relationships, and secondly by the rise of Protestantism. To what extent was the evolution of the economic environment itself affected by the Church's loss of unity and of power? Was there any causal connection between certain doctrinal aspects of Protestantism (in particular of Calvinism) and the rise of capitalism? It may be remarked immediately that, seen in relation to such test-cases as usury, poverty, and the concept of vocation or calling, which we shall examine in an English context, the radicalism of the Protestant Reformers in doctrinal matters was often matched by the conservatism of their social and economic teachings, which showed a striking continuity with those of the Catholic Church.

The teachings of any one Church might be influenced by the degree of complexity and commercialization of its economic environment, its relations with the State, and the extent to which it kept the power of enforcement of its precepts. One school of thought would explain any difference between Lutheran and Calvinist economic codes by reference to the contrast between the rural society within which Luther could declare approvingly that 'in olden days, God caused the children of Israel to dwell far from, the sea, and did not allow them to engage in much commerce',[3] and the more commercialized background of Geneva or the Netherlands.

More frequently expressed is the belief that the control of the Churches as a whole over economic issues and values simply went by default, that the Reformation so weakened Church authority that the questions of the just price or of usury ceased to be subject to ecclesiastical authority and became secularized.

[1] J. W. Baldwin, *The Medieval Theories of the Just Price*; J. T. Noonan, *The Scholastic Analysis of Usury*.

[2] In the sixteenth century some Catholic authorities, including Luther's adversary Johann Eck, strongly defended interest-taking.

[3] *An Appeal to the Ruling Class of German Nationality*, in Woolf, i, 196.

Some Catholic historians have saddled the Reformation with a negative contribution in a double sense; urging that the Protestants' denial of any necessary relation between conduct in this world and reward in the next led to a separation of faith and morality, and that although their economic precepts remained admirable the Protestant Churches were unable to enforce them. By smashing Church unity they had undermined the foundations of the only power which might have held man's self-interest in check.

A letter from Calvin to Somerset in 1548, reminding him that the troubles of England have sprung 'not from lack of preaching, but from failure to enforce compliance with it',[1] points to the contemporary grasp of the need for effective sanctions, and indeed to the fundamental question of the nature and extent of the social and economic responsibilities of government. The enhanced importance of the State, both in political philosophy and in practical affairs, was a characteristic feature of the Renaissance. Now contemporary economic developments, the disunity of the Christian Churches, and in certain cases the fact that the Church had, in a significant sense, been taken over, all combined to present the nascent State with a complex problem.

For whether or not the Church could come to terms with evolving economic forces, the State had to do so, partly because of the obvious connection between economic strength and political power, and partly because of the growing influence of commercial interests upon policy. Meanwhile the weakening of the Church meant that the only power now left with any pretensions to the authority needed to enforce a traditional code of ethics in the conduct of social and economic affairs was the State. Out of a conjunction of religious, political and economic circumstances there thus evolves the concept of the secular saviour. In the source-material of the mid-Tudor decades we find a constant appeal to the State to uphold a code of economic and social morality which the Church cannot enforce. But alongside it, most significantly, we sometimes find the more novel appeal to government to take action on what one might fairly describe as grounds of economic efficiency.

The concept of the commonwealth was, in effect, the focal

---

[1] Cited in R. H. Tawney, *Religion and the Rise of Capitalism*, 98.

point of such discussion, upon which religious and political, as well as social and economic, themes converged. In the following chapters we shall first consider the nature and fortunes of the ideal of the Commonwealth itself, in relation to those who, in thought or in statecraft, professed to serve it. Next we shall examine, in turn, the political and the religious themes. Finally, we shall consider in some detail the social and economic problems of the commonwealth, and the ideas advanced as to the objectives and methods of governmental action to deal with them.

CHAPTER TWO

The Ideal of the Commonwealth

I F the mid-Tudor ideal of the Commonwealth emerged from the conjunction of forces and circumstances described in the last chapter, it is equally true that this development occurred within the context of traditional thought. It is symbolic that the ideal of the Commonwealth was so frequently related to the completely medieval analogy of the body politic. This device was admirably suited both to the continuity and to the metamorphosis of economic and social thought at this time. *Per se* it expressed the medieval ideal of an organic society, and served both for exposition of the social and economic values inherited from medieval religious teaching and for criticism of the ills of the body politic and of the shortcomings of its various members. Yet at the same time increasing emphasis upon the power and duties of the head could express growing realization of the responsibilities of the prince in economic and social spheres, and of the transfer to the secular ruler of the onus of enforcement of the desired code of conduct.

While it has been suggested that the 'dream of a perfectly co-operating commonwealth' of the idealists only developed as a reaction against the trends of the latter part of the reign of Henry VIII,[1] expressions of the general concept, indicating its continuity in association with the organic analogy of society, occur much earlier. Edmund Dudley's *The Tree of Common Wealth* (1509–10) enunciates the duty of the prince 'to maintain and support, as far as in him is or lieth, the common wealth of his subjects', to protect the poor from oppression, to preserve the commons in tranquillity and not suffer them to fall into idleness, and to keep all degrees in concord and unity beneath the shelter of the tree of the

[1] J. W. Allen, *A History of Political Thought in the Sixteenth Century*, 134.

commonwealth.[1] 'Lady Publike wele' was a chief character in the interlude of John Roo which so enraged Wolsey,[2] while Barlow, in 1528, made it one of his criticisms of the religious that they brought about 'the common weal's hindrance' rather than its 'furtherance'.[3]

Sometimes the term *public* wealth' was preferred, probably because of the potential connotations of the word 'common'. Sir Thomas Elyot discerned a 'like diversity to be in English between a public weal and a common weal, as should be in Latin between Res publica and Res plebeia', and rejected the chaotic implications of the term 'common weal' that 'every thing should be to all men in common, without discrepancy of any estate or condition', and that 'all men must be of one degree and sort'. A 'Public Weal' he defined as 'a body living, compact or made of sundry estates and degrees of men, which is disposed by the order of equity and governed by the rule and moderation of reason'.[4]

But the term *common* wealth' was the more usual, the normal implication being that of the mutual necessity and interdependence of all parts or estates of the body politic. The conventional analogy was that which likened the realm to a human body, but sometimes the imagery varied, as when Hooper described the commonwealth as a ship and lamented the number of Jonases aboard,[5] or Elyot compared the 'public weal' to a garden, its rulers to the gardeners, its degrees of people to the beds, and its vices and abuses to moles.[6] The ideal of mutual service, expressed through the performance of economic functions within a religious and organic context, each individual being bound to 'refer his craft and occupation unto the commonwealth, and serve his brethren as he would do Christ himself', was clearly set forth by Tyndale.[7] Hugh Latimer advised his congregation to 'consider that no one person is born into the world for his own sake, but for the commonwealth sake. Let us, therefore, walk charitably; not seeking our own commodities.'[8] In his 'Godly Meditations',

[1] E. Dudley, *The Tree of Common Wealth*, 31–2 and 102–3.
[2] Edward Hall, *Chronicle*, 719.
[3] J. Barlow, *Burial of the Mass*, 68, 78 and 91.
[4] *The Boke named the Governour*, i, 1–3.
[5] *Early Writings*, 459–60 ff.   [6] *The Governour*, ii, 445.
[7] *Works*, i, 138.   [8] *Sermons and Remains*, 88.

written while in prison awaiting martyrdom, John Bradford regretted 'transgressing the politic laws for apparel and meats', and declared that 'this is a sin, dear Father, that I always have been a private more than a commonweal man; always I seek for mine own commodity, contemning that which maketh to the commodity of others'.[1]

Indeed, this implication of a prior or transcendent claim of the communal interest appears as the title of an anonymous work published c. 1548: *The prayse and commendacion of suche as sought comenwelthes; and to the contrary, the ende and discommendacion of such as sought priuate welthes.* Its author attributes the decay of the commonwealth to 'men so given to insatiable covetousness, in procuring their own private wealths; . . . by like in these days the higher Powers study private wealths for all men study the same, and no man passeth upon the commonwealth'.[2] Clement Armstrong had earlier referred bitterly to those 'wretches . . . that for their own singular weal worketh against God's will and ordinance, to destroy the common weal of the whole realm', so that 'for the less profit they destroyed the more'.[3]

The popularity of the medieval device of the corporeal analogy in order to stress the mutual interdependence of all the members of the body politic, and to explain and justify differences of rank, of function, and of rewards, continued right through the decades studied. An extended use of the analogy is found in an English translation of *The booke whiche is called the body of Polycye,* by Christine de Pisan, published in 1521 and apparently well known at the English court. The Commonwealth idealist John Hales was completely representative in declaring that 'it is no perfect body that lacketh any member. It is a monster that hath arms, and lacketh feet . . . [But] as nature hath not ordained that the foot should have so much blood as the arm, so all men may not be like, nor of like substance in a common wealth.'[4] Equal stress was laid upon the sinews of obedience, through which the whole body was directed, and upon the folly of feet or legs setting themselves up against the head. At the same time, the higher members were warned not to disdain the lesser; even the very poor were necessary members of a Christian body politic.

[1] *The Writings of John Bradford,* 163.   [2] Pp. A.iv–A.v.b.
[3] *Treatise,* in *T.E.D.,* iii, 90–1 and 98.   [4] 'Defence', in *Discourse,* p. lx.

But in regard to diseased members, even the Homily of 'Christian Love and Charity' (1547) felt constrained to advise that 'such evil persons, that be so great offenders of God and the commonweal, charity requireth to be cut off from the body of the commonweal, lest they corrupt other good and honest persons; like as a good surgeon cutteth away a putrified and festered member for love he hath to the whole body, lest it infect other members adjoining to it'.[1] In a letter referring to the Pilgrimage of Grace, in December 1536, Henry VIII had declared his intention to resort to such surgery and to 'cut away all those corrupt members that with wholesome medicines will not be recovered and brought to perfect health'.[2]

Indeed, the analogy of disease in the human body was often used to depict the defects of the body politic. Thomas Starkey was particularly fond of this device; lack of good government he likened to a frenzy, depopulation to consumption, excess of idlers to dropsy, and idle craftsmen or ploughmen to gout![3] The extension of the figure to include the treatment of ills gave rise to some familiar imagery: John Hales pointed to the need for 'a tent ['teynte' in the original—an obsolete term meaning 'probe'] that must enter further into the sore, if we mind to have it perfectly cured, that it shall not fester underneath',[4] while Sir John Cheke warned that 'desperate sickness in physic must have desperate remedies, for mean medicines will never help great griefs. So if ye cast your selves into such sharp diseases, ye must needs look for sharp medicines again at your physicians hands.'[5]

The same parallel was employed at length, and in very striking fashion, by John Ponet in his Shorte Treatise of politike power, in 1556.

A child born besides Oxford in the year M.D.LII. with two heads and two parts of two evil shaped bodies joined in one. A child born in Coventry, in the year M.D.LV. without arms or legs. A child born at Fulham by London even now this year, with a great head, evil shaped, the arms with bags hanging out at the Elbows and heels, and feet

---

[1] In The Two Books of Homilies Appointed to be Read in Churches, ed. J. Griffiths, 72.
[2] The Letters of King Henry VIII, 156.
[3] Dialogue, 76, 79–80, 86 and 87–8.
[4] 'Defence', in Discourse, p. lxiii.
[5] The hurt of sedition, in Holinshed, Chronicles, iii, 1004–5.

lame. .... The child by Oxford, what did it betoken, but that our sweet head, King Edward should be taken away (as he was indeed) and that there should be in his place two heads, diverse governors, and a toward division of the people, but not all together: ... The child of Coventry without the principal members to help and defend the body, must needs signify, that the natural body, that is, the people of England shall be helpless. ... The child of Fulham, what can it signify, but the natural body of England shall be weak, the chief members (the arms and legs) which is the nobility, so clogged with chains of gold, and bags of money, that the hand shall not be able to draw out the sword nor the heels to spur the horse to help and defend the body, that is, the commons. And as the head of it is the greatest part, and greater than it ought to be, with too much superfluity of that it should not have, wherefore it must pull from the other members to comfort it, and lack of that good proportion it ought to have: so shall the governors and heads of England suck out the wealth and substance of the people (the politic body) and keep it bare.[1]

Ponet's fellow-exile, William Turner, sometime physician to the Duke of Somerset, used the device with professional expertise. *A new book of spirituall Physik for dyuerse diseases of the nobilitie and gentlemen of Englande*, was published in 1555—possibly at Basle, despite its jesting claim to have been 'imprinted at Rome by the vatican church'. He diagnosed a number of failings in conduct and in faith: 'the whole Palsy or numbness through all the body', that is, 'unlearnedness'; 'the Dropsy', which is 'to be swelled & puffed up, with wind and water, and to be exceeding thirsty' with pride and greed; 'the Romish Pox', brought back by 'Doctor Steven' from his sojourn with 'the whore of Babylon'; and 'the Leprosy', or infection with shameless conduct by 'proud start-ups, or self made gentlemen'.[2]

Thus the general agreement, in principle, that 'no man may abuse his own things to the prejudice of the common weal',[3] was matched by an equal consensus of opinion that in reality this precept was blatantly ignored. This posed the problem of how 'singular' interests might be brought into harmony with, or at least prevented from injuring, the common good, which in turn

[1] Pp. K.iii.b–K.v.
[2] Fols. 46, 46.b, 48, 48.b, 72, 76, 76.b, 82.b, 83, 83.b, 95.b.
[3] *Discourse*, 52; below, 36–7, on the question of authorship.

led to the question of the social and economic functions of government. In his 'Discourse on the Reformation of Abuses', in 1551, of which the corporeal analogy once more provided the framework, the young Edward VI himself essayed an answer. He defined 'the temporal regiment' as consisting 'in well ordering, enriching, and defending the whole body politic of the commonwealth, and every part of the whole, so one hurt not th'other',[1] and condemned infractions of the traditional, inherited code in social and economic affairs as symptomatic of weakness or disease in the body politic, whose health it was the duty of government to preserve.

This theme of the responsibility of rulers was common, though the bluntness with which it was expressed might vary. William Tyndale and John Rastell concurred in justifying the land, wealth and income of governors and officers on the ground that they 'minister peace'[2] and 'take pain for the common wealth'.[3] An English translation of Erasmus's *Enchiridion militis Christiani* (1533) (apparently highly praised by More and Fisher until the discovery that it was Tyndale's), which enjoyed great popularity and had been reprinted seven times by 1550, directed the 'Christian prince' that he should 'turn not to thine own profit things which are common, but bestow those things which be thine own and thine own self altogether upon the commonwealth. The common people oweth very many things to thee, but thou owest all things to them.'[4] Elyot reminded rulers 'that by their preeminence they sit, as it were on a pillar on the top of a mountain, where all the people do behold them', and compared their responsibilities for the health of the body politic with those of the 'physicians attending on their cure'.[5]

An anonymous 'Discourse addressed to the King' (*c.* 1532) portrays an almost mystical unity of king and people:

Your Grace, in form of Son of Man, shall be a lively King in your kingly image like as an earthly man, to have all your people as members in your kingly body of your realm, in as sensible knowledge in the soul in

---

[1] In J. G. Nichols, *Literary Remains of King Edward the Sixth*, 480.
[2] W. Tyndale, *Works*, i, 131.
[3] J. Rastell, *Gentleness and Nobility*, ll. 790–1.
[4] Printed by W. G. Zeeveld, in E. M. Nugent, *The Thought and Culture of the English Renaissance*, 181 and 184–7; see also J. K. McConica, *English Humanists and Reformation Politics*, 145.
[5] Sir T. Elyot, *The Governour*, i, 248; ii, 6, 405–10.

your kingly head in Christ's heavenly man, as every earthly man has sense and knowledge of all his bodily members in his soul in his head, so as never man nor woman in England shall live out of cure nor out of knowledge, never to have no insurrection nor riot in this whole realm.

But combined with this cloying adulation is a clear and relatively advanced conception of the economic and social duties of the prince. By ensuring that all the people have employment, while those who cannot work have livings to keep them out of need, the king will be the best-loved monarch that ever was in England, which in turn will be the richest of realms. In a blending of religious zeal and concern for social justice the Crown is urged to set up a right order of faith, to put all the people to work at husbandry, clothing, etc., and not to suffer vagabonds or workers of sin. The whole reformation of right order in the commonweal rests only in the ministration of the 'kingly head right'.[1]

The sentiments and phraseology are almost conclusively reminiscent of Armstrong's 'How the (co)men people may be set aworke. An order of a comen welth.'[2] This also compares the realm to a 'mystical' body, in which the king, as head, should suffer no harmful members such as lawyers who promote strife, merchants who contrive scarcity, or 'friar, monk, canon nor other cloaked hypocrite' who will not work. The king must enforce tillage to produce victual, regulate cloth manufacture within the towns, and prohibit the import of articles we might make for ourselves.

The definition of the task of the ruler as being 'constantly to proceed forth to the advancement of the commonweal: that is, truly to administer justice, to restrain extortion and oppression, to set up tillage and good husbandry, whereby the people may increase and be maintained',[3] is developed at length in such works as William Forrest's *Pleasaunt Poesye of Princelie Practise*, dedicated to Somerset in 1548, and Starkey's *Dialogue*. The *Dialogue* compares the function of the king in the state or commonwealth with that of the heart in the body, and urges that a healthy realm

---

[1] *L. and P. Henry VIII*, v, No. 1501, 635–6. If this is by Armstrong, 1535 is a more likely date.

[2] *L. and P. Henry VIII*, *Addenda*, i (Part II), No. 1382, 470–1.

[3] Thomas Cooper, address to Edward VI, in Strype, ii (Part II), 124.

depends on good order and policy established by laws and enforced by rulers who, 'observing a certain reasonable mean, ever have their eyes fixed to the common weal'.[1] Also specifically concerned with the powers and duties of governance are Bullinger's *Treatise or Sermon . . . concernynge magistrates and obedience of subiectes* (1549), and Baldwin's compilation, *A Myrroure For Magistrates* (1559). Henry Bullinger deprecates excessive taxation and court expenditure, since taxes 'be public and not private goods', and describes a realm as stronger 'with less abundance, and more concord betwixt the superiors and inferiors, than with infinite treasures, where magistrates & subjects do not agree'.[2] William Baldwin warns that offices are not 'gainful spoils for the greedy to hunt for, but painful toils for the heedy to be charged with', for 'the goodness or badness of any realm lieth in the goodness or badness of the rulers . . . the wealth and quiet of every common weal, the disorder also and miseries of the same, come specially through them'.[3]

Hooper's injunction that if princes err and 'their offence be hurtful and slanderous to the word of God, and pernicious to the commonwealth, the preacher of God's word must not dissemble to correct it by the word of God plainly, without colour or circumlocution',[4] was abundantly discharged in the contemporary pulpit. Becon reminded magistrates that 'they are the ministers of God, appointed to bear rule not for their own profit and commodity, but for the wealth and profit of God's people', and attacked excessive taxation, failure to punish the wicked, and the search for personal enrichment.[5] Alluding to these latter charges, Latimer defined 'a princely kind of thieving . . . the noble theft of princes and of magistrates. They are bribe-takers.'[6] Thomas Lever pleaded for 'Godly governors, which . . . shall be ready, not only to serve the markets with corn, but also to serve God and the king with lands and goods, bodies and lives'; instead, the people were confronted with the spectacle of the magistrates dividing a bishop's land as the soldiers had divided Christ's coat. Little wonder that 'therefore now the most part of men lacking teachers and rulers, do without grief of conscience, or fear of

---

[1] *Dialogue*, 46–8, 50–1, and 157–64.
[2] Pp. D.viii.b–E.i.b.
[3] Pp. ii–iii.a.
[4] *Early Writings*, 360.
[5] *Catechism*, 114, 107, and 310; *Early Works*, 253.
[6] *Sermons*, 139.

punishment abuse every thing unto the ruin and destruction, which God hath ordained unto the upholding and increase of a christian common wealth'.[1]

The significance of good and bad government in social and economic terms served as the basic plot of two works of particular interest: Robert Crowley's *The Fable of Philargyrie. The Great Gigant* (1551) and the anonymous *Respublica* (1553), tentatively ascribed to Nicholas Udall. The first is a bitter, and barely veiled, expression of the disillusionment of the radical Protestant idealists with the selfish scramble for wealth and power which followed the break from Rome. It describes the coming of Philargyrie ('love silver'), under whose promptings self-interest and greed replace, and outdo in covetousness, the hypocrisy of the old (Catholic) order. All the wealth that Hypocrisie has gathered is now gobbled up by Philargyrie until, after an open clash between them, the former's rule is replaced by that of Philaute ('self-love')—a change to which parliament agrees. Economic mismanagement and shameless pandering to Philargyrie's greed, by such steps as the raising of rents, the decision to 'make right fine gold of brass', and the sale of Boulogne, continue until at last the king answers the appeal of Truth and awakens to his responsibilities.[2]

Respublica, performed in London at Christmas 1553, is also concerned with the economic and social impact of misgovernment under the regime of Edward VI, or, more specifically, of Northumberland. It contains many clear contemporary allusions, and while one can only speculate whether particular statesmen are personified in the four Vices of the interlude—Oppression, Insolence, Avarice and Adulation—Northumberland and Cecil seem to be indicated at certain points.[3]

The Lady Respublica, despairing at the lack of good men to rule her realm, consoles herself with the thought that

> like as by default, quick ruin doth befall.
> So may good government at once recover all.[4]

---

[1] *Sermons*, 96–8.
[2] *Philargyrie*, pp. D.v.(a), D.vi.(a), D.vi.(b), and D.vi.(a) and (b).
[3] Anon., *Respublica*, ed. L. A. Magnus, p. xxvii.
[4] Ibid., p. 15, ll. 459–60.

But unfortunately she entrusts her land to a clique headed by
Avarice, who has crept into her Council posing as 'Policy'.
Their malpractices provoke from poor People—who is presented
as speaking in dialect—the complaint that he, and the realm, have
been made 'thread bare'. Indeed,

> we Ignoram people, whom itche doe perzente,
> wer ner zo I-polde, zo wrong, and zo I-torment.
> Lord Ihese Christe whan he was I-pounst & I-pilate
> was ner zo I-trounst as we have been of yeares Late.[1]

Unabashed, the Vices reckon up their gains, including the past
and future proceeds of raids on the lands and incomes of the
bishops; true,

> some of them were aged & yet would not die,
> and some would in no wise to our desires apply.
> But we have Rods in piss for them every one,
> that they shall be fleeced if we reign, one by one.

But their complacency is disturbed by an uneasy awareness that
People 'with a wide throat doth . . . roar' against them, that he
complains to Respublica, and is 'sturdy'. They advise Respublica
to pay no heed to this disobedient 'maintainer of wrong opinions'
and to suppress any criticism of ministers, and indulge in a dia-
tribe against People himself for daring to meddle in such high
matters, even his plaintive 'yele geve volke leave to thinke?' being
snubbed.[2]

At last the arrival of 'the general Verity, Old time's daughter'
—Mary Tudor, daughter of Henry VIII—rescues Respublica,
and the Vices are overthrown. People, rejoicing at the improvement in his conditions, remarks that

> iche am hable sens to bie me anewe cote,
> And, Is thanke God, chave in my purse a Zilver grote.
> I wis iche cowlde not zo zai these zixe yeares afore.[3]

Peace charges Avarice and his colleagues with the poisonous
effects of their misrule:

---

[1] Ibid., pp. 23–4, ll. 648–76.
[2] Ibid., p. 27, ll. 794–825, p. 31, ll. 934–41, p. 37, l. 1113, and p. 38, l. 1152.
[3] Ibid., p. 42, l. 1291, and p. 52, ll. 1599–1602.

Call ye it peace, sirrah, when brother & brother
cannot be content to live one by another:
when one for his house, for his land, yea for his groat
is ready to strive & pluck out an other's throat?

Avarice is handed over to People to 'be pressed as men do press a sponge', while Adulation promises to repent and serve the Commonweal.[1]

Respublica is an outstanding example of contemporary realization of the evil social and economic consequences of misgovernment—and of an attempt to use such realization for propaganda purposes through presentation as stage entertainment. But its clear statement of the duty of the ruler to redress economic and social grievances is in no way unrepresentative—indeed this was sometimes made a necessary complement of the subject's duty of obedience.[2] Nor was the point missed that the power of the Crown itself rested upon the well-being of its subjects, that 'it is the king's honour that the commonwealth be advanced'.[3] Armstrong observed that

the king and his lords hath need to minister right order of common weal, or else they must needs destroy their own weal by the very ordinance of God, for they are upholden and borne upon the body. If they will be rich, they must first see all common people have riches, that out thereof must rise their riches and all the people be out of need. A rich, wealthy body of a realm maketh a rich, wealthy king being the head thereof, and a poor, feeble, weak body of a realm must needs make a poor, feeble, weak king.[4]

[1] Ibid., p. 54, ll. 1689–92, and pp. 61–2.
[2] Cf. below, Baldwin, 49, and Tyndale, 50–1.
[3] H. Latimer, *Sermons*, 99.
[4] C. Armstrong, *Reforme*, in *T.E.D.*, iii, 115.

CHAPTER THREE

'Commonwealth's Men'

IN attempting to trace the fortunes, and significance, of the ideal of the Commonwealth during the period 1529 to 1559 some caution is needed. As to the existence of that ideal in mid-Tudor England, and its expression in sources of all types—the sermons of divines, declarations of public figures, suggested projects of legislation or action as well as statutes and proclamations, the writings of radical pamphleteers and authors of verse and stage interludes—there is no doubt. But to what extent may we speak of any conscious pursuit of that ideal in the work of specific writers or statesmen? On the one hand, individuals' interpretations of its nature would vary; on the other, its implications for practical policy would mean far more in the proposals of a Cromwell or of a Hales than in the writings of an Armstrong or of a Simon Fish. Nonetheless, the near-ubiquity of lip-service to the ideal is itself of significance, and to divest it of all practical influence upon policy is to fly in the face of far too much evidence.

Considered advocacy of the concept of service of the Commonwealth has, broadly, been attributed to three groups of particular import: the More Group, the Cromwell Group, and the later 'Commonwealth Party' in which Somerset, Hales and Latimer were outstanding figures. Between the membership and ideas of these groups a significant degree of continuity or interconnection exists, and the careers of several individuals preclude any rigid classification. But the undoubted elements of continuity must not blind us to those of diversity. We might with equal validity suggest the existence of a fourth group: the radical Protestants such as Frith and Tyndale, distinguished by their approach from a specific religious viewpoint and by their combination of hope for radical religious reform and for social and economic amelioration.

From the outset the members of this group fell foul of More, in regard to the possible social implications of their teachings as well as on doctrinal issues. Any attempt to include all the fore-going within one unified, continuous 'Erasmian polity'[1] courts the danger of attenuating the adjective, and sometimes almost of equating it with 'Erastian'.

The More group has been characterized as representing the application both of such inherited medieval concepts as that of measure, and of the Erasmian ideal of public service, to the emergent Renaissance State, with a typically Humanist emphasis upon the importance of education in order to attain the desired objectives.[2] In this circle have been included More himself, John Rastell, John Heywood, Starkey, Pole, Lupset and Elyot. It has been suggested that the members of this group equated good government with applied Christianity, and combined two meanings of the term commonweal: 'first, the common well-being, general good, or welfare of a group of people; second, the whole body politic, the state, community, or the common-wealth'.[3] Indeed, this integration of meaning applies, effectively, throughout our chosen period—with occasional exceptions, in-cluding incidentally Elyot himself.[4]

Of the stature of Sir Thomas More there is no doubt—whether as centre of a circle of Humanist thought and culture, as practical statesman whose experience, including that as Chancellor, had made him aware both of the realities of social and economic problems and injustices and of the responsibility of the ruler, or as a martyr for his religious beliefs. But the meaning and significance of his most famous work, *Utopia*, has been much debated. Al-though genuine concern with the economic and social bases of society is clearly evident, it may be significant that More refused to publish an English version of the book which would make it easily accessible to many who might misconstrue its meaning.[5]

[1] See J. K. McConica, *English Humanists and Reformation Politics*, Chapters 5 and 6, and the critique of this interpretation by A. G. Dickens in *History*, lii (1967), 77–8.
[2] J. K. McConica, loc. cit., and W. G. Zeeveld, *Foundations of Tudor Policy*, 116.
[3] P. Hogrefe, *The Sir Thomas More Circle*, 98.
[4] Above, 14.
[5] W. G. Zeeveld, in E. M. Nugent, *Thought and Culture of the English Renais-sance*, 217.

For in the realm of practical politics, whether in opposition to a king who would rend the unity of Christendom or, as in his *Supplicacion of soules*, to radical elements who, he feared, would overturn the whole concept of due degree and order, More showed himself to be fundamentally conservative. J. W. Allen argues that, beyond its validity as 'a simple indictment of society . . . More knew that his Utopia was nowhere and proved nothing',[1] Christopher Morris sums up the work as 'a satire, a fantasia, a *jeu d'esprit*, . . . not a communist nor even a liberal manifesto',[2] and J. H. Hexter concludes that 'the author of *Utopia* was no Utopian'.[3]

As we have seen, Sir Thomas Elyot explicitly rejected the term *common* weal because of its alleged egalitarian or subversive implications, and preferred the phrase *public* weal. Elyot's great hope lay in the education of rulers—the theme of *The Boke named The Gouernour*—and of the nobility, to whom *The Image of Governance* (1541) was specifically addressed, so that they could fulfil their functions within the existing social hierarchy. Unlike his friend More, he came to terms with the Henrician revolution and served his king as ambassador and propagandist.

John Rastell, printer, pamphleteer and dramatist, is, in several ways, a particularly interesting member of this circle. His *Gentleness and Nobility* (1529) exemplifies the interlacing of the themes of due order and degree, measure, the nature of true nobility, and the idea of service of the commonweal, which distinguishes the approach of this group. His personal relationships—he was brother-in-law to More, father-in-law of John Heywood, and friend of Clement Armstrong—demonstrate the close links between members of the More and Cromwell groups. Both in the socio-economic criticism of his verse-dramas and in the projects for reform of the law and the judicial system of his prose works,[4] Rastell's deep concern for social justice within the commonwealth is evident. As to how radical his views became, opinions differ;[5] certainly he broke with More after about 1530, but the degree to

---

[1] J. W. Allen, *Political Thought in the Sixteenth Century*, 154–6.
[2] C. Morris, *Political Thought in England. Tyndale to Hooker*, 19.
[3] J. H. Hexter, *More's Utopia. The Biography of an Idea*, 131.
[4] Below, 92–3, 170, 184, 210.
[5] A. W. Reed, *Early Tudor Drama*, 6, and K. W. Cameron, *Authorship and Sources of 'Gentleness and Nobility'*, 33.

which this may be attributed to differences on social and economic issues as distinct from his conversion by Frith remains unknown.

Also closely associated with More, to whom unlike Rastell he remained loyal, was the dramatist John Heywood. Certain personal references have been read into his most remarkable work, *The Spider and the Flie*, commenced *c.* 1536 but not completed and published until twenty years later; it is suggested that Cranmer is the Spider and Rastell the Fly, while the resemblance is pointed out between the Ant's fate and Heywood's own in having to recant, with a halter round his neck, at Paul's Cross after involvement in a conspiracy against Cranmer.[1] But the play is concerned far more with social and economic than with personal or doctrinal issues.[2] Before his execution the Head Spider delivers a homily against tyranny and ambition, and appeals for honest government in the interest of the commonwealth.[3]

Basic congruence and continuity of thought on economic and social problems were cut across by the religious and political circumstances of the 1530s. Of the two members of the More group whose views Thomas Starkey professed to represent in his *Dialogue*, Reginald Pole fled abroad and resisted all efforts to persuade him to return and support the Henrician religious changes. The other, Thomas Lupset, had died in 1530, but his very conservative attitude on religious and social issues would place him alongside More and Elyot, and quite out of sympathy with a radical agitator such as Simon Fish.[4] But Rastell's attacks on Fish provoked a reply from John Frith which converted him to Protestantism, and he joined the camp of Thomas Cromwell. Starkey himself in many ways represents a major thread of continuity. His service with Cromwell marks a clear link between the group around that minister and the humanist tradition of the More circle; Starkey's *Dialogue* is woven around a debate on an issue which was a characteristic theme of that circle—the duty of the individual, especially if of ability and learning, to serve the commonweal. At the same time, he anticipates the later Commonwealth Party.

---

[1] A. W. Reed, op. cit., 54 and 62–3; also R. de la Bere, *John Heywood, Entertainer*, 108.

[2] Below, 47–8, 91–2, 142–3.   [3] J. Heywood, *Spider and Flie*, 397–404.

[4] J. K. McConica, op. cit., 197; also J. A. Gee, *The Life and Works of Thomas Lupset*, 180–1.

We have noted that the religious background to discussion and development of these ideas cannot be ignored. It would be wrong to move on to consider the Cromwell group without pausing to stress the significance of the concern shown for the economic and social aspects of the commonwealth in the work of a number of radical Protestants at this time, in particular, of William Tyndale, John Frith and Simon Fish. While some might hesitate to envisage them as a clearly defined group, there was a personal link between them, they all suffered exile and martyrdom or death in prison, and they all expected economic and social improvements in society as a corollary of religious changes. We shall return to their views in a later context,[1] but it is worth observing here that the 'Commonwealth's men' of the reign of Edward VI probably derived as much from the radical Protestant urge to social amelioration of these men as from the Erasmian humanism of More's associates.

Assessment of Thomas Cromwell's place in constitutional history is still subject to debate,[2] but there seems to be general agreement as to his keen interest in economic and social questions. Professor Elton has brought out the significance of the term 'commonwealth' within the context of the ideas of Cromwell and his adherents where it occurs almost as often as 'empire': 'together these two—national sovereignty and paternalism—make up Cromwell's philosophy of the state which matters so much because he actually impressed it upon the realm and government of England'.[3] A letter of Cromwell to Henry VIII, in January 1534, reporting the fortunes of a proposal to control sheep-rearing, expresses his concern for 'the Common wealth of this your realm and . . . your most loving and obedient subjects'.[4] Indeed, his 'Injunctions to the Clergy' of August 1536 are as preoccupied with social and economic as with doctrinal issues. The clergy should, by personal example and by exhortation, bring their parishioners to conduct tending to the 'profit of the common weal'—in particular, to hard work rather than to pilgrimages, to

[1] Below, Chapter 5.
[2] For recent statements of the position see *Past and Present*, Nos. 25 (July 1963); 29 (Dec. 1964); and 32 (Dec. 1965).
[3] G. R. Elton, *England under the Tudors*, 185; see also G. R. Elton, 'The Political Creed of Thomas Cromwell', 88.
[4] *Life and Letters of Thomas Cromwell*, i, 373.

genuine charity,[1] to training of youth 'to Learning or to some other honest exercise occupation or husbandry . . . to the great commodity and ornament of the common weal' and the avoidance of idleness to which they might 'be driven for lack of some mystery or occupation . . .'[2] It is ironical that Aske should report of the Pilgrims of Grace that 'their especial great grudge is against the Lord Cromwell, being reputed the destroyer of the commonwealth'.[3]

How important was any continuity between More and Cromwell? J. K. McConica believes that 'Erasmian reform is very clearly the chief inspiration' of Cromwell's 'Injunctions';[4] W. G. Zeeveld asserts that Cromwell deliberately turned to the humanist school in order to clothe his policy of expediency with a cloak of tradition.[5] Certainly there was recruitment of humanist writers in order to present the government's case to the public eye. But we may credit several members of More's entourage with entering the service of Cromwell out of genuine conviction. Professor Dickens describes the Cromwellians as 'humanists with the background of poor scholars rather than that of great officials; they were charged by their employer to write in English and aim their arguments at the reading-public and even at the mass of the English nation. Their social outlook squares with this approach; also with the bourgeois forces which had come to play an increasing part in English public life . . .'[6] Members of this group included Starkey, Rastell, John Bale, William Marshall, Clement Armstrong and Sir Richard Morison.

Rastell became an enthusiastic supporter until he clashed with Cranmer, as a result of his opposition to payment of tithes in London, and was committed to prison, where he died in 1536.[7] In a number of rather pathetic letters to Cromwell in 1534 he complains bitterly that his work is opposed by 'some who are called priests and spiritual men' and pleads for Cromwell's attention, telling him that 'I have leaned to you more than to any other of the King's Council this four or five years, and shall do so

---

[1] Below, 111.   [2] *Life and Letters*, ii, 26–9.
[3] M. Bateson, *The Pilgrimage of Grace. Aske's Narrative*, 342.
[4] McConica, op. cit., 160.
[5] *Foundations of Tudor Policy*, 113.
[6] A. G. Dickens, *Thomas Cromwell and the English Reformation*, 88.
[7] A. W. Reed, op. cit., 21–2; P. Hogrefe, op. cit., 118–19.

as long as I see you inclined to good causes. I am an old man and cannot live long, but I desire to spend my time for the commonwealth.'[1]

Associated with Rastell was John Bale, who had left the Carmelite order of friars and become a secular priest. Bale was encouraged and rewarded by Cromwell as a propagandist, and organized a company of players. His own works have been described as perhaps the earliest instances of the use of the play exclusively for controversial purposes, and as 'peerless examples of the limitless bitterness aroused by the religious struggles in the sixteenth century'.[2] But he expressed genuine concern with the social implications of religious reform, and on the fall of Cromwell went into exile, where he deplored the misuse of confiscated monastic wealth, returning c. 1547-8.[3]

The humanist William Marshall, who had had some acquaintance with More, was advanced £20 by Cromwell for his translation of Marsiglio's *Defensor Pacis* which appeared in 1535. In the following year he complained to the minister that 'the "Defence of Peace" cost over £34; though the best book in English against the usurped book of the Bishop of Rome, it has not sold'.[4] Another very important aspect of Marshall's work related to the problem of poor relief; he was the translator of the Ypres *Forma Subventionis Pauperum* and very probable author of a detailed draft project for relief of poverty in 1535.[5]

As for Clement Armstrong, while his literary gifts and ability as an analyst of economic problems have been questioned, his sincerity and his anticipation of many of the preoccupations of later 'Commonwealth-men' are undoubted.[6] After an 'exchange of grocery for high-class interior decorating' in his career, he became a friend of John Rastell and followed his lead. Professor Bindoff considers that it was the influence of a religious conversion that made Armstrong turn to social pamphleteering. He appears to have shared Rastell's opposition to payment of tithes.[7]

[1] *L. and P. Henry VIII*, vii, Nos. 1071-3, 417-18.
[2] J. W. Harris, *John Bale*, 27-8 and 63-4.   [3] Ibid., 28.
[4] *D.N.B.*, xii, 1135; also J. K. McConica, op. cit., 134-6.   [5] Below, 129-30.
[6] On Armstrong see S. T. Bindoff, 'Clement Armstrong and His Treatises of the Commonweal', also A. G. Dickens, op. cit., 86, and G. R. Elton, *England under the Tudors*, 186.
[7] An anti-tithe tract of his is calendared in *L. and P. Henry VIII*, viii, No. 453, 177.

But when he forwarded two well-known tracts of his to Cromwell they evoked no interest or response.[1]

Far more important were Sir Richard Morison and Thomas Starkey—the fact that they were both recruits of Cromwell from the service of Pole is yet another link with the More circle. Morison, who translated the *Introduction to wisedome* of the Spanish humanist Juan Luis Vives, published several works of significance in regard to political thought which will concern us later.[2] Starkey became chaplain to Henry VIII in 1535, and a year later published *An Exhortation to the people, instructynge theym to Unitie and Obedience*. But his most interesting work, the *Dialogue*, written *c.* 1538, which has been termed a restatement of many of the basic ideas of More, Erasmus and Vives about law and government,[3] was never published in his own time. Professor Dickens describes Starkey as 'a forerunner of the liberal "Commonwealth Party" . . . a fundamental thinker . . . the champion of an enlightened social policy',[4] and J. W. Allen attaches particular weight to his view 'that redress [of social evils] is largely a question of organization and that governmental action can do much to create the very and true commonweal'.[5]

Thus it is suggested that the 'commonwealth's men' of the 1540s had their predecessors in 'the Clement Armstrongs and Rastells [who] though more obscure . . . were no less active in thought than the Haleses and the Levers', with Hugh Latimer as a close link between them.[6] The nature of the ideas advanced by men such as these does much to support the case that the Cromwellians represented a 'fund of social liberalism on the Protestant side', though the extent of Cromwell's commitment thereto may be queried and his influence was, in any case, cut short.[7] Any tendency towards social liberalism, whether this took the form of recommendation of governmental intervention to redress what were considered social and economic injustices and to enforce equity between rich and poor, or of 'relatively democratic emphases'[8] in relation to education and selection for office,

[1] S. T. Bindoff, op. cit., 71–3.   [2] Below, 57–8.
[3] P. Hogrefe, *The Sir Thomas More Circle*, 126.
[4] A. G. Dickens, *Thomas Cromwell*, 84.
[5] *Political Thought in the Sixteenth Century*, 142–3.
[6] G. R. Elton, 'Parliamentary Drafts, 1529–1540', 118.
[7] A. G. Dickens, *Thomas Cromwell*, 89.   [8] Ibid.

or social mobility, was all too likely to be identified, by its opponents, with religious extremism and Anabaptist egalitarianism during the reaction after the fall of Cromwell.

Meanwhile we must beware of equating or identifying the Commonwealth ideal too closely with any specific doctrinal attitude. It is often expressed, in the context of much valuable social and economic criticism, in the work of men whose conduct in regard to political and religious changes, in the phrase of the times, 'smacked more of the willow than the oak'. Men such as William Forrest, priest, one-time retainer of Wolsey, who dedicated his *Princelie Practise* to Somerset but was later chaplain to Queen Mary; the schoolmaster of erratic habits, Nicholas Udall, who could pen an attack on the Rising in the West against the Prayer Book of 1549 and yet retain favour under Mary, as the probable author of *Respublica*; or Thomas Paynell, translator of *The preceptes teachyng a prynce or a noble estate his duetie* (*c.* 1528–30), a former friar who became and remained a royal chaplain under Henry VIII, Edward VI and Mary. Much interesting material indeed is found in works such as *The prayse and commendacion of suche as sought comenwelthes* (*c.* 1548), and *Policies to reduce this realme of England vnto a prosperus wealthe and estate*, addressed to Somerset in 1549, whose authorship remains, as yet, quite unknown, or in memoranda on economic policy by merchants such as William Lane and William Cholmeley.[1]

It remains true that the accession of Edward VI,[2] the 'Young Josiah' of the hopeful Protestants, of whom Somerset was all-too-prophetically to write that 'in Scripture, Josiah was no old king even when he died',[3] saw a great resurgence of the ideals and hopes of the Commonwealth men. Among the Commonwealth Party which looked to Somerset for patronage were John Hales and a number of divines, including Latimer, Lever, Bradford, Ridley, Becon and Hooper. Hales and Latimer were apparently accounted leaders of the group, while on the Council Somerset and Cranmer displayed sympathy enough with their ideals to

---

[1] Below, 41 and 144–5.

[2] The first volume of Professor W. K. Jordan's biography, *Edward VI: the Young King* (London, 1968), unfortunately appeared too late for me to draw upon its extensive documentation and percipient comments.

[3] Letter to Pole, 4 June 1549, printed in N. Pocock, *Troubles connected with the Prayer Book of 1549*, p. viii.

find themselves denounced as Commonwealth men, radicals and rabble-rousers.[1] Cecil and Sir Thomas Smith were perhaps more cautious adherents than many of the above, but represent a line of continuity into the reign of Elizabeth I, while establishment of Smith's authorship of the *Discourse*[2] would make him of pre-eminent significance in the evolution of Commonwealth economic and social analysis. The favour of Protector Somerset made this group far more influential and held out the prospect of translating into action projects of reform which had formerly been matters of literary speculation.[3]

Immediately before his execution Somerset described himself as having been 'ever glad of the furtherance and helping forward of the Common Wealth of this realm'. It is true that he had a keen eye for augmenting his personal lands and fortune, but his genuine sympathy with the poor during his period of office is acknowledged. Apart from his establishment of the Enclosure Commission, and his reluctance to deal harshly with Ket's Rebellion, this is evidenced by his parliamentary enactment of 1548 which gave tenants at will on certain of his demesne lands the security of copyholders which was not theirs by common law, making it impossible for his successor to expel them 'contrary to equity and conscience'.[4] On one occasion a complaint from his brother, the lord admiral, drew forth the rebuke that 'if you mean it, that for our part we are ready to receive poor men's complaints, that findeth or thinketh themselves injured or grieved, it is our *duty and office* to do so'.[5]

Such attitudes aroused concern, and later anger, among some of his colleagues. Even Paget, who had been instrumental in establishing his power, questioned the wisdom of Somerset's liberalism, alleging that

your pardons have given evil men a boldness to enterprise as they (have done), and cause them to think you dare not meddle with them ... I told your Grace the Truth, and was not believed: well, now your Grace seeth it what sayeth your Grace? Marry, the King's

---

[1] Conyers Read, *Mr. Secretary Cecil and Queen Elizabeth*, 42.
[2] Below, 36-7.
[3] A. F. Pollard, *England under Protector Somerset*, 215–16.
[4] 2 & 3 Edw. VI, c.12; see also A. F. Pollard, op. cit., 232, 310 and 316.
[5] Letter printed in Tytler, i, 121.

subjects out of all discipline, out of obedience, caring neither for Protector nor King, and much less for any other mean officer. And what is the cause? Your own levity [lenity?], your softness, your opinion to be good to the poor. The opinion of such as sayeth to your Grace, 'O Sir, there was never man that had the hearts of the poor as you have. Oh! the Commons pray for you, Sir. . . .'

In consequence the law is not enforced, 'the foot taketh upon him the part of the head, and commons is become a king, appointing conditions and laws to the governors . . .' To lack of firmness some were prepared to add a more sinister charge: 'some evil men list to prate here that you have some greater enterprise in your head, that lean so much to the multitude'.[1]

Indeed, in the crisis of 1549 the Council were to accuse Somerset of 'extreme ambition', of having 'subverted all Laws, Justice and good order' and of having 'laboured to sow [division] between the Nobles, the Gentlemen, and the Commons', hoping 'to have destroyed the nobility and other honest personages of the realm and after to have aspired to his majesty's place'.[2] A handbill published in support of the Protector urged the people to rise in his defence, and that of the king, 'because we, the poor Commons, being injured by the extortions of gentlemen, had our pardon this year by the mercy of the King and the goodness of the Lord Protector; for whom let us fight, for he loveth all just and true gentlemen which do no extortion, and also the poor commonalty of England'. Another handbill, with like intent, attacked the Council on several counts, including that of base birth,[3] and called for God's vengeance upon them. The comment of Lord Russell and Sir William Herbert, in a letter to Somerset, that 'your grace's proclamations and billets put abroad for the raising of the Commons we mislike very much',[4] is hardly surprising.

Another blamed for the disorders of 1549 was John Hales—perhaps the most zealous supporter of Somerset and of Commonwealth ideals among those who held official positions. Hales is first noticed as a dependant of Cromwell and a subordinate of Sir

[1] Letter to Somerset, in F. W. Russell, *Kett's Rebellion in Norfolk*, 16–17; also A. F. Pollard, op. cit., 58.
[2] Documents printed in N. Pocock, *Troubles*, 95–118.
[3] Below, 89.
[4] Tytler, i, 209–11 and 219; N. Pocock, *Troubles*, 90–92; also A. F. Pollard, op. cit., 248–9 and 252.

Ralph Sadler, whose favour helped him in the acquisition of lands and of the post of clerk of the hanaper. It is ironic that, like Somerset himself, he seems to have been keenly active in augmenting his private fortunes at this stage of his career.[1] But under Edward VI he was both propagandist and practical worker for the ideals of the Commonwealth. In 1547 he became one of the Members of Parliament for Preston. He acted, if not as chairman, at least as chief spokesman of Somerset's Enclosures Commission and was accused by its opponents of having instigated the whole investigation—a charge which he rebutted in his 'Defence', while stating defiantly that if true it would have been no cause of shame.[2] He was attacked as an 'anabaptist' and a 'libertine' who would have all things in common.[3]

In his letter to Somerset, written while on circuit with the commissioners, we find a clear statement of the hope which characterized the Edwardian Commonwealth group that religious and socio-economic reform would be accomplished together:

If there be any way or policy of man to make the people receive, embrace, and love God's word, it is only this,—when they shall see that it bringeth forth so goodly fruit, that men seek not their own wealth, nor their private commodity, but, as good members, the universal wealth of the whole body ... and what wealth will thereby universally grow to the whole realm; albeit these worldlings think it but a money matter, yet am I fully persuaded, and certainly do believe in your Grace's sayings, that, maugre the Devil, private profit, self-love, money and such-like the Devil's instruments, it shall go forward, and set such a stay in the body of the commonwealth, that all the members shall live in a due temperament and harmony, without one having too much, and a great many nothing at all, as at this present it appeareth plainly they have.[4]

Hales's claim to authorship of the *Discourse of the Common Weal of this Realm of England* has now once more been subjected to serious question, in the context of a convincing advocacy of that of Sir Thomas Smith, in whose favour the weight of evidence

---

[1] A. J. Slavin, *Politics and Profit. A Study of Sir Ralph Sadler 1507–1547*, 133, 169–71, and 203; on Somerset see M. L. Bush, 'The Lisle-Seymour Land Disputes: A Study of Power and Influence in the 1530s'.

[2] 'Defence', in *Discourse*, p. liv.

[3] C. Read, *Mr. Secretary Cecil and Queen Elizabeth*, 50.

[4] Printed in Tytler, i, 114–17.

now seems to lie.[1] But he most certainly drew up several papers analysing contemporary social and economic ills and drafted proposals for actual reforms. These were not without influence upon policy: apparently all the suggestions in his 'Causes of Dearth' were carried through both houses during the second session of Parliament in November 1548, including the tax on sheep which angered the lord admiral, and which was nullified by Somerset's fall.[2] Hales himself gives a graphic account of the fate of some of his other legislative proposals.[3]

Opposition to the activities of the Enclosure Commission was backed by the open or secret support of the majority in the Council, and in 1550, after Somerset's opponents had used his failure to suppress Ket's Rebellion with sufficient speed and rigour to overthrow him, Hales actually suffered a short term of imprisonment. In 1551 he went abroad on an embassy to the Imperial court, and it has been suggested that he despaired of his efforts at social reform, but his interest in affairs of state did not altogether cease, for he presented a composition to Elizabeth at the time of her coronation.[4]

Also very closely linked with Somerset was Sir Thomas Smith. Already a distinguished classical scholar and regius professor of civil law at Cambridge, Smith entered the service of Somerset early in 1547. He became clerk of the Privy Council and, significantly, acted as master of the Court of Requests for poor men's cases which the Protector set up in his own house. From 1548 to 1549 he was one of the two secretaries of state. His biographer, Mrs Mary Dewar, describes him as having staked all on Somerset.[5] Inevitably, he fell with him, and suffered imprisonment in the Tower between October 1549 and March 1550.

Smith submitted a memorandum to Somerset in which he pointed out the disastrous effects of debasement of the coinage. There followed some loss of favour, and it is suggested that in the enforced leisure which resulted during the summer of 1549 Smith composed what is probably the most highly thought-of piece of Commonwealth literature: *A Discourse of the Common Weal of*

---

[1] Below, 36-7.
[2] 2 & 3 Edw. VI, c. 36; 3 & 4 Edw. VI, c.23; A. F. Pollard, op. cit., 224-6.
[3] Below, 203-4.
[4] Below, 201; C. Read, op. cit., 71; A. F. Pollard, op. cit., 231.
[5] *Sir Thomas Smith*, 3.

this Realm of England. The case for Smith's authorship as against that of Hales is impressive. The concentration upon the cumulative effects of coinage debasement which is the major theme of the *Discourse* is not present elsewhere in Hales's writings, but tallies closely with two other works for which Smith's authorship is claimed.[1] Sir Thomas Smith would thus emerge as possibly the most significant thinker among those who wrote on the application of Commonwealth ideals to the economic and social problems of mid-Tudor England. Certainly the author of the *Discourse* was, as we shall see, in some ways perhaps the most original and forward-looking analyst of the rationale of governmental intervention in economic affairs.

The number of divines associated with the Commonwealth party exemplifies the revival under Somerset of the hope that religious reform and remedial social and economic action would be combined. For a short while, men such as Latimer, Ridley, Bradford, Lever, Becon and Hooper looked for the realization of their ideals. The first of these had expressed the most radical socio-religious views in his early days, even after his appointment as bishop of Worcester in 1535, and was always outspoken in his sympathy for the poor and his condemnation of economic exploitation or injustice.[2] He has been described as nominal leader of the Commonwealth men in the 1540s,[3] and after Ket's Rebellion Sir Anthony Aucher referred bitterly to 'that Common Wealth called Latimer' as having obtained the pardon of some of those implicated.[4] The sympathy of the young King Edward VI himself with the Protestant religious teachings of this group almost certainly extended also to their socio-economic ideals. His interest in economic and social problems led him to compose a 'Discourse on the Reformation of Abuses'. Professor Jordan describes this work, written early in 1551, as 'clearly reflecting . . .

---

[1] M. Dewar, op. cit., 49–55; also her articles, 'The Memorandum "For the Understanding of the Exchange": its Authorship and Dating', and 'The Authorship of the "Discourse of the Commonweal" '. See also E. Hughes, 'The Authorship of "The Discourse of the Commonweal" ', and E. Lamond's edition of the *Discourse* which attributes it to Hales.

[2] *L. and P. Henry VIII*, x, No. 462, 189–90; see also H. S. Darby, *Hugh Latimer*, 115.

[3] G. R. Elton, *England under the Tudors*, 186.

[4] A. F. Pollard, *England under Protector Somerset*, 281.

the thought and aspirations of the Commonwealth Party' and in particular Latimer's Lenten Sermons of 1549.[1]

Among Latimer's close friends were Nicholas Ridley and John Bradford. Ridley, a classical scholar, had served as chaplain to Cranmer and became bishop of Rochester in 1547 before succeeding Bonner at London three years later. He was to be actively and successfully engaged in efforts to improve the city's provision for relief of poverty.[2] Bradford, after conversion by a sermon of Latimer's, became chaplain to Ridley, and apparently devoted much of his time to personal charity.[3] Another of Ridley's chaplains, Thomas Lever, came close to Latimer in the power of his preaching against economic and social injustice, which won the approval of Knox.[4] Thomas Becon had been forced to recant at Paul's Cross in 1542 and his writings had been condemned as heretical four years later. But on Edward VI's accession he was made chaplain to Cranmer and to Somerset himself, in whose household he lived for some time. Publications of Becon's sermons were particularly successful.[5] John Hooper, who became the Lord Protector's chaplain in 1549, and was appointed to the bishopric of Gloucester in 1550, was as radical and uncompromising in the field of economic and social criticism as in that of religion. His record of active concern for the well-being of the people of his diocese was to be impressive.[6]

Cranmer himself is believed to have been in sympathy with the Commonwealth group,[7] and we shall meet with evidence of his support of liberal ideals.[8] But, like Somerset himself, he was charged with feathering his nest, and Cecil wrote to warn him of court gossip about his wealth and covetousness.[9] His recent biographer suggests that he showed rather less sympathetic understanding than did Latimer or Lever to the rebels of 1549.[10] He survived the Protector's fall without disgrace. One of Cranmer's chaplains, who became bishop of Winchester in succession

[1] W. K. Jordan, *The Chronicles and Political Papers of King Edward VI*, p. xxv.
[2] Below, 128-9; J. G. Ridley, *Nicholas Ridley*.
[3] Below, 113.　　　　[4] *D.N.B.*, xi, 1021-2.　　　　[5] Below, 65.
[6] F. D. Price, 'Gloucester Diocese under Bishop Hooper 1551-3'.
[7] C. Read, *Mr. Secretary Cecil*, 41-2; A. F. Pollard, op. cit., 216.
[8] Below, 104.
[9] W. S. Hudson, *John Ponet (1516?-1556), Advocate of Limited Monarchy*, 34.
[10] J. Ridley, *Thomas Cranmer*, 293-7.

to Gardiner, was John Ponet, His main significance clearly lies in
the field of political theory,[1] but the nature of his statements on
economic and social issues[2] makes it a fair inference that his
sympathies lay with the Commonwealth men. W. S. Hudson
stresses his insistence that 'every law must meet the primary test
of the effect it produces on the commonwealth and that it shall
be evaluated as to whether or not it serves the common good'.[3]

Two other particularly zealous propagandists for the commonweal must be mentioned: Henry Brinklow and Robert Crowley.
Brinklow, a former Grey Friar who became a mercer and citizen
of London and author of several pamphlets which were printed
in the 1540s, was a radical Protestant reformer in the tradition of
Tyndale, Fish and Frith. He was especially concerned with the
social reforms which he believed should follow the break from
Rome—the use of former church property for the common good,
such as provision of hospitals for the sick poor and of free schools
for poor men's children—as well as with abuses in administration
of the law and with economic exploitation. Crowley, who had
been at Oxford, became a printer in London in 1549, and after
starting to preach was ordained deacon by Ridley two years later.
His publication of several editions of *Piers Plowman* is symbolic,
and his own works leave no doubt as to his social and economic
sympathies. Indeed, J. W. Allen has singled him out as perhaps
the most typical exponent of the contemporary concept of the
'very and true commonweal', urging the continuity of his views
with medieval philosophy, in regard both to his concept of society
as a whole and to his contempt for profit-seeking commercialism
in particular.[4]

Whether their ideals and ideas be interpreted as looking back
nostalgically to medieval values and assumptions or forward to
mercantilism,[5] all those who would check the unbridled operation
of private profit to the common hurt were denounced as rabble-
rousing Anabaptists by those who felt their interests to be opposed.
Sir Anthony Aucher, whose gibe at Latimer we have already
noticed, was typical. In September 1549 he urged Cecil to 'be
plain with my Lord's grace, that under the pretence of simplicity

---

[1] Below, 60-2.   [2] Below, 61, 116, 140.   [3] Op. cit., 146-7.
[4] J. W. Allen, *Political Thought in the Sixteenth Century*, 137-8.
[5] Below, 191-2.

and poverty there may rest much mischief. So do I fear there doth in these men called Common Wealths and their adherents.'[1] Indeed, he hinted darkly that 'some think my Lord Grace rather to wish the decay of the gentlemen than otherwise'.[2]

The fall of Somerset saw the abandonment of his projects of reform and the disgrace of some of his supporters. Ponet's *Treatise of politike power* (1556) contains a scathing account of the clique that overthrew the Protector, led by 'the ambitious and subtle Alcibiades of England'—Warwick.[3] The attitude of the regime has been characterized as 'one of tyranny tempered by corruption'; Sharington, guilty of frauds at the Bristol mint, was released and pardoned, while Aucher, also guilty of malversation and hence the more fearful of the application of Commonwealth principles, kept his office.[4] Policy with regard to enclosures was temporarily reversed and the Statute of Merton was re-enacted,[5] while the taxes imposed on sheep and on woollen cloths were abolished.[6] Latimer, in a 'Sermon before Edward VI' in Lent 1550, spoke bitterly of the re-enactment of the Statute of Merton, deriding its provision that in any enclosures 'sufficient' should be left for the tenants.[7]

It was made felony for twelve or more to meet for the purpose of abating rents or the price of victual, or for breaking down enclosures (whether lawful or not) or enforcing rights of common or rights of way over such enclosure.[8] In 1551 two Suffolk men were 'committed to the Tower on Whitsun-even, by the commandment of the Lord Wentworth' because, with others, they had 'made supplication to the King against Robert Syder and William Rouse for the destroying their corn'. They were, apparently, sent to execution.[9] Conyers Read describes as 'infamous' the third session of Edward VI's first Parliament, from November 1549 to February 1550, which passed the legislation referred to,[10] while R. H. Tawney believed that the effect of 'the tyranny of the oligarchy which ruled from 1549 to 1553' was to bring to its nadir the situation of the sixteenth-century peasantry.[11]

It has been suggested, however, that the contrast between the

[1] A. F. Pollard, op. cit., 216. [2] C. Read, op. cit., 55. [3] Pp. I.iii–I.iv.
[4] A. F. Pollard, op. cit., 267–8. [5] 3 & 4 Edw. VI, c.3.
[6] 3 & 4 Edw. VI, c.23. [7] *Sermons*, 248.
[8] 3 & 4 Edw. VI, c.5. [9] Tytler, i, 271–2. [10] *Mr. Secretary Cecil*, 66.
[11] *The Agrarian Problem in the Sixteenth Century*, 372.

regime of Northumberland and that of Somerset has been painted too much in terms of black and white.[1] Between 1550, when he was released from the Tower, and 1552, when he was executed, certain of Somerset's former supporters, including Smith and Cecil, seem to have concluded—rightly or wrongly, and from whatever motive—that his zeal for the commonwealth was not free from a strong taint of personal ambition. It was under Somerset that the most savage statute for repression of vagabondage had been passed,[2] and under Northumberland that it was repealed.[3] By 1552 a return to the traditional policy of preservation of tillage had taken place.[4] Northumberland's pose as an enlightened Protestant reformer secured the support of those divines referred to earlier.

But for them the cup of bitterness was soon to be twice-filled. Realization of the real motives and nature of Northumberland's religious policy, and his ruthless political ambition and self-seeking greed, made them despair of socio-economic reform from such a quarter.[5] Their disillusionment forms the background of Crowley's *Philargyrie* and of the anonymous *Respublica* with its implied contrast with what was expected in the reign of Mary. But during that reign the religious issue was dominant, and some of the Commonwealth men, including Latimer, Ridley, Hooper and Bradford, suffered martyrdom for their doctrinal beliefs, while others, such as Hales and Ponet, were in exile.

The careers of Cecil and Smith suggest an important element of continuity—in terms of experience, of economic and financial acumen, and of a cool and cautious sympathy for Commonwealth ideals—through these troubled years into the reign of Elizabeth I. Cecil had served Somerset but, despite a period of imprisonment, had survived his fall with some dexterity, not being of the stuff of a martyr for the poor against the gentry. In September 1550 he became a principal secretary, and it was to him that William Lane, a London merchant, sent an extremely interesting analysis of the effects of coinage debasement upon our overseas trade in the following year.[6] When the shift back towards the normal

---

[1] M. W. Beresford, 'The Poll Tax and the Census of Sheep, 1549', 21–2.
[2] 1 Edw. VI, c.3. Below, 131.   [3] 3 & 4 Edw. VI, c.16.
[4] 5 & 6 Edw. VI, c.5.   [5] Below, 79–81.
[6] Below, 144–5. C. Read, op. cit., 67 and 474.

restraints upon enclosure took place in 1552 a projected bill for converting pasture into tillage was placed in his hands, and in Mary's Parliament of 1555 two bills designed to check enclosures were handed to Cecil after their first reading.[1]

Smith, while harder hit by the fall of Somerset than his friend Cecil, also survived the regimes of Northumberland and of Mary. Mrs Dewar believes that his continued interest in economic problems found expression in the composition, c. 1554, of the memorandum 'For the Understanding of the Exchange', formerly attributed to Sir Thomas Gresham.[2] As we shall see in a later setting, constructive concern with economic problems was certainly not lacking in the reign of Mary, but its expression in a context of Protestant religio-social idealism is clearly not to be expected!

Against the background of the *via media* religious settlement established by Elizabeth I, several of the ideals and projects of the Commonwealth men were echoed in the 'Considerations delivered to the Parliament 1559'.[3] Professor Bindoff describes this programme as 'conservatively, even reactionarily, paternalistic in outlook', questions its previous ascription to Cecil, and suggests the interest, and possible influence, of Sir Nicholas Bacon or even of Sir Thomas Smith, in economic policy at this time.[4] The selection of 1559 as a terminal date for this study must, then, inevitably appear somewhat arbitrary. Neither the concept of the commonwealth, nor all the ideas and projects associated with it, disappeared at this time. But the date is chosen as marking the end of the 'crisis period' which had given to discussion of the Commonwealth ideal particular urgency. The validity of the assumption that thereafter that urgency waned[5] may well be open to question. But there remains a very strong impression that when the aftermath of Ket's Rebellion and the fall of Somerset had been followed by the martyrdom of several outstanding Protestant social reformers in the reign of Mary the edge of idealism was blunted.

[1] Ibid., 80 and 109.
[2] M. Dewar, 'The Memorandum "For the Understanding of the Exchange" '.
[3] Printed in *T.E.D.*, i, 325-30.
[4] S. T. Bindoff, 'The Making of the Statute of Artificers', 80-1, 84, and 89-91.
[5] Below, 217-19.

CHAPTER FOUR

'Good Order and Obedience'

IT has been suggested that contemporary discussion of the commonwealth during the period 1529–59 is of particular interest because of the conjunction of critical developments during those decades.[1] While we are here concerned primarily with the evolution of ideas relating to the social and economic problems of the commonwealth and the responsibilities of government in that sphere, this cannot be isolated from developments in political and religious thought. Indeed, any attempt at over-rigid separation would be an anachronism, for good government was conceived of very much in economic and social terms, while social and economic relationships were often thought of as an aspect of religious morality. We shall therefore consider first the duty of obedience of the subject and the power of the prince—an issue deriving an immediate and urgent relevance from the fear that several of the specific ailments of the body politic might give rise to the greatest ill of all, rebellious strife between its members.

The maintenance of 'good order and obedience' was accepted as the essential basis of the very existence of the commonwealth. A royal proclamation of 1536 is typical in 'considering that there is nothing more odious to God nor more pernicious and hurtful to the commonwealth than the contempt and inobedience of people against their sovereign lord. . . .'[2] We may trace the emergence of a semi-divine attribute of kingship, in the anonymous 'Discourse addressed to the King' in 1532, describing 'Your Grace, in form of Son of Man' as head of the realm in quasi-mystical terms,[3] in the transition from the designation 'Your Grace' to that of 'Your Majesty', and then 'Your Sacred Majesty', and in Cromwell's 'Injunctions to the Clergy' to preach 'that the

---

[1] Above, 1–5.   [2] *Proclamations*, No. 168, 244–5.   [3] Above, 18–19.

43

king's power is within his dominion the highest potentate or power under god'.[1]

The stress on loyalty to the Crown as a fundamental principle becomes the more readily understandable when related not only to the arrogation by the Crown of headship of the Church, on the one hand, but also to the endemic memory and fear of rebellion and disorder on the other. The preamble to the statute of 1534 'for the establishment of the King's succession'[2] exemplifies the dread of a reversion to anarchy. Advocacy of the paramount duty of obedience to an anointed king derived, to a marked degree, from the stark realization that acceptance of authority was the guarantee of the stability of the commonwealth and its preservation against external attack or internal disintegration. We might therefore expect to find discussion of this topic related to empirical developments rather than to theoretical debates as to origins. And in fact the great bulk of publications in this field were occasioned by such events as Henry's break from Rome (with its implied dangers of internal or external opposition) and by specific rebellions caused by religious, social or economic factors.

In examining the views expressed we may, at the outset, usefully distinguish two major issues: the one, connected with religious developments, involving the question of the power of the king over the Church and hence, ultimately, the problem of the right of disobedience and even of resistance; the second, analysis of the duty of obedience to duly constituted authority as the only safeguard of social order. As we shall see, certain conclusions on these two themes differ, but the second takes its peculiar urgency not only from contemporary economic and social developments but also against the background of potential political and religious discord, while the two are further linked by the fear that religious radicalism will lead to social revolution—an issue to be considered in Chapter Five.

Sometimes the two themes might conveniently be fused, as in the spate of government-inspired propaganda of the 1530s. Typical is Starkey's *An Exhortation to the people, instructynge theym to Unitie and Obedience* (1536) which laments the discord in the country as undermining 'a quiet common weal', frightens its readers with the spectre of what has happened in Germany, and

[1] *Life and Letters*, ii, 26.   [2] 25 Hen. VIII, c.22.

counsels avoidance of extremes likely to lead to 'the ruin of all civil order'.[1] Starkey was joined in the literary offensive in which Cromwell engaged at the time of the Pilgrimage of Grace by Sir Richard Morison, whose work may show the influence of Machiavelli in its realism and its stress on the criterion of efficiency in the service of the ruler.[2] In *A Remedy For Sedition* (1536) he describes realms without laws as 'forests of wild beasts', for 'when every man will rule, who shall obey? [Therefore] an order, an order must be had, and a way found, that they rule that best can, they be ruled, that most it becometh so to be.' Rebels are reminded that since 'God maketh kings' it is their plain duty to obey their ruler and accept the officers of his choice.[3] This was the main theme of a work of more limited scope which he published in the same year: *A Lamentation in whiche is showed what Ruyne and destruction cometh of seditious rebellyon.* Here he turns the Lincolnshire rebels' advocacy of the principle of degree in their attack on 'low-born' royal ministers by pointing out that 'it far passeth Cobbler's craft' to discuss affairs of state. Fear of God and love of the commonwealth are joined with loyalty to the prince; 'obedience is the badge of a true christian man'.[4] In *An Invective Ayenste the great and detestable vice, treason* (1539), he argues that since God defended even Nero he is unlikely to abandon Henry VIII, his chosen king; for 'God hath joined with the majesty of a king, such a fear' that successful treason is unthinkable. Indeed, not being content that so few were punished after the late 'Northern insurrection' God has visited the north country with a pestilence, while loyal London has been spared.[5]

It is not surprising that Christopher Morris attributes to Tudor propagandists 'an almost hysterical attitude towards rebellion'.[6] This, and the fear which caused it, is strikingly expressed in 'An Exhortation Concerning Good Order and Obedience to Rulers

[1] Pp. a.iv.(b), 4, 32, 40 (ii), and 72–72 (ii).
[2] On Starkey: C. Morris, *Political Thought in England, Tyndale to Hooker*, 40–1, 51; J. W. Allen, *Political Thought in the Sixteenth Century*, 142–53; on Morison: C. Morris, op. cit., 64–7; F. Raab, *The English Face of Machiavelli*, 34–40; on both, W. G. Zeeveld, *Foundations of Tudor Policy*, and F. le V. Baumer, *The Tudor Theory of Kingship*.
[3] Pp. A.ii–A.ii. b, and B.iii.
[4] Pp. A.iii–A.iiii. b.
[5] Pp. a.v.(b)–a.vi.(b), D.iii.(b), and D.viii.(a) and (b).
[6] Op. cit., 72–4.

and Magistrates' in the first *Book of Homilies* of 1547. Without
obedience to kings and magistrates 'the goodly order of God:
without the which no house, no city, no commonwealth can
continue and endure' would collapse into 'Babylonical confusion
. . . no man shall keep his wife, children, and possessions in
quietness; all things shall be common; and there must needs follow
all mischief and utter destruction both of souls, bodies, goods, and
commonwealths'. Therefore 'it is not lawful for inferiors and
subjects in any case to resist the superior powers. . . . Christ taught
us plainly that even the wicked rulers have the power and
authority from God. . . . The violence and injury that is committed
against authority is committed against God, the common weal,
and the whole realm.'[1]

Among the writings evoked by the disorders of 1549 was Sir
John Cheke's *The hurt of sedition how greeuous it is to a common
wealth*. Examining the motives and effects of the actions both of
the rebels for religion in the West and of 'the other rabble of
Norfolk rebels' who would 'pretend a common-wealth', Cheke
reiterates the maxim that 'in countries some must rule, some must
obey', for as 'the child is bound to the private father . . . be we not
all bound to the common-wealth's father? . . . If the members of
our natural body all follow the head, shall not the members of the
political body all obey the king?' He derides those who would
shift their obedience 'from a king to a Ket', but 'who can persuade
when treason is above reason . . . and commotioners are better
than commissioners, and common woe is named commonwealth?'[2]

Nicholas Udall produced *An answer to the articles of the commoners of Devonshire and Cornwall*, whose rising he attributed to
'two sorts of beasts'—'idle, loitering ruffians that will not labour'
and 'rank Papists'. His arguments closely resemble those of
Morison and Cheke:

Were there never so many private griefs . . . yet if every private person should be officer for himself . . . as him lusteth: then where is a king
without whose power no common weal can long prosper? Where is
the force of laws without which no policy can flourish? Where is the
authority of magistrates without whom the public peace and tran-

---

[1] In *The Two Books of Homilies*, ed. J. Griffiths, 105–14.
[2] *The hurt of sedition*, in Holinshed, iii, 988–91.

quillity cannot be preserved? ... Take these things away and what surety or safety may any man be in?[1]

The point made by both Cheke and Udall, that by their disorders the rebels have themselves deepened the economic distress of which they complain,[2] is repeated in Cranmer's 'Sermon Concerning the Time of Rebellion'. Cranmer, incidentally, inverts the common argument that evil rulers are a scourge of God for wicked subjects: because 'we have suffered perjury, blasphemy, and adultery ... gluttony and drunkenness, vagabonds and idle persons', now there 'suddenly cometh upon us this scourge of sedition, the rod of God's wrath, to teach us how sore God hateth all wickedness, and is displeased with his ministers that wink thereat'. But his main theme is not that slack magistrates must expect the plague of God, but the folly of such as 'out of all rule and order ... say, gentlemen have ruled aforetime, and they will now rule another while. A goodly realm shall that be, that shall be ruled by them that never had experience to govern, nor cannot rule themselves.'[3]

In 1554, possibly in response to Wyatt's rebellion, to which it refers, appeared *An exhortation to all menne to take hede and beware of rebellion: wherein are set forth the causes that commonlye moue men to rebellion*, by John Christopherson, chaplain to Mary Tudor. The similarity of ideas and approach, and sometimes even of imagery,[4] to those of Cheke and Cranmer is striking. After reviewing the economic, personal, and religious causes of rebellion, Christopherson rejects the validity of them all because of the disastrous effects; subjects may not resist even an evil prince, for they may have deserved a 'naughty ruler'.[5]

John Heywood's *The Spider and the Flie*, published two years later, contained a significant reservation in accepting the duty to reverence

> All authority not against the great God,
> In spiders under him placed as potentates,[6]

---

[1] Printed in N. Pocock, *Troubles*, 146–7.
[2] *The hurt of sedition*, 988; *An answer*, 145–6.
[3] In *Miscellaneous Writings and Letters*, ii, 191–5.
[4] Cf. Christopherson, p. B.ii.(b), and Cheke, iii, 1004—image of the sore.
[5] Pp. A.iiii.(b), A.a.iiii.(b), D.vii.(b), and L.i.(b).
[6] See below, 91–2, for the plot of this allegory, in which the Spiders represent the gentry and the Flies the commons.

and stressing that it is the authority that is worshipped, not the person, especially if the latter 'lacketh honest use of authority'.[1] But even more important is the Ant's warning that

> Flies have had ever cause to mislike war most
> Whoever had the right, the flies the field lost.
> To one score spiders slain, flies twenty score,
> And much of their offspring lost for evermore.

The moral is that 'well framed flies will suffer and not resist'.

The Ant goes on to explain that even if the Flies should win, their own ruin would follow that of the Spiders, for

> When flies have killed spiders that stay the rude rout,
> Then fly against fly common cut-throat most stout;

momentarily the Fly army is checked by this spectre of anarchy and the dissolution of the whole social order.[2] The arguments of the allegory are laced with clear contemporary allusions: the Fly army, like Ket's camp on Mousehold Heath, is camped around the 'tree of reformation', while the events of 'time passed six year' serve to point the lesson for Flies that God's law enjoins

> You base inferiors to work your lord's will,
> Obey your superiors, be they good or ill.[3]

This assertion that all power is of God, this insistence on obedience to authority as the linch-pin of the whole order of society, runs right through the period studied, from Stephen Gardiner's *Oration of True Obedience* (1535), through the writings of his bitter opponent, Hooper, to John Aylmer's *An Harborowe For Faithfull and Trewe Subiectes* in 1559.[4] Indeed, it must be set within the context of contemporary European as well as of inherited traditional teachings—Luther's almost frantic reaction to the Peasants' Revolt typified the fear that any claim forcibly to resist lawful authority menaced the very existence of ordered society.[5] We may, however, pose certain questions. First, what of the responsibilities of the prince or magistrate towards the

---

[1] *Spider and Flie*, 171.   [2] Ibid., 238–9 and 242.   [3] Ibid., 222, 262–3.

[4] S. Gardiner, op. cit., in P. Janelle, *Obedience in Church and State, Three Political Tracts by Stephen Gardiner*, 89; J. Hooper, *Later Writings*, 103; and J. Aylmer, op. cit., pp. M.ii.b–M.4.

[5] J. W. Allen, *Political Thought in the Sixteenth Century*, 9, 16 and 19.

governed? Secondly, are there any circumstances which justify either passive disobedience or even active resistance in face of a ruler's commands?

With regard to the first, the subject's duty of obedience to the prince was, as we have seen,[1] increasingly balanced by emphsis on the positive duties of the ruler to his subjects. The king's moral responsibility to God and society, the obligation to govern well, in conformity with natural and divine law, were clearly stated: 'the law is God's and not the king's. The king is but a servant to execute the law of God, and not to rule after his own imagination.'[2] Princes hold power of God, and must see 'that they furnish the people with good laws, that both openly and privately they procure the weal, commodity and rest of their dominions'.[3] William Baldwin, in *A Myrroure For Magistrates* (1559), echoed Cranmer's point that 'when kings and chief rulers suffer their under officers to misuse their subjects, and will not hear nor remedy their people's wrongs when they complain, then suffereth God the Rebel to rage. . . . And therefore what soever prince desireth to live quietly without rebellion, must do his subjects right in all things.'[4]

Nonetheless, despite—or because of—this stress on the prince's moral responsibility to God, there was general agreement that 'though the magistrates be evil, and very tyrants against the commonwealth, and enemies to Christ's religion; yet the subjects must obey in all worldly things'.[5] (The qualification is significant.) Wicked rulers were a punishment for the sins of the people and must be suffered patiently, lest God 'so multiply the number of evil governors [that] the images of good magistrates may all be graven in one ring'.[6] Such ideas were commonplace, and in practical terms must certainly be related to fear of the floodgates that might open if the people took into their own hands 'the rod of correction'.[7] The humanist Starkey declared that 'the people in every common weal be rude and ignorant, having of them selves

---

[1] Above, 18–23.
[2] W. Tyndale, *The Obedience of a Christian Man*, in *Works*, i, 369.
[3] R. Taverner, *A Catechisme . . . of the Christen Religion*, 84–6.
[4] Pp. iii.(a), H.i.(a) and (b).
[5] T. Cranmer, *Miscellaneous Writings and Letters*, ii, 188.
[6] B. Gilpin, *Sermon . . . before King Edward VI*, 43–4.
[7] J. Rastell, *Gentleness and Nobility*, ll. 1006–11.

small light of judgement, but ever in simplicity, as sheep follow the herd, so follow they their masters'.[1] But sometimes the metaphor was harsher and 'the vulgar people', 'the rude multitude', emerged as 'a beast of many heads, which doeth nothing as reason and right judgement would'.[2]

One of the frankest expressions of this combined contempt for and fear of the multitude is William Thomas's 'Discourse' for Edward VI, 'whether it be better for a commonwealth, that the power be in the nobility or in the commonalty'. To these orders of society Thomas ascribes 'two repugnant desires: the one to rule, and the other not to be ruled'; the acceptance of anarchy as the natural aspiration of the commons, rather than participation in government (which would be unthinkable), is most significant. He concedes the danger of abuse of power by nobleman or magistrate, 'wherefore Machiavelli . . . determineth that in cases of extremity . . . the commotions of the people are necessary, to mitigate the excess of the great men's ambitions'— a familiar point now secularized! But if the commons should 'prevail once in power, all goeth to confusion: the estate is subverted, every man's property, his possession and goods are altered'. The wise monarch will therefore protect the commons from any tyranny of the nobles, but will keep them 'void of power'.

Neither do I mean, that for the dangers rehearsed, the commons should be so kept down, as the wretched commons of some other countries be. But I would their discipline and education should be such, that the only name of their prince should make them to tremble. . . . For if they have but so much liberty as to talk of the prince's causes, and of the reason of laws, at once they shew their desire not to be ruled: whereof groweth contempt, and consequently disobedience, the mother of all errors.[3]

But alongside such views we must now set the awkward questions put to princes by Tyndale in *The Practice of Prelates* (1530):

concerning that the hypocrites put you in fear of the rising of your commons against you, I answer; If ye fear your commons, so testify ye

[1] T. Starkey, *An Exhortation*, 34.
[2] J. L. Vives, *Introduction to wisedome*, trans. Sir R. Morison, pp. B.i and C.i.(b)–C.ii.   [3] Printed in Strype, ii (Part II), 372–7.

against yourselves that ye are tyrants. For if your consciences accused you not of evil doing, what need ye to fear your commons? For what commons was ever so evil that they rose against their heads for well doing?[1]

Bishop Hooper, in 1550, took this uncomfortable line of thought still further in describing the trouble and danger that could arise

among the unlearned and ungodly people by ignorance: for when they see such deformities and confusions rise and chance ... in kingdoms, courts, judicials, laws, governors, that more fancy private profit and singularity than the profit of the whole commonwealth ...; they suppose verily (for lack of knowledge in God's word) that all orders, policies, kingdoms, and dominions be no other thing than cruel tyranny and oppression of the poor; and also to have their beginning and original either of the devil, or of pride and covetousness of men.[2]

This passage is strikingly reminiscent of Raphael Hythlodaye's stark questioning of the whole basis of society:

therefore when I consider and weigh in my mind all these common wealths, which now a days any where do flourish, so god help me, I can perceive nothing but a certain conspiracy of rich men procuring their own commodities under the name and title of the common wealth. They invent and devise all means and crafts, first how to keep safely, without fear of losing, that they have unjustly gathered together, and next how to hire and abuse the work and labour of the poor for as little money as may be. These devices, when the rich men have decreed to be kept and observed under colour of the commonalty, that is to say, also of the poor people, then they be made laws.[3]

These passages bring into focus the endemic nightmare of Tudor England—that economic distress might express itself in rebellion against the existing social order. It is true that England suffered nothing to equal the Peasants' Revolt of 1524–5 in Germany, which cost perhaps 100,000 lives, but the nightmare became reality in 1536[4] and again in 1549. Even the sympathetic Hooper pictured how 'the poor man, partly provoked by necessity

---

[1] W. Tyndale, in *Works*, i, 388–9.   [2] J. Hooper, *Later Writings*, 78.
[3] Sir T. More, *Utopia*, 112.
[4] For the Pilgrimage of Grace was, for the commons, motivated predominantly by economic and social grievances; see A. G. Dickens, 'Secular and Religious Motivation in the Pilgrimage of Grace', and R. R. Reid, *The King's Council in the North*, 113–44.

and need, and partly of unchristian hatred and disdain he hath at his neighbour's wealth and prosperity, conspireth, worketh, provoketh, and desireth by all means to oppress and rob his richer neighbour', to oppose 'magistrates and superior powers, take away and usurp every man's goods, he careth not how'.[1]

While insurrection itself was never condoned, recognition of the existence of genuine social and economic distress as a potential or actual cause of revolt, and a willingness at least to understand the actions of those provoked beyond endurance, are clearly evidenced. A letter to the emperor in July 1548 speaks of growing sympathy for the 'just cause' of the peasants who 'say that the violent usurpation of their rights committed by the nobles compels them to seek some remedy for the extreme need in which they now are, having no pastures for their cattle and sheep as they once had, and many being reduced to a diet of bread and water, having tasted neither flesh nor fish for a long time past'; it is only too likely that 'the common people of the towns, who can no longer bear the dearness of food stuffs . . . will rise in revolt as well as the peasants'.[2]

Latimer, alluding to Ket's rebellion, made the plea: 'for God's love restore their sufficient unto them, and search no more what is the cause of rebellion'.[3] Hales distinguished three 'sundry causes' of the risings: 'Some be papists, and would have again their old popery. Some be Anabaptists and libertines, and would have all things common. And the third be certain poor men that seek to have again their revenues that have been by power taken from them, and to be relieved of the great dearth and prices of victual.'[4] The causes diagnosed are significant: religious reaction; religio-social extremism; and plain economic distress, which clearly enlists Hales's sympathies.

An anonymous work addressed to Somerset in 1549, pointing to unemployment, poverty and hunger as inevitably occasioning disorder, cites the East Anglian troubles of 1526[5] as proving that 'there cannot a greater occasion be given to make tumult and Insurrection than suddenly to drive a great tumult together out of

---

[1] *Later Writings*, 97.

[2] Admittedly, a highly-coloured account for foreign consumption; printed in R. L. Palmer, *English Social History in the Making. The Tudor Revolution*, 33–4.

[3] *Sermons*, 249.   [4] 'Defence', in *Discourse*, p. lvii.   [5] Below, 108.

their work into Idleness'. For 'surely there is nothing that will
sooner move the people unto Sedition than the dearth of victual.
What fair means or what threatening, what strait Laws or what
weapons can pacify or keep quiet the hungry multitude . . . what
Faith and allegiance will those men observe towards their prince
and governor which have their children Famished at home for
want of meat.'[1]

Crowley's *The Way to Wealth, wherein is plainly taught a most
present Remedy for Sedicion* (1551) contains an impassioned statement of the pressures that drove men to resistance, and of the
bitterness of the poor towards great farmers, graziers, rich
butchers, lawyers, merchants, gentlemen, and

men that have no name because they are doers in all things that any
gain hangeth upon. Men without conscience. Men utterly void of God's
fear. Yea, men that live as though there were no God at all! Men that
would have all in their own hands; men that would be alone on the
earth . . . Cormorants, greedy gulls; yea, men that would eat up men,
women & children, are the causes of Sedition!

Neither custom nor law can prevent them from enforcing
extortionate rents and fines, enclosing commons, taking lands and
houses.

Very need therefore constraineth us to stand up against them! In the
country we can not tarry, but we must be their slaves and labour till
our hearts burst, and then they must have all. And to go to the cities we
have no hope, for there we hear that these insatiable beasts have all in
their hands [and levy double and treble rents]. . . . No remedy therefore, we must needs fight it out, or else be brought to the like slavery
that the French men are in! These idle bellies will devour all that we
shall get by our sore labour in our youth, and when we shall be old
and impotent, then shall we [be] driven to beg. . . . Better it were therefore, for us to die like men, than after so great misery in youth to die
more miserably in age.[2]

But 'if I should demand of the greedy cormorants what they
think should be the cause of Sedition, they would say:

The peasant knaves be too wealthy, provender pricketh them! They
know not them selves, they know no obedience, they regard no laws,

---

[1] *Policies to reduce this realme of England vnto a prosperus wealthe and estate*, in
T.E.D., iii, 325, 335–6.
[2] *Works*, 132–3. See More's *Utopia*, 112, for a striking similarity.

they would have no gentlemen, . . . they would have all things common! . . . But as they like their fare at the breakfast they had this last summer [an allusion to the repression of the risings of 1549] so let them do again. . . . We will teach them to know their betters. And because they would have all common, we will leave them nothing. And if they once stir again, or do but once cluster together, we will hang them at their own doors![1]

Against such a background of economic distress and mutual hatred, and in the absence of good leadership and example from gentry and spiritualty, 'it cannot much be marvelled, if the simple and ignorant people, by some wicked heads and firebrands of hell, be sometimes seduced to rebel against their prince and lawful magistrates'.[2] Gilpin's condemnation of those who deliberately promoted strife was echoed by Christopherson, who described their ostensible aims 'to deliver the poor commons from oppression, to restore them to their old liberties, to cause the farms that be enhanced, to be let for the old rent, and the common pastures, that be taken in by gentlemen, to be laid open again' as but 'goodly painted words to blind the simple people'.[3] Cranmer indeed asserted that

the great part of them that be the chief stirrers in these insurrections be ruffians and sturdy idle fellows, which be the causes of their own poverty, commonly resorting to tippling and to alehouses, much drinking and little working, much spending and little getting; and yet will they be clad gorgeously, fare daintiously, and lie softly. . . . These fellows make all this hurly-burly in one place, then they run to another.[4]

This tendency to ascribe the guilt of insurrection itself to the spectre of the professional agitator was reflected in governmental action. The troubles of 1549 evoked several proclamations against 'renegades, tale-tellers, and seditious persons . . . running and posting from place to place' stirring up riots under pretence that 'they seek to redress the commonwealth'.[5] Some offenders were set in the pillory, with the words 'Movers of Sedition and Spreaders

---

[1] Ibid., 142–3.
[2] B. Gilpin, *Sermon . . . before King Edward VI*, 27.
[3] *An exhortation*, pp. B.iiii.a and b.
[4] *Miscellaneous Writings and Letters*, ii, 194.
[5] *Proclamations*, No. 337 (8 July 1549), 469–70; see also No. 341 (16 July 1549), 475–6.

of False Rumours' placarded on their backs, while others had their ears cut off.[1] A letter of Sir Thomas Smith to Cecil, in July of that year, contains a project for crushing any such danger at the outset by organizing the gentlemen and head yeomen in every shire so that they be able 'where they hear tell of any evil rule, or beginning of stir to be, there suddenly in the night to come with a sixty or a hundred horse, and take and lead away the stirrers before any more company be come unto them'.[2] The idea has a close, and interesting, resemblance to one put forward in the *Discourse of the Common Weal.* The Knight, discussing the danger of disorder from unemployed industrial workers, recounts that 'in fraunce they have divers bands of men of arms, in divers places of the realm, to repress such tumults quickly . . . if we had the like here, we might be bold to have as many artificers as they have'. But both Husbandman and Merchant reject this with horror, the latter remarking that 'the stomachs of Englishmen would never bear that, to suffer such injury and Reproach' as the French peasants, while the Doctor 'would not have a small sore cured with a greater grief'.[3]

A letter to the emperor on 21 April 1551 described how

five or six nights ago a gathering of ruffians and serving men was discovered in London, whose object was to excite the people to revolt. . . . At the same time, some peasants at different places thirty or forty miles away from London had formed a project to get together a force of 10,000 or 12,000 to finish off all the gentry of the neighbourhood, and march to London to the assistance of the people of that city. . . . There are plenty of folk ready to rise . . . for they are saying openly that they can abide privation no longer and had rather die than live in such a plight.[4]

The acute concern of government was evidenced in the appearance, a week later, of a proclamation 'Enforcing Statutes against Vagabonds, Rumor Mongers, Players, Unlicensed Printers, etc.' This deplored the 'great number of idle persons and masterless men' in London, and ordered them to leave and make for their last domicile, travelling at least eight miles per day, in groups of

---

[1] F. Aydelotte, *Elizabethan Rogues and Vagabonds,* 54 and 63; R. L. Palmer, *English Social History,* 78–9.　　　　[2] Printed in Tytler, i, 186–7.
[3] *Discourse,* pp. 94–5.　　　　[4] R. L. Palmer, op. cit., 79–80, also 80–1.

not more than four. It also forbade all tales or rumours touching king, council, magistrates or officers.[1]

In these circumstances humanitarian sympathy with those driven by misery to revolt tended inevitably to be swamped by the fear that—apart from its innate illegality—any uprising would in practice give free rein to the more desperate elements of the population and to the nightmarish aspirations of those who would 'have all in common'. Such fears are very clearly expressed in the works of More. In *Utopia* Hythlodaye's argument in favour of the abolition of private property receives the answer that

men shall never there live wealthily, where all things be common. For how can there be abundance of goods, or of any thing, where every man withdraweth his hand from labour? Whom the regard of his own gains driveth not to work, but the hope that he hath in other men's travails maketh him slothful. Then when they be pricked with poverty, and yet no man can by any law or right defend that for his own, which he hath gotten with the labour of his own hands, shall not there of necessity be continual sedition and bloodshed? Specially the authority and reverence of magistrates being taken away, which, what place it may have with such men among whom there is no difference, I cannot devise.[2]

In *The supplicacion of soules* . . . *Agaynst the supplicacion of beggars* (1529), a work of a rather less detached and academic character, More paints a frightening picture of the danger from those who behave

with contempt of God and all good men, and obstinate rebellious mind against all laws, rule, and governance, with arrogant presumption to meddle with every man's substance, with every man's land, and every man's matter nothing pertaining to them. . . . For they shall gather to-gether at last, and assemble themselves in plumps and in great routs, and from asking fall to the taking of their alms themselves, and under pretext of reformation . . . shall assay to make new division of every man's land and substance, never ceasing if ye suffer them, till they make all beggars as they be themself, and at last bring all the realm to ruin, and this not without butchery and foul bloody hands.[3]

The claim to have all in common was condemned as the cause and excuse of idleness, and as threatening not only property

---

[1] *Proclamations*, No. 371 (28 April 1551), 514–18.   [2] *Utopia*, 44–5.
[3] In *The workes of Sir Thomas More Knyght*, 313.

rights but the whole concept of due order and degree. Elyot argued that 'where all thing is common, there lacketh order; and where order lacketh, there all thing is odious and uncomely',[1] while Cheke asked the rebels of 1549: 'Would ye have all alike rich? That is the overthrow of labour, and utter decay of work in this realm. For who will labour more, if when he hath gotten more, the idle shall by lust without right take what him lust from him, under pretence of equality with him. This is the bringing in of idleness, which destroyeth the common-wealth.'[2]

Perhaps the fullest and frankest analysis of those forces that were felt to threaten the bases of society is that of Morison in *A Remedy For Sedition*. He concedes that poverty is an undoubted cause of disorder, that 'it can not be chosen, but men will steal, though they be hanged, except they may live without stealing'. But those who identify poverty as the sole cause of crime and rebellion are over-simplifying. The root of poverty must be sought in lack of education, of training and of honest crafts, and in idleness, which may 'provoke men, or things like men, to rebellion'.[3] Even this does not probe deeply enough. There remains what he characterized in *A Lamentation* as 'some other wild worm, that would not suffer mad brains to be at rest':[4] the deep-seated jealousy of 'the worser sort' of those who were their superiors in possession or degree.

The thesis that an attack upon property rights and due obedience to superiors would subvert the foundations of civilized society, and recoil upon the heads of those who made it, is a major theme in the *Remedy*. 'How can there be any common wealth', asks Morison, 'where he that is wealthiest, is most like to come to woe? Who can be rich, where he that is richest is in most danger of poverty? . . . We love to be deceived, we imagine a certain common wealth in word and in outward appearance, which if we baptize right . . . we must needs call a common woe. We think it is very evil, that so many of us be poor, we think it were a good world, if we were all rich.' But what would such equality entail?

I as good as he, why goeth he before, I behind? I as rich as he, what needeth me to labour? The maid as proud as her dame, who milketh

<hr />

[1] *The Governour*, i, 7.   [2] *The hurt of sedition*, in Holinshed, iii, 990.
[3] Pp. D.ii–D.ii.b, and E.iii.b.   [4] P. B.iiii.b.

the cow? ... To my purpose, Lords must be lords, commons must be commons, every man accepting his degree, every man content to have that, that he lawfully may come by. We must, if we purpose ever to come to wealth, which we oft lose in wrong seeking for it, all agree, that the laws have their place. ... Cheese is no medicine to drive away rats: neither sedition a means to make men wealthy. What end of misery shall there be where no man weareth rich, but an other is made a beggar? ... What end of robbing and spoiling shall there be, if the poor may evermore rob the rich? If the stronger may pull from the weaker? Must not you abide the same law, that you make your self? Must not you, when you have spoiled them that are rich, and so made your selves wealthy, suffer that they now being poor, spoil you rich? And then must not ye be poor again?[1]

These last few pages point to a harsh practical reason why, although degrees of understanding and sympathy might vary, no writer would countenance the attempted redress of social and economic grievances by insurrection: it was the fear of a peasant jacquerie. But it is fair to observe also the validity of the distinction made between the voicing of a legitimate protest and taking the law into one's own hands. Wrongful actions by rulers or gentry were indeed censured as violating accepted ideals of social obligation, but this did not give the lower orders of society the right to usurp power which was not theirs.

Hales warned those aggrieved by enclosures not to 'go about to take upon you to be executors of the statutes; to cut up men's hedges, and to put down their enclosures or by any ways to hurt them. For this is not your office to do. ... Be ye not breakers of the law, while ye go about to have vices reformed by the law.'[2] Ket and his followers, while ignoring this advice, were at great pains to profess to be acting in the king's name. In their Petition they 'pray your grace to give licence and authority ... to such commissioners as your poor commons hath chosen, or to as many of them as your majesty and your council shall appoint and think meet' to enforce the laws which existing officers neglect,[3] while a 'Commission' of 5 August refers to its signatories, R. Kett and T. Aldrich, as 'commissioners of the ... King's Great Camp at

---

[1] Pp. A.ii–A.iii.b, and B.iv–B.iv.b.
[2] J. Hales, 'Charges', in Strype, ii (Part II), 364.
[3] Printed in F. W. Russell, *Kett's Rebellion in Norfolk*, 55.

Moushold'.[1] But Cheke's scornful word-play on 'commotioners' and 'commissioners' typifies the reaction of authority.

Rebellion against economic and social injustice might then be understood but never condoned. Those whose greed and oppression provoked insurrection were censured, but so too were the rebels themselves because, in every sense, their action upset the fundamental order of the body politic. In the last analysis, the offences of both sides stood condemned by reference to the same organic ideal of society. In order to find any attempt at justification of disobedience or active resistance we must turn to an issue still generally held to transcend and comprehend all economic, social and political considerations: that of religious truth. Rebellion against the prince was normally denounced as breaking a fundamental assumption of society, but what if the prince himself should attempt to subvert the truths upon which society itself was built? Despite contemporary adulation of the monarch the reservation of the right to disobey, or even to resist, his commands if these were against 'the law of God' always lay beneath the surface, and both its general quiescence and its occasional obtrusion must be related more to circumstance than to theory.

Thus while the exiled Pole advanced a belief in limited obedience,[2] the early English Protestants preached non-resistance. Tyndale's dying prayer that the king's eyes should be opened is symbolic: the anointed ruler might not be resisted, but neither must his commands against God's law be obeyed, for the king is but the servant of that law.[3] In the context of European discussion of this issue it is instructive to recall Luther's recognition that 'no Christian authority is valid when exercised contrary to Christ'.[4] For Luther did not teach 'an umitigated doctrine of non-resistance. . . . The duty of the subject is not really a duty owed to the magistrate: it is a duty to God.'[5] It has been observed that Tyndale's attitude should most properly be described as one of 'Passive Disobedience',[6] and certainly the troubled middle years of the century were to validate the distinction. Hooper stated

[1] Ibid., 107.
[2] W. G. Zeeveld, *Foundations of Tudor Policy*, 107.
[3] Above, 49.
[4] *Appeal to the Ruling Class of German Nationality*, in Woolf, i, 124.
[5] J. W. Allen, *Political Thought in the Sixteenth Century*, 19–23.
[6] C. Morris, *Political Thought in England. Tyndale to Hooker*, 38.

explicitly that 'if the higher powers command anything contrary to God's word, they should not be obeyed . . . [but] without all violence, force and rebellion'.[1] Latimer agreed that 'I may refuse to obey with a good conscience yet for all that I may not rise up against the magistrates, nor make any uproar; for if I do so, I sin damnably . . . yet I may not obey their wicked laws to do them.'[2]

While Latimer, Hooper and Cranmer suffered martyrdom for their principles, Bishop Ponet fled into exile where he wrote *A Shorte Treatise of politike power, and of the true Obedience which subjectes owe to kynges and other ciuile Gouernours* (1556). This went much further than any source thus far considered in advocating non-obedience to certain commands of an unjust prince; indeed Ponet's arguments were based on such broad constitutional principles that he has been described as a precursor of Locke.[3] Ponet considers 'Politike power' as established by God, and its exercise as subject to 'the law of nature'. If God is forsaken tyranny follows, through rulers 'that make unrighteous laws, and devise things which be too hard to be kept, whereby the poor are oppressed on every side'. A 'mixed state' of government is best, and any claim to an 'absolute power' is an 'usurpation', since 'Kings, princes, and other politic Governors be subject to God's laws, and the positive laws of their countries'. But if laws are the sinews of the body politic, extremes of racking or of shrinking must be eschewed, 'for too much maketh the governors to forget their vocation, and to usurp upon their subjects: too little breedeth a licentious liberty and maketh the people to forget their duty'. These two extremes are seen in the Papists and the Anabaptists: 'for the anabaptists mistake christian liberty, thinking that men may live without sin, and forget the fall. . . . And the papists neither consider the degrees of powers, nor over what things civil power hath authority, nor yet how far subjects ought to obey their governors.'[4]

Since rulers may err, 'men ought to have more respect to their country, than to their prince: to the common wealth, than to any one person. For the country and common wealth is a degree above

---

[1] *Later Writings*, 109.   [2] *Sermons* (Everyman), 311.
[3] C. Morris, op. cit., 146–7, and 151–2.
[4] Pp. A.i–A.viii.b, B.iii–C.vi.b, C.viii–C.viii.b.

the king.' While he ascribes the origin of private property to the fall, and rebuts the naïve Anabaptist belief that 'all things ought to be common', Ponet points out that since the right to property is coupled with the duty of charity, rapacious princes compare unfavourably with 'the common Anabaptists' who 'not only take other men's goods as common, but are content to let their own also be common, which hath some smack of Charity'. The monarch who taxes unjustly, debases the coinage, or seizes his subjects' property forgets that he 'is but God's minister or steward. . . . The prince's watch ought to defend the poor man's house, his labour the subject's ease, . . . his trouble the subject's quietness.'[1]

Having prepared the ground Ponet now puts the question: 'Whether It Be lawful to depose an evil governor, and kill a tyrant.' He replies that 'Kings, Princes and governors have their authority of the people', that 'all laws do agree, that men may revoke their proxies and letters of Attorney' when abused, that 'Kings, Princes and other governors, albeit they are the heads of a politic body, yet they are not the whole body. And though they be the chief members, yet they are but members: neither are the people ordained for them, but they are ordained for the people.' Hence he does not shrink from invoking in a novel context the familiar point that it is a law of nature to cut away an incurable member lest it destroy the whole body politic, since 'common wealths and realms may live, when the head is cut off, and may put on a new head'.[2]

Ponet's views are of obvious relevance not only to the immediate question of obedience seen in relation to the religious crisis, but also to the wider theme of the nature of the social and economic obligations of government in the commonwealth. A comparison with Morison is instructive. Whereas the latter accepts complete and unquestioning obedience to authority as the only safeguard of existing liberties and property rights against the arbitrary action of the 'monster with many heads', Ponet would make the ruler's accordance of respect for such individual rights one condition of the continuance of his power. In this respect perhaps Morison was to Ponet as Hobbes to Locke. But finally,

[1] Ibid., pp. D.vi, E.viii–E.viii.b, and F.i–F.viii.
[2] Ibid., pp. D.vi and G.i.b–G.vi.b.

despite his condemnation of injustice and the low ebb of contemporary morality, Ponet deplores the existence of 'inward grudge, and secret malice between the members, that is, the Nobility and Commons', and counsels avoidance of the attempts of traitorous priests to rouse the commons against lords and gentry.[1]

Christopher Goodman, Knox's fellow-exile in Geneva, displays obvious affinities of thought with Ponet in his *How Superior Powers Oght to be Obeyd* (1558). He attacks 'the preaching of unlawful obedience and yielding to ungodly Rulers', for 'obedience against God is disobedience'. The commons must not follow their superiors if these neglect their obvious duty, for 'it appertaineth not only to the Magistrates and all other inferior officers to see that their Princes be subject to God's Laws, but to the common people also'. Therefore the people 'ought not to suffer all power and liberty to be taken from them, and thereby to become brute beasts, without judgement and reason, thinking all things lawful, which their Rulers do', and they 'may lawfully punish their Magistrates as private persons transgressing the Lord's precepts'.[2]

It is, then, most significant when he goes on to chide the populace with their readiness 'to arm your selves against your superiors, to defend your commons and earthly commodities with holden from you, by the greedy desire of new upstart gentlemen', and their reluctance to do so to defend 'spiritual possession'. When God entrusts the sword to the people's hands they must beware of pursuing private aims or gain in their resistance to authority. Finally, when governors 'be so shamefully corrupted, and so mindless of their charge and office, that neither the Citizens can be comforted, nor succoured by their Mayors, Sheriffs, and Aldermen: neither the poor Townsmen and Tenants by their Justices and Landlords, but all given over as it were to Satan, and to serve the lusts of their chief Rulers, care not whether the poor people sink or swim', then the people must turn to God for help, remembering that 'tyrants can go no farther than God permitteth'.[3]

Thus, despite the revolutionary implications of what they wrote in regard to the subject's right to rebel on religio-political

---

[1] Ibid., pp. K.vii–L.i.   [2] C. Goodman, op. cit., 28, 43, 142, 148 and 175.
[3] Pp. 176–7, 197, and 215–18.

grounds, both Ponet and Goodman seem very chary of being interpreted as justifying revolt against economic abuses. Indeed, both Catholic and Protestant propagandists accused their opponents of exploiting the people's sense of grievance in this sphere.[1] Despite the circumstances of the accession to the throne of Mary Tudor, Christopherson rather ungratefully condemned 'the rebels of Norfolk' and identified them with those 'blindly persuaded that all men's goods ought to be common'. As to poor men 'oppressed with taxes, and tributes, with polling and pilling, with rents raised, and with pastures enclosed: such perhaps have cause to complain, but no cause at all to make rebellion'. Those who rise because they say they can endure such poverty no longer 'have forgotten God'.[2]

On this, all were agreed. Becon, while teaching that the magistrate must not be obeyed if he gave orders contrary to God's word,[3] and while fully conscious of the justice of the poor's complaints, still deplored the events of 1549: 'The inferior members to envy the principal parts of the body! . . . The servant to rule the master, the inferior to rise against his sovereign, the subject to disobey his governor! . . . The brainsick, yea rather the brainless head to attempt redress of matters in a commonweal, unsent, uncalled! O preposterous order!'[4] Despite his obvious sympathy with the commons and readiness to state their case, even Crowley states plainly in the last resort that 'the devil should never have persuaded thee that thou mightest revenge thine own wrong! . . . to revenge wrongs is, in a subject, to take and usurp the office of a king, and consequently, the office of God'.[5] Indeed, not least of the crimes of the exploiter and oppressor is to have driven his victims into the sin of rebellion.[6] The commons should 'commit their cause to God & quiet them selves in their vocation, being contented with oppression, if God's will be so; then shall ye be sure that God will fight for them'.[7]

In sum, despite the occasional recognition of a possible right to disobey or, less frequently, even to resist a ruler on religious grounds, mid-Tudor England believed revolt against economic or

---

[1] Above, J. Christopherson, 54, and J. Ponet, 62.
[2] *An exhortation*, pp. B.viii–B.viii.b, C.v, and D.v.
[3] *Catechism*, 90 and 327.   [4] *Fortress of the Faithful*, 593–4.
[5] *Works*, 134.   [6] Ibid., 117–18.   [7] Ibid., 149.

social wrongs to be both illegal and damnable. It may be contended that even in writers as radical and forward-looking as Ponet and Goodman a consideration of their reasons for advocating the one type of resistance but rejecting the other reveals the enduring medieval basis of their thought. For action against a monarch who endeavoured to subvert religious truth, and patient sufferance of economic distress without revolt against one's superiors, were both commended as leading to the fulfilment of God's purpose for society. The subordination of economic to religious considerations which this implies is typical of the medieval scale of values.

The eagerness to charge one's religious opponents with fomenting social disturbance testifies to the common dread among the well-to-do of what might happen if the lower orders took the bit between the teeth. It has been shrewdly observed that 'the attempts at revolution, when not stirred from without, were always conservative in purpose and for the most part aimed against new measures or conditions'.[1] But although the declared aims of the rebels, in regard to specific social or economic issues, might indeed be conservative or even reactionary, the very action of banding together and taking up arms against their superiors threatened both the obvious self-interest of the propertied classes and the inherited medieval belief in due order and degree symbolized in the concept of the body politic. The most radical of Commonwealth idealists, savagely though he might attack the conduct of the noble, the magistrate, the landowner, the merchant, the prelate and the priest, never sought to undermine the structure of society or to achieve social and economic reform by means of revolution.

[1] L. Einstein, *Tudor Ideals*, 96.

CHAPTER FIVE

The Voice of Religion

IN approaching the relationship between religious developments and the social and economic aspects of the commonwealth, two main lines of inquiry may be suggested. First, the nature of any relationship between Protestantism and social and economic change; secondly, the effects, both empirical and as reflected in social theory, of the Crown's administrative take-over of the Church in England—as distinct from any theological innovation. The first has itself two different aspects. The suggested causal connection between doctrinal changes and the development of economic rationalism[1] has provided modern historians with a wide and fiercely-contended field of debate. Contemporaries were more immediately concerned with the narrower, but frighteningly deeper, issue of the alleged relationship between religious innovation and the spectre of revolt inspired by economic grievances.

The significance of the pulpit in Tudor England, in the formation and leadership of public opinion and in the full and frank expression of social criticism, derived directly from the medieval tradition.[2] After the break from Rome its influence was clearly realized by government and utilized—particularly in the Paul's Cross sermons[3]—for propaganda purposes in the religio-political and social and economic spheres. As we shall see, authority was equally sensitive to the dangerous potentialities of religious oratory. Apart from direct oral influence, preaching in print had great impact upon the literate section of the population, the works of Becon apparently being especially popular.[4]

Religious moralizing was also closely linked with another great

---

[1] M. Weber, *The Protestant Ethic and the Spirit of Capitalism*, 26.
[2] G. R. Owst, *Literature and Pulpit in Medieval England*, 98–100, and 236.
[3] M. Maclure, *The Paul's Cross Sermons. 1534–1642*, 13–14, and 20.
[4] J. Ayre, Introduction to T. Becon, *Early Works*, p. xv.

mirror of, and influence upon, public opinion: dramatic representation. As the interlude evolved from the medieval morality the issues portrayed became increasingly topical and secular, but the moral undertone remained; responsiveness to public opinion found expression in a dramatization of popular preaching.[1] Of this type were John Skelton's *Magnificence*, the lost play of 'Lord Governance and Lady Public-Weal', by John Roo,[2] and the anonymous *Respublica* and *A Newe Interlude of Impacyente pouerte*. The taste for moralizing expressed itself not only in the printing of these dramatic productions but also in many of the pamphlets of the time which resembled religious sermons. Indeed, the closeness of the connection between the spoken and the printed word may well go far to explain the strain of at-first-sight surprising scurrility which runs through the works of writers as diverse as More, Tyndale, Barlow, Fish, Bale and Christopherson.

Despite his allegedly dominant influence in both expression and admonition of public opinion, the Tudor preacher himself was far from happy as to reception of his message. Becon alluded glumly to those who 'if they have a ghostly or learned curate, . . . him do they hate, they wish the pulpit a coal-pit. They think it a hundred year, if he preacheth but half an hour.'[3] (The customary length of a Paul's Cross sermon was apparently two hours.[4]) This reluctance was not confined to the common sort: Bernard Gilpin complained bitterly, in 1552, that 'I am come this day to preach to the king, and to those which be in authority under him. I am very sorry they should be absent. I am the more sorry for that other preachers before me complain much of their absence. . . . I will speak to their seats, as if they were present.'[5]

Tyndale, depicting the unpopularity of the honest preacher, remarked that 'if we preached not against pride, covetousness, lechery, extortion, usury, simony, and against the evil living both of the spiritualty, as well as of the temporalty, and against inclosing of parks, raising of rents and fines, and of the carrying of wool out of the realm, we might endure long enough'.[6] Latimer, perhaps best-known of all who preached on social and economic

---

[1] G. R. Owst, op. cit., 478; also W. Farnham, *The Medieval Heritage of Elizabethan Tragedy*, 209 and 246; and C. F. T. Brooke, *The Tudor Drama*, 69–71.
[2] See E. Hall, *Chronicle*, 719.   [3] *Early Works*, 39.
[4] M. Maclure, op. cit., 8.   [5] *Sermon . . . before King Edward VI*, 20.
[6] *Works*, i, 284.

issues, concluded despairingly: 'Let the preacher preach till his tongue be worn to the stumps, nothing is amended.'[1] True, his preaching on the theme of covetousness in high places, and commendation of restitution as well as contrition, caused such remorse in one of his hearers that repayment of the sums embezzled was actually made through Latimer, the penitent being, surprisingly, none other than John Bradford.[2] But other listeners were made of sterner stuff. Ridley described how the preachers' exhortations were 'spurned privily' even by the 'greatest magistrates', while 'as for Latimer, Lever, Bradford, and Knox, their tongues were so sharp, they ripped in so deep in their galled backs, to have purged them . . . of insatiable covetousness . . . of intolerable ambition and pride, of ungodly loathsomeness to hear poor men's causes, and to hear God's word, that these men, of all other, these magistrates then could never abide'.[3]

Resentment of the criticisms expressed was made sharper by fear as to the conclusions which might be drawn from them by a discontented populace—a fear which led to the description of Latimer as 'a seditious fellow'.[4] For while the preachers' expression of opinion upon social and economic issues was no new phenomenon, it was evidently of heightened importance during an age which was characterized by innovation in both doctrinal and administrative aspects of religion, on the one hand, and by an accelerated process of economic and social change, on the other. In regard to our first main theme, the relationship between religious developments and the evolution of ideas on social and economic affairs, the connection predicated, and dreaded, by many contemporaries was that religious innovation would lead to social revolution. More's refusal to translate *Utopia* into English may symbolize the fear that ideas literally interpreted against a background of social distress could become the slogans of rebellion. For close to the surface lay the disquieting thought expunged at publication from the manuscript copy of Morison's *Remedy for Sedition*: 'In time of peace, be not all men almost at war with them that be rich?'[5]

[1] *Sermons*, 101.
[2] T. Sampson, Introduction to *The Writings of John Bradford*, 32–3; H. Latimer, *Sermons* (Everyman), 206; H. S. Darby, *Hugh Latimer*, 179.
[3] *The Works of Nicholas Ridley*, 58–9.   [4] *Sermons*, 134.
[5] W. G. Zeeveld, *Foundations of Tudor Policy*, 216.

The fourteenth century had seen an apparently innocuous theme such as 'Adam dalf and Eve span' become a popular watchword of revolution.[1] So, now, statements such as that of Tyndale, that 'among Christian men, love maketh all things common; every man is another's debtor, and every man is bound . . . to supply his neighbour's lack of that wherewith God hath endowed him',[2] were clearly open to misinterpretation. A list of heresies proscribed in 1530, in which the work of Tyndale and of Simon Fish is specifically attacked, includes the following: 'Every man is lord of another man's good.' 'He that is rich, and liveth of his rents, may not use nor spend his goods as he will, but thy goods belong as well unto the poor as to thee.' 'God hath not given riches to the rich men for to boast and brag therewith . . . but to the intent they should be servants to all the world.' 'A man shall be reproved for no other thing at the day of judgement, but for forgetting the poor.'

Although rather bluntly phrased, these appear to be expressions of the wholly traditional concept of stewardship in the use of one's goods, with especial emphasis on the duty of charity. But they were obviously considered far too susceptible to misinterpretation, the more understandably so in view of the unfortunate juxtaposition of the assertion that: 'Four manner of people, or four parts of people, liveth and are fed by one part, that is to say, by citizens, artificers; and husbandmen which laboureth and getteth their own expenses, and the expenses of the other four parts, of priests, monks, of lord councillors, old people and children; and of men of war, thieves, murderers, ruffians, common women, etc. that getteth nothing but spendeth all.'[3]

But apart from any question of misunderstanding or deliberate distortion of the expression of traditional Christian ethics by misguided sections of the populace or, worse still, by those who deliberately incited them to revolt, Protestantism was subject to the charge that it inevitably led to, or even consciously sought, social upheaval. The fear of a correlation between religious heresy and ideas subversive of the existing political and social

---

[1] G. R. Owst, *Literature and Pulpit in Medieval England*, 236, 291–4.
[2] *Works*, i, 131.
[3] 'A publick instrument made . . . in an assembly of the archbishop of Canterbury . . .' Printed in D. Wilkins, *Concilia Magnae Britanniae et Hiberniae*, iii, 727–32.

order was not new. It derived directly from the belief of the medieval church that its doctrines were so inextricably interwoven with the whole social order that the heretical beliefs that fretted at the one would inevitably rend the whole fabric of the other.[1]

In the late fourteenth and early fifteenth centuries Lollardy had been equated with sedition since some, at least, of its adherents believed that 'all goods should be held in common, and no one ought to be allowed to have property'.[2] Persecution drove the movement underground, but recent research has shown that its role was still vital and important at a popular level in early Tudor England, until in the 1530s this surviving force of a 'diffused but still inveterate Lollardy [was] revivified by contact with continental Protestantism'. This influence took first the form of Lutheranism, and later—and possibly more congenially—that of the Anabaptism, under which name its adherents might sometimes find themselves charged, which infiltrated from the Netherlands.[3]

Anabaptism, in its multiplicity of forms, displayed both pacific and apocalyptic tendencies. Although its outstanding leaders did not preach sedition or violence, several instances where these characteristics were much in evidence sufficed to discredit the movement in all moderate—let alone conservative— eyes. The adventure of Thomas Müntzer in 1525, the tragedy of Münster under the fanatical leadership of Jan van Leiden and Jan Matthijs a decade later, and some of the demands for economic and democratic reform put forward during the Peasants' Revolt in Germany, were enough to give credence to the usually unjustified allegation of a wish to have all in common, and to make the charge of Anabaptism completely damning.[4]

It has been asserted that in England some of the Christian social radicals, including Anabaptists, desired the abolition of the magistracy.[5] In the nature of things, little trace of this can be

---

[1] On this issue see W. K. Jordan, *The Development of Religious Toleration in England*, i, 25–33.

[2] M. E. Aston, 'Lollardy and Sedition. 1381–1431', 23, 27 and 36.

[3] A. G. Dickens, *Lollards and Protestants in the Diocese of York, 1509–1558*, 7–11 and 243; A. G. Dickens, *The English Reformation*, 22–37 and 236–8.

[4] J. Lecler, *Toleration and the Reformation*, i, 193–209; G. H. Williams, *The Radical Reformation*, 401–3, 778–90.

[5] H. C. White, *Social Criticism in Popular Religious Literature of the Sixteenth Century*, 30.

found in published works of the time and, as we shall see, the extremist views ascribed to the Anabaptists in political, social and religious matters were condemned by the mass of their fellow-Protestants, but in the bitterly controversial atmosphere of the age such a handy tar-brush was not likely to be ignored by the more Catholic or conservative faction. Bale alludes to this in *John King of England,* when he makes the spokesman of the papist clergy exclaim delightedly that

> If your true subjects impugn their treacheries,
> They can fetch them in, man! for Sacramentaries,
> Or Anabaptists.[1]

At the same time, criticism of one's superiors, or of the social order in general, could conveniently be met with the rejoinder of Heywood's Spider to the Fly:

> And sure thou holdest perilous opinions;
> Were thou opposed pithily to the quick,
> I durst lay my life thou art an heretic.[2]

One of the most vehement statements of the alleged connection between religious innovation and social subversion is that of More in his reply to Simon Fish: *The supplicacion of soules . . . Agaynst the supplicacion of beggars* (1529). As to whether in fact More's real views had changed between the writing of *Utopia* and that of this work there is some disagreement,[3] but there is little doubt that by the later date the humanistic speculation which characterized the first work was strictly subordinated to the immediate dread of religious heresy, civil disorder and social anarchy. More describes Fish's ideas as 'sedition under the colour of counsel . . . and under the pretence of favour unto poor folk, a devilish desire of noyance both to poor and rich, priests, religious, and lay man prince, lord, and people as well quick as dead'. He sketches the chaos which will ensue if the unruly elements among the lower orders are thus encouraged to break out,[4] and the consequences if the clergy are uprooted:

---

[1] Op. cit., in *Dramatic Writings*, ed. J. S. Farmer, 287.
[2] *Spider and Flie*, 201.
[3] See W. E. Campbell, *More's Utopia and his Social Teaching*, 9 and 96–7; J. H. Hexter, *More's Utopia. The Biography of an Idea*; W. K. Jordan, op. cit., 43–4.
[4] Above, 56.

Then shall all virtue be had in derision: Then shall all vice reign and run forth unbridled: Then shall youth leave labour and all occupation: Then shall folk wear idle and fall to unthriftiness: Then shall whores and thieves, beggars and bawds increase: Then shall unthrifts flock together and swarm about, and each bear him bold of other: Then shall all laws be laughed to scorn: Then shall the servants set nought by their masters, and unruly people rebel against their rulers.[1]

Another who set his face, in more uncompromising and unquestioning fashion than More, against any conjunction of religious moralizing and social criticism was Stephen Gardiner. In his *Answer to Bucer* (1541) he warned preachers 'not to cite to the people such texts from Scripture, as not being brought forward in their proper place, or not being unfolded fully, beguile the people into the refusal of obedience'. Such statements as that 'subjects are only entrusted to the prince's fostering care and protection, and are not subject to princes in any other way than for the sake of God' are not altogether false, 'but they are spoken in such a way as to seem in favour of the people, and to tend to anarchy; which latter is not without cause suspected of many, to be the aim of this sect, which, under colour of godliness, endeavours meanwhile to confound all things human'.[2] We shall find that the resolve to bar all possible means of entry to radical religio-social ideas led him to propound a limited concept of the function of government in society, which might fairly be described as running counter to the general trend of his era.[3] Meanwhile, his immediate aim is to crush subversion: 'as to the people, that must of necessity apply themselves to obedience, let them not revolve in their minds how the prince governs, but how they themselves may obey and show compliance'.[4]

Starkey shared this apprehension of the danger from 'unwise masters, foolish teachers of religion, indiscreet preachers' whose ideas would lead to 'the ruin of all civil order, and of all good worldly policy, whereof good and true religion is the most stable and sure foundation'.[5] Paget, attempting a diagnosis of the disorders of 1549, urged that 'society in a realm doth consist and is maintained by means of religion and law', and traced the evils that followed when 'the use of the old religion is forbidden by a

[1] Op. cit., 290 and 313.   [2] In *Obedience in Church and State*, 205.
[3] Below, 87.   [4] Op. cit., 183.   [5] *Exhortation*, 34, 72–72.ii.

law, and the use of the new is not yet printed in the stomachs of the eleven of twelve parts in the realm'.[1] In the *Discourse of the Common Weal* the Capper expresses the view that the religious contentions of the learned might be a contributory cause of 'these uproars of the people', and indeed the last section of the book is devoted to the harmful effects of doctrinal controversy.[2] Christopherson, naturally, ascribed 'discord and disobedience' to the new religion and cited the hideous examples of events in Germany and Bohemia.[3]

It is hardly surprising that the Protestants, for whom considerations of doctrinal purity were reinforced by those of sheer self-defence, joined in the scathing condemnation of extremists in order to dissociate moderate doctrinal reform from any attack on the social order and temporal power which, they hastened to stress, was of God. Thus Bale, while deriding the papists' use of the charge of Anabaptist tendencies against patriotic Protestants, was careful to make 'Imperial Majesty' (Henry VIII) allude to Münster and promise the destruction of the seditious sect.[4] The persecution caused by the Münster episode apparently gave rise to a wave of Anabaptist migration to England, and the warnings sent to Henry VIII and Cromwell led to a harsher policy.[5] A proclamation of March 1535, declaring that 'of late many strangers . . . are arrived and come into this realm', ordered Anabaptists to depart within twelve days, on pain of death.[6] The order was repeated in November 1538,[7] and a statute of 1542 referred specifically to the spread of 'divers naughty and erroneous opinions' among the king's subjects 'most specially of the lower sort'.[8]

Anabaptist activity in England perhaps reached its peak under Edward VI. Hooper, in 1550, described Kent and Essex as 'troubled with the frenzy of the anabaptists more than any other part of the kingdom',[9] while John Veron, in the introduction to his translation of an anti-Anabaptist tract by Bullinger (1551),

---

[1] Letter to Somerset, in F. W. Russell, *Kett's Rebellion*, 17.
[2] *Discourse*, 21 and 131–41.   [3] *An exhortation*, pp. Aa.iiii.b and R.v.
[4] *John, King of England*, in *Dramatic Writings*, 291; also 293.
[5] I. B. Horst, 'Anabaptism in England', 215–16.
[6] *Proclamations*, No. 155, 227–8.
[7] Ibid., No. 186, 270–6. See also Nos. 188, 191, and 272, on Anabaptism, contentious debate of scripture, and so forth.   [8] 34 & 35 Henry VIII, c.1.
[9] H. Robinson, ed., *Original Letters Relative to the English Reformation* (Cambridge, 1846), i, 87.

warns that 'these Libertines and Anabaptists, are running in hugger mugger, among the simple and ignorant people' of the latter county.[1] In 1551 also appeared *A preseruatiue, or triacle, agaynst the poyson of Pelagius*, by William Turner, which attacked 'murdering Anabaptists: which destroyed the noble city of Munster . . . : and rose up against the Magistrates, in Amsterdam . . . [and] destroyed Groningen, in West Friesland . . .'[2] In the last months of the reign the Council again commanded Cranmer to suppress unlawful sects in Kent. Baptist and Catholic historian alike contend that many of the Marian martyrs in south-east England came from 'these radical sectaries',[3] but there is very little evidence to support this assertion.[4]

Becon and Lever condemned 'the jay-like janglers of God's word, and brainless babblers of the gospel',[5] as 'clouds without any moisture of gods grace, tossed about with contrary winds of strange doctrine; trees passing summer time without any fruits of good works . . . wild waves of the sea frothing forth unshamefast brags, and wandering stars without constancy in judgement and opinion'. Lever explained the doctrinal errors of those who 'labour by wresting of the scripture to pull themselves from under due obedience': 'to have all things common' in the sense of giving all superfluity to the poor, this 'doth derogate or take away nothing from the authority of rulers. But to will to have all things common, in such sort that idle lubbers . . . might take and waste the gains of labourers without restraint of authority, or to have like quantity of everything to be given to every man is under a pretence to mend all, purposely to mar all.'[6] Veron attacked those who sought in scripture 'but a carnal and fleshly liberty' and licence to defy 'temporal rulers & magistrates'.[7]

Yet Lever hotly denied that 'this error is the fruit of the scripture in English',[8] echoing Tyndale's rebuttal:

Even so now (as ever) the most part seek liberty;[9] they be glad when

---

[1] H. Bullinger, *A most necessary & frutefull Dialogue*, p. C.iii.

[2] P. F.ii, also p. I.vi.b.

[3] I. Horst, op. cit., 216–17, and P. Hughes, *The Reformation in England*, ii, 261–3.

[4] A. G. Dickens, *The English Reformation*, 267.

[5] T. Becon, *Early Works*, 347.   [6] T. Lever, *Sermons*, 105 and 27–8.

[7] J. Veron, in H. Bullinger, op. cit., p. B.iiii.   [8] *Sermons*, 28–9.

[9] In this context, and as just used by Veron, the word 'liberty' must be taken in a pejorative sense, as in 'Libertine'. On the dreaded heresy known as 'Spiritual Liberty' see N. Cohn, *The Pursuit of the Millennium*, 177 ff.

they hear the unsatiable covetousness of the spiritualty rebuked; ...
when tyranny and oppression is preached against; when they hear
how kings and all officers should ... seek no other thing save the
wealth of their subjects; and when they hear that they have no such
authority of God so to pill and poll as they do, and to raise up taxes and
gatherings to maintain their fantasies and to make war they wot not
for what cause: and therefore because the heads will not so rule, will
they also no longer obey, but resist and rise against their evil heads, and
one wicked destroyeth an other. Yet is God's word not the cause of
this, neither yet the preachers.[1]

Incitement to revolt comes not from preachers of the truth but
from the corrupting example of self-seeking and evil-living
rulers.[2]

Latimer scorned his detractors' accusations: 'Well now, if
covetousness be the cause of rebellion, then preaching against
covetousness is not the cause of rebellion. ... Forsooth, our
preaching is the cause of rebellion, much like as Christ was the
cause of the destruction of Jerusalem.'[3] Brinklow, Crowley and
Becon conceded the mischief done by false prophets, 'preaching
uncalled, unsent', but ascribed the outbreaks of rebellion to a lack
of sufficient 'preaching of God's Word sincerely and truly', a
result, in part, of pillage of church income.[4] Becon and Cranmer
hurled back their opponents' charge, holding the 'massmongers'
responsible for the origin of the troubles of 1549.[5]

It may be instructive to trace the interaction of the fears and
hopes of the two sides in the dispute. In the Catholic or conservative camp, Wolsey, More and Gardiner appear to have been at
one in their dread as to the social consequences of doctrinal
innovation and attacks on the established religious order. The last-
named relates disapprovingly how the radical Robert Barnes
'began ... to exercise railing ... (and to please such of the lower
sort as envieth ever authority) chiefly against my Lord Cardinal.
... And yet that railing, in a friar, had been easily pardonned, if

---

[1] *The Obedience of a Christian man*, in *Works*, i, 199–200.
[2] T. Lever, *Sermons*, 28–9; W. Tyndale, *Practice of Prelates*, in *Works*, i, 390.
[3] *Sermons*, 249–51.
[4] H. Brinklow, *Supplycacion to ... Henry VIII*, 25; R. Crowley, *Works*, 134,
140; T. Becon, *Fortress of the Faithful*, 595–6.
[5] T. Becon, loc. cit.; T. Cranmer, *Miscellaneous Writings and Letters*, ii, 189.

Barnes had not fondly persisted in the Anabaptists' opinion, denying suits to be lawful among Christian men.'[1] L. B. Smith describes the conservatives as primarily administrators and states-men so that, despite their ecclesiastical titles, they viewed religion mainly as a divinely sanctioned bulwark of the social order; 'for the graduates of Wolsey's school, the sagacious ministers of state, the most powerful of all fears, that of social revolution, was to cloud the clear air of religious controversy'.[2]

In marked contrast with the forebodings of this group were the early hopes of the Protestant-radical faction that religious reform and social and economic amelioration would march hand in hand —hopes exemplified perhaps in Tyndale. The fact that the Protestants saw the power of the king as the one hope against religious darkness on the one hand, and social injustice on the other, explains their obdurate belief in non-resistance, despite Henrician persecution. It might be argued on their behalf that their radicalism, on both social and theological issues, lay in an appeal to what they conceived of as the values of the early Christian Church, and that the only innovations in dispute were those of papist prelates and covetous worldlings, which they wished to clear away. But the savagery of the attacks made by such as Barlow and Fish inevitably aroused revulsion in some who might share their concern, for example, with the problem of poverty.

Among those early Protestants who attacked the covetousness of the clergy themselves, and the way in which the Church had become corrupted by wealth, was John Frith. In an unusual adaptation of the corporeal analogy he argued 'that the body [of the Church] is cankered long ago, and now are left but certain small members, which God of his puissant power hath reserved uncorrupted; and because they see that they cannot be cankered as their own flesh is, for pure anger they burn them, lest, if they continued, there might seem some deformity in their own cankered carcase, by the comparing of these whole members to their scabbed body'.[3] Perhaps the most splenetic attacks were those of Simon Fish, of Jerome Barlow in his *Burial of the Mass*,

[1] *The Letters of Stephen Gardiner*, 165–6. See *The Acts and Monuments of John Foxe*, 415–21, for Barnes, Wolsey and Gardiner.
[2] *Tudor Prelates and Politics*, 104–5; also 5, 43, 110 and 280.
[3] *On the Sacrament of the Body of Christ*, in *Works*, iii, 340–2.

of the anonymous author (probably Barlow)[1] of *A proper dyaloge betwene a Gentillman and a husbandman, eche complaynynge to other their miserable calamite, through the ambicion of the clergye* (c. 1530), and of John Bale.

Barlow's gibe at evil-living clergy that 'through covetousness they make their merchandise . . . of bodies and souls', with friars 'copy holders of hell, And fee farmers of purgatory',[2] was later developed at length in the anonymous *The boke of Marchauntes* (1547). The 'merchants' of the title are mercenary-minded clerics who bargain for parsonages and 'hook benefices', and hold great fairs 'on high feast days, clean contrary to the other Merchants'. Neither are they content with one trade, 'but these wolfish grossers, gross up all at once and ravish everywhere'. The Pope himself is brought into the merchandising analogy as the 'hatmaker' and 'hatseller' of Rome, the 'sovereign haberdasher'.[3]

The charge of greed and inefficiency among the clergy was still made after the break from Rome. In 1546 Brinklow deplored the continued existence of pluralists and non-residents and attacked 'each ravening wolf that cometh with a sheephook in his hand'.[4] Cranmer himself, in 1552, answering a letter from Cecil which warned of court gossip about his wealth and covetousness, had to rebut the charge of greed, protesting that 'if I knew any bishop that were covetous, I would surely admonish him; but I know none, but all beggars, except it be one'.[5] Gilpin, in the same year, referred to patrons who 'think as good to put in asses as men'. Indeed 'the bishops were never so liberal in making of lewd priests; but they are as liberal in making lewd vicars. I dare say, if such a monster as Dervel Gatherel, the idol of Wales, burnt at Smithfield, should have set his hand to a bill to let the patron take the greatest part of the profits, he might have had a benefice.'[6]

The spectacle of lack of genuine religious zeal coupled with misappropriation of church wealth under colour of reformation angered sincere reformers, who had eagerly projected a correct

[1] On Barlow, see E. G. Rupp, *Studies in the Making of the English Protestant Tradition*, 52–72. [2] *Burial of the Mass*, 22 and 72.
[3] Pp. A.vi.a–A.vii.b, B.i.a, C.iv.a and C.v.a.
[4] *Supplication of the Poore Commons*, 79 and 92.
[5] *Miscellaneous Writings and Letters*, ii, 437; see W. S. Hudson, *John Ponet*, 34.
[6] *Sermon . . . before King Edward VI*, 16.

use of church income. Disappointed hopes of the institution of a 'godly order in Church and State' had provoked the rebellion of the 'Puritan ecclesiast' Sir Francis Bigod in 1537.[1] His *Treatise Concernynge Impropriatiqns of Benefices* (1534) had condemned 'the crafty juggling . . . & lewd legerdemain' by which 'my masters impropriated or improper masters' had 'almost through England, destroyed these holy and godly provisions' for preaching, hospitality and charity. His assertion that 'it is not meet that any man . . . should receive the benefit or fruit of a preacher, unless he do his duty therefor',[2] was echoed two decades later in some acid comments on lay impropriations by William Turner, in a letter to Cecil.[3] Referring back to the spoliations, by 'King Henry the eight, with his covetous council', of church lands given by benefactors to maintain alms and preaching, Turner derided Gardiner and Tunstall for condoning them: 'were not these good shepherds, that suffer Christ's flock thus so many ways to be robbed and spoiled'.[4] Whether or not one accepts the judgement that Henry VIII, by his actions, 'had once for all shackled together the cause of dogmatic reform and the self-interest of a grasping and unprincipled new nobility',[5] it remains true that, in the event, the Protestant movement was throughout this period hag-ridden by those who seized every opportunity of turning any alteration in religious structure or dogma to their own pecuniary advantage.

The fall of Cromwell has much significance within this context. Thus far the Crown had enforced a jurisdictional and administrative revolution upon the Church, had acquired much of its property, and had thrust out the Pope and the monastic orders. But neither the hopes of Protestant doctrinal reform nor the suggestions as to fruitful employment of confiscated monastic wealth had received much encouragement. Now came the 'Catholic Reaction', and the Six Articles of 1539 were followed within a year by the execution of Barnes and of the great political hope of supporters both of religious reform and of ameliorative socio-economic legislation, Thomas Cromwell.

Thus, while the Catholic group accused the Protestants of

[1] Introduction to *Tudor Treatises*, ed. A. G. Dickens, 9–17.
[2] *Tudor Treatises*, 43–51.
[3] Printed in Tytler, i, 335–6.
[4] W. Turner, *The Huntyng of the Romyshe Wolfe*, pp. D.vi–D.vi.b.
[5] H. F. M. Prescott, *Mary Tudor*, 110–11.

exacerbating the discontent caused by the apparent increase in social distress, the latter realized that their hopes as to the social and economic results of the break from Rome were illusory. Their bitterness is exemplified in the writings of Brinklow, who pointed to the disposition of church wealth by 'the godly and politic order of the Christian Germans. . . . Which divided not such goods and lands among the princes, lords and rich men, that had no need thereof; but they put it to the use of the common wealth, and unto the provision for the poor, according to the doctrine of the Scripture'.[1] 'The fault will be laid to all those of the parliament house, specially to those which bear the greatest Swing.'[2] By now, the anti-monastic vituperations of earlier days had given way to nostalgic contrasts with the grasping new landlords.[3]

The regime of Edward VI illustrates well the complexity of the relationship between religious and economic and social developments. The sermons of Latimer and Lever, high in favour with the king, complained that traditional standards in economic and social relationships were being abandoned, and regretted the failure to seize the great opportunity to bring in a religious and social millennium and to enforce truly Christian rules of conduct. Lever stressed the need to 'take good and diligent heed when ye be chasing the wild (wily) fox of papistical superstition, that the greedy wolf of covetous ambition, do not creep in at your backs: For surely he will do more harm in a week, than the fox did in a year'.[4] The anonymous author of *The prayse and commendacion of suche as sought comenwelthes* (c. 1548) put the question: 'I pray you, who in these days are such oppressors, such grasiers, such shepherds, such enhancers of rents, such takers of incomes, as are those which profess the Gospel?'[5]

In a sadly retrospective letter from prison, in 1555, Ridley confessed that 'we pastors, many of us were too cold, and bare too much, alas, with the wicked world; our magistrates did abuse, to their own worldly gain, both God's gospel and the ministers of the same'.[6] Hales conceded the justice in the sneer that 'we be talkers of God's word and no followers'.[7] Secretary Petre—at

---

[1] *Complaynt of Roderyck Mors*, 48.   [2] *Lamentacyon of a Christen*, 116.
[3] Below, 112.   [4] *Sermons*, 58.   [5] P. A.iv.b.
[6] Printed in *The Acts and Monuments of John Foxe*, vii, 435.
[7] 'Charges', in Strype, ii (Part II), 354.

heart a Catholic—wryly pointed to the contrast with the Apostles, who 'left their fishing of fishes, and became fishers of men' while we 'which talk much of Christ and his holy word . . . leave fishing for men, and fish again in the tempestuous seas of this world for gain and wicked mammon'.[1]

Of the extent and success of such activity there is only too much evidence. In May 1549 Somerset's brother, whose own conscience was not over-tender, described his colleagues in authority as 'at this point now, that there can neither Bishopric, Deanery, nor Prebend fall void, but one or other of them will have a fleece of it'.[2] In a letter to Cheke in July 1551 Ridley describes how his wish to present a prebend to a worthy person (Grindal) is hindered by 'such as do not fear God. One Master William Thomas, one of the clerks to the council, hath in times past set the council upon me, [to get] the said prebend unto him and his heirs for ever.'[3]

Cold figures support the allegations of shameless plunder. Many of the appointments to bishoprics were accompanied by 'adjustments' which stripped church revenue for the benefit of those in authority or favour. Bath and Wells, Westminster, London, Winchester, Exeter, Worcester and Gloucester were all subject to pillage—sometimes facilitated by amalgamation. Finally a bill was passed (fortunately rendered inoperative by Northumberland's fall) which suppressed the diocese of Durham, sub-divided it into two separate, meanly-endowed sees, and annexed the greater part of its revenue to Northumberland. In 1552–3 'superfluous' church plate was collected to the value of over £10,000.[4]

It is ironic that the fall of Somerset, who was moderate in religious views and would-be paternalist in economic affairs, should have been secured—at least in part—by an alliance between those who, for not very admirable reasons, disliked his attempts to stem the tide in the latter sphere, and those who disapproved of such innovations as he had made in the former. The disgrace of Somerset once achieved, Warwick (Northumberland) abandoned

[1] Sir William Petre, letter to Cecil, in Tytler, i, 427.
[2] Tytler, i, 170.   [3] T. Ridley, *Works*, 331–2.
[4] See F. C. Dietz, *English Government Finance, 1485–1558*, 193–4 and 200–1; J. D. Mackie, *The Earlier Tudors, 1485–1558*, 502 n. and 518; and P. Hughes, *The Reformation in England*, ii, 160.

any pretence of sympathy with the Catholic group, and doctrinal innovation and self-seeking greed proceeded at an accelerated pace, further confiscation of church property and income providing an uneasy point of contact.

The significance has been remarked of what was in effect an inversion of 'conservative' and 'revolutionary' in the social and economic context.[1] The discontented peasantry, and Somerset their sympathizer, had fought to conserve, or return to, what they considered a desirable set of economic and social standards; but the 'innovators' now controlled the machinery of government. An avowedly Protestant regime was now as ready as had been the Catholic-conservative of a previous era to make use of the device of identifying the sympathetic attitude or preaching of such as Hales and Latimer, or attempts to protect the peasantry against any harmful effects of economic developments, with sedition and the wish to 'have all in common'. Indeed, after Somerset's fall we find on the one hand more extreme developments in doctrinal matters, symbolized by the prominence of Hooper and Knox, while on the other, in the economic and social sphere, shameless furtherance of sectional interests was backed up by stern suppression of any discontent. Thus both the fears of such as More, that religious and doctrinal innovation would *per se* be conducive and sympathetic to social revolt, and the hopes of such as Tyndale and Brinklow, that religious reform would proceed hand in hand with social and economic amelioration, were proved in the event over-simplifications.

Under Northumberland the Protestants were given a looser rein in respect of dogma, but their protests against social injustice went unheeded. By 1552 disillusion had led to distrust and bitterness. In a sermon before the Court, in April of that year, Knox, naming Northumberland and Winchester, deplored that often

the most godly princes had officers and chief counsellors most ungodly, conjured enemies to God's true religion. . . . Little wonder is it then, that a young and innocent King be deceived by crafty, covetous, wicked and ungodly counsellors? I am greatly afraid that Achitophel be counsellor, that Judas bear the purse, and that Sobna be scribe, comptroller, and treasurer.[2]

[1] W. G. Zeeveld, *Foundations of Tudor Policy*, 172–3, and 196; L. Einstein, *Tudor Ideals*, 96.   [2] Strype, ii (Part II), 69–71.

The depth of Northumberland's religious convictions was soon to be demonstrated in circumstances which made even more remote any hope of a radical-Protestant millennium! A final irony derives from the fact that the surge of support which swept aside Northumberland's house of cards and put Mary Tudor on the throne came from that same region—the eastern counties—whose combination of economic and social conservatism with a Protestant religious ethos he had crushed in 1549.

It is fair to conclude that in an analysis of the reaction—at least in practical terms—to social and economic issues under Edward VI, the interplay of personalities, sectional interests, and the cherished principle of respect for legitimate authority, sheds more light than any question of theology. Indeed, turning to the problem of the nature of any relationship between Protestantism and social and economic change during the period 1529–59 as a whole, we must reiterate that the Protestants saw themselves not as innovators but as advocates of a return to the purity of the truly Christian belief and code of behaviour, alike in religious, social and economic spheres, of an earlier age. Certainly, on the evidence of the material studied, there seems little doubt of the basic continuity, in England, between Catholic and Protestant teachings on social and economic relationships.

The popularity of the analogy between society and the human body, the stress on the organic interdependence of all its members and on the paramount importance of due degree and order, continued unbroken. So too did the ideal of measure, and dislike of excess in any type of appetite or action, together with the concept of stewardship and its derivative beliefs on the nature, obligations and limitations of property rights.[1] Economic issues were still evaluated within the context of the broader subject of general social morality. The conduct of owners or occupiers of land, of craftsmen and of merchants, was, by and large, still assessed by medieval standards. Indeed, M. M. Knappen cites Tyndale, Frith, Brinklow, Crowley and Hooper as characterizing the 'early, semi-medieval phase of Puritanism', and finds the early Puritan's social and economic doctrine practically indistinguishable from that of his rivals in its derivation from the teaching of the scholastics. He concludes that 'in Edward's reign the Puritan continued

[1] Below, Chapter 6.

to speak on social issues in the language of medieval clericalism, opposing, so far as he had the power, the economic changes of the time'.[1] This basic continuity and congruence of ideals and of function is exemplified in the Marian bishop of Winchester's commendation, in his funeral sermon for the queen, of the 'lively preacher in the church' and the 'lively officer or magistrate in the commonweal, that dareth to speak against injuries, extortions, seditions, rebellions, and other discords . . . to the decay of Christian religion, and the subversion of the public wealth'.[2]

In short, Catholic and Protestant preacher were as one in their rejection of many of the implications of contemporary economic developments—a rejection embittered by failure to secure enforcement of the old standards to which they clung. When we face the question of whether any modifications of traditional medieval views on specific issues did in fact occur, it is difficult to avoid the conclusion that any such were caused by circumstances and pressures that were practical rather than theological. Indeed, even if it be accepted that Calvinism contributed much that was new in this respect, it has been pointed out that effectively Calvinism in England dates only from the reign of Edward VI.

The evolution of ideas upon particular social and economic problems and relationships will be examined in later chapters. But briefly to anticipate certain of their conclusions, first, in regard to the vexed question of vocation or calling[3] we shall meet with evidence which supports the contention that Protestant ideas remained, as yet, essentially medieval.[4] Alongside this, examples may be found of Protestants who took a rather more liberal view of social mobility and, perhaps even more significantly, taught that the path of advancement may be the calling of God for particular individuals.[5] But, on balance, the picture which will emerge is one of continuity, rather than of divergence, between medieval and early Protestant teaching. At most one discerns perhaps a certain change in emphasis; whereas in the former stress was laid on patient and faithful acceptance of one's lot, especially if that involved poverty, in the latter more is heard of conscientious performance of tasks given, of striving as much as

[1] *Tudor Puritanism*, 401, 406.   [2] Strype, iii (Part II), 544; see also 545.
[3] For a brief survey see R. W. Green, ed., *Protestantism and Capitalism. The Weber Thesis and its Critics.*   [4] Below, 97–100, 100–1.   [5] Below, 104.

of acceptance, with the possibility of advancement to serving God by performing those tasks at a higher level.

In regard to trade and industry, Protestant preachers continued to advocate medieval standards,[1] and in their teaching on the crucial question of usury the same tendency appears.[2] It is true that Brinklow, in 1542, suggested that some of the confiscated church wealth should be loaned at 3 per cent interest to 'poor occupiers'; but the first year was to be interest-free, and proceeds thereafter were to be devoted to charity.[3] (In this context it is instructive that public institutions—the *montes pietatis*—lending to the poor at very low interest rates had been most successfully established in fifteenth-century Italy.[4]) Hooper is described as taking 'on balance . . . the Swiss attitude of tolerating limited "charitable" usury'.[5] But these would seem to be special cases; we shall find that Bucer's advocacy of the general rectitude of lending money at interest received little support in Edward VI's England.[6]

As to the nature and obligations of charity, it has been suggested that the 'redefinition of charity is one of the more arresting manifestations of the Protestant spirit'. C. H. and K. George, writing of the period after 1570, find the Protestant view of charity 'an assertion of equality, of brotherhood, quite distinct in emphasis from that of Catholic theory', in fact 'a kind of welfare-state approach'. They relate the increasingly discriminating approach to the 'objects of charity' to the Protestant ethic of work and its implications.[7] Indeed, it has been urged that in the long run the puritan stress on the duty of work as an expression of salvation, together with rejection of works as a means of salvation, led to a harsher attitude towards the poor.[8] As far as mid-Tudor England is concerned, one may cite expressions of opinion which seem to indicate such tendencies.[9] But the evidence of continuity of traditional concepts is far more impressive.[10] Certainly continued emphasis on the possibly blessed function of poverty, and on both the duty of charity and the blessing which it bestows on the giver,

---

[1] Below, 170–1.   [2] Below, 152–3.
[3] *The Complaynt of Roderyck Mors*, 50–3.
[4] J. T. Noonan, *The Scholastic Analysis of Usury*, 294–309.
[5] M. M. Knappen, op. cit., 418.   [6] Below, 153–4.
[7] *The Protestant Mind of the English Reformation, 1570–1640*, 154–9.
[8] M. M. Knappen, op. cit., 404; C. H. and K. George, op. cit., 158.
[9] Below, 125–6.   [10] Below, 109–111.

is clear, while recognition of the need for discrimination in the exercise of charity to secure the most beneficial effects for the recipient in particular and society in general, and the evolution towards a 'social welfare' approach which we may indeed clearly perceive in many commentators, may fairly be attributed to empirical rather than to doctrinal influences.

The impression gained from the sources is that in England, during the period 1529–59, the continuity of traditional concepts regarding economic and social standards and obligations remained almost wholly unaffected by any doctrinal innovation, but that the question of observance or enforcement of these standards was greatly affected by actual economic and social developments. Furthermore, while on the one hand the Reformation in England shattered the unity of the Church, diminishing any remaining hope of such enforcement by a body coextensive with Christendom, on the other it conferred more power and, by implication, more responsibility upon the State. Early Tudor puritanism has indeed been charged not with responsibility in a positive, doctrinally causal sense, for innovations in social conduct and economic practice, but with failure to adjust its teaching thereto in an attempt to assimilate new problems or functions within a Christian code of relationships. Its contribution to the dissolution of the traditional economic and social code lay in splitting the Church and 'was therefore negative rather than positive, destructive rather than constructive'.[1] But it may with equal justice be urged that many of the Protestant moralists were realists in their clear perception that the only institution with the coercive power necessary to enforce such a code was the emergent State to which their appeals were often addressed.

This raises a final and most crucial aspect of the interrelationship between religion and social and economic problems, one which derived from the growing complexity and urgency of those problems and the Crown's assumption of the headship of the Church rather than from the realm of theology. This was the realization that the implementation or enforcement of those norms of conduct sanctioned by religion must become, to an increasing degree, the province of the temporal power. Thus Latimer could pray, 'for God's sake make some promoters'.[2]

[1] M. M. Knappen, op. cit., 422. [2] Below, 153, n. 3.

The Protestant Reformation may have split the organizational and doctrinal unity of the Church, but the concept of a code of social values and standards of universal applicability remained. The Protestants appealed to the prince not only to rescue the realm from what they considered spiritual enslavement but also to enforce that code. In this also they acted in the medieval tradition; for the notion of enforcement by secular authority of values defined by the Church was itself a result of the inter-dependence of Church and civil power in the Middle Ages. While the Protestant Reformers were accused of tearing the robe of uniformity of religious faith, they strove to preserve and bind closely together the threads of social interdependence and respon-sibility in the commonwealth, stressing the paramount leadership in this regard of the secular saviour.

CHAPTER SIX

The Social and Economic Problems of the Commonwealth

I. DUE DEGREE; THE PROBLEM OF SOCIAL STABILITY

IN the last two chapters we have seen first, that the duty of obedience of the subject and the responsibility of the ruler were conceived of very largely in social and economic terms, and secondly, that true religion was believed to be not only a prerequisite of social stability but also the arbitrator of social justice. Men of religion were expected to speak out frankly against abuses and exploitation and to remind government of its obligations in this sphere. We turn now to a more detailed consideration of the social and economic problems of the commonwealth, with specific reference to contemporary discussion of the objectives and methods of State intervention.

We shall find that the ideas and comments put forward were often conservative or reactionary, clinging to an idealized version of an outworn order, blindly rejecting what could not be understood, and void of any constructive proposals. But sometimes they were forward-looking, anticipating the doctrine of enterprising self-interest controlled by the State to the advantage of society as a whole.[1] It may be urged that the implied dichotomy should not be over-emphasized; certainly the problems were discussed within the matrix of an inherited Christian code of morality touching economic transactions and social relationships. In regard to the nature and application of this code, we must repeat that the great question at issue was not the influence of any doctrinal innovation upon the content of social and economic

[1] Below, Chapter 10.

moral teaching, but rather the difficulty of harmonizing an accepted body of precepts with developments in the sphere of actual transactions which, in an increasingly complex economy, tended to become ever more impersonal and amoral. Interest and success in the formulation of constructive proposals owed more to the practical and business experience of the individual than to his religious sympathies.

Before examining opinions as to the objectives of governmental action in social and economic affairs we must note one significant voice which ran counter to the general trend. Stephen Gardiner's main purpose in his *Answer to Bucer* (1541) appears to be the defence of a relatively circumscribed concept of the functions of government against the attempts of some doctrinaire Protestants—typified by Bucer—to load the temporal authority with the duty of enforcement of the moral precepts of the Church in economic and social matters, and to persuade princes to 'proclaim a penal law against every sin forbidden by divine law'.[1] Princes, he argues, must chastise heretics, murderers, and thieves, 'but as for the covetous, the drunkards, the liars, the slothful, the proud . . . their effect does not extend to the ruin of the whole community, and so they leave those men to be taught by the church'. Again, 'slothful, sluggish and idle fellows spoil themselves by their laziness; they infringe God's law, yet they do not touch the commonwealth, nor do they disturb it, still less do they cast it into confusion'; rather is it Bucer who does this by striving to impair the authority of princes.[2] P. Janelle attributes this argument to Gardiner's dislike of the Calvinist theocracy,[3] but it is fair to relate it also to his concern that the people should 'not revolve in their minds how the prince governs', his dread of a combination of religious heresy and social revolution,[4] and his fear of the implications if the regimen of the prince should itself be subject to judgement by those of radical religio-social beliefs. But Gardiner's attitude is the exception rather than the rule; in general, the intervention of government was eagerly sought by the religious moralist.

For what purposes, then, was the State expected to take action in the economic and social sphere? Perhaps we should place first

---

[1] In *Obedience in Church and State*, 193; see also 175.
[2] Ibid., 179 and 209.　　　[3] Ibid., Introduction, p. lxvi.　　　[4] Above, 71.

the maintenance of due degree and order—the basis of the security of government itself and of the very existence of society as a whole. The dread of instability and lack of balance was often expressed in relation to such concepts as Due Degree and Order, Gentility, Measure and Vocation. The first of these, to which the corporeal analogy was so admirably suited, is clearly set out in the 'Exhortation Concerning Good Order and Obedience to Rulers and Magistrates':

Almighty God hath created and appointed all things, in heaven, earth, and waters, in a most excellent and perfect order. . . . Every degree of people, in their vocation, calling, and office, hath appointed to them their duty and order. So that in all things is to be lauded and praised the goodly order of God: without the which no house, no city, no commonwealth can continue and endure. . . .[1]

The theme recurs repeatedly in economic, political and religious contexts, though occasionally a different device is used—as when society is likened to the pieces on a chess-board or a delicately tuned harp. Indeed, the concept of hierarchy lay at the heart of the social philosophy of the whole Tudor period.[2] Yet despite ubiquitous lip-service to this ideal the sources suggest a marked tendency to ignore it when opportunity offered. Perhaps it is in precisely such a period as this, when a previously accepted ideal is, in practice, subject to attack, that we might expect to find it extensively discussed.

It is at least certain that few themes are dealt with more bitterly than that of the upstart. Edmund Dudley's general warning that 'the commonalty' should not 'presume above their own degree, nor let any of them presume or counterfeit the state of his better',[3] was channelled by the poet John Skelton into a series of vicious personal attacks upon that most hated of all upstarts, Wolsey. Skelton rages disgustedly at the power and position achieved by this fat hog, this mastiff cur, this butcher's dog, of base progeny and greasy genealogy,

> Brought up of poor estate,
> With pride inordinate,

---

[1] *The Two Books of Homilies*, ed. J. Griffiths, 105.
[2] See E. M. W. Tillyard, *The Elizabethan World Picture*, 3, 7, 82–4, and 87–91.
[3] *The Tree of Common Wealth*, 45–6.

> Suddenly upstart
> From the dung-cart.[1]

It is ironic that this furious resentment of a conservative—both in religion and politics—and defender of the old order should be matched, with a striking similarity of tone and phrase, in an attack on Wolsey from a very different quarter. In his scurrilously anti-clerical *Burial of the Mass*, Barlow addresses Wolsey as

> Carter of York, the Vile butcher's son.
> The mastiff Cur bred in Ipswich town.

and derides his 'noble stock'.[2] Even the far nobler Tyndale marvels that 'a misshapen monster should spring out of a dunghill into such a height', and goes on to refer to 'the chiefest of all his secretaries [Cromwell?], one nothing inferior unto his master in lying, feigning, and bearing two faces in one hood'.[3] Cromwell was himself to be the subject of the same type of charge when the Pilgrims of Grace attacked him because of his low birth—he is the 'Crim' of 'Crim crame and riche'.[4]

Henry VIII's concern at the making of this type of allegation led him, in a letter of November 1536 'to the Rebels in Yorkshire', to rebut in detail the assertion that there were now fewer nobler counsellors than at the start of his reign. Already in October he had, in an 'Answer to the Petitions of the Traitors and Rebels in Lincolnshire', written scornfully of 'one shire, and that one of the most brute and beastly of the whole realm, and of least experience, to find fault with your Prince for the electing of his counsellors', and accused its inhabitants of extreme presumption beyond their degree in attempting to do so.[5] A hand-bill published by Somerset's supporters in the crisis of 1549 hurled the same charge of base origins at his enemies in the Council, 'come up but late from the dunghill; a sort of them more meet to keep swine than to occupy the offices which they do occupy'.[6] William Turner, explaining how the obvious occupational derivation of certain names exploded pretensions to gentility,

---

[1] *Complete Poems*, 269, 292, 317, and 322.   [2] *Op. cit.*, 20 and 57.
[3] *The Practice of Prelates*, in *Works*, i, 465 and 480.
[4] *Life and Letters of Thomas Cromwell*, i, 181–4.
[5] *The Letters of King Henry VIII*, 141–3, and 150–3.
[6] Printed in Tytler, i, 209.

included among his examples that of his *bête noire*, 'Steven Gardiner'.[1]

Apart from its use as a peg on which to hang such personal attacks, the case of the upstart was a subject of general complaint and will recur in the context of discussion of the nature of true gentility. It is but one aspect of what seems to have been a fear of general social insubordination. A sermon of 1545 complained that 'a prentice admonished will make answer again churlishly, and if his master go about to correct, he will withstand him and take the staff by the end'.[2] The concept of due degree and order between master and servant was the main theme of *The Boke of Nurture, for Men, Servauntes, and Chyldren*, by Hugh Rhodes (*c.* 1554), which warned masters not to dress their servants or children too sumptuously, 'for it increaseth pride and obstinacy', and instructed servants to take off caps and stand up straight when spoken to.[3]

Christopherson included 'discord and disobedience' among the evil effects of the new religion, so that 'servants control their masters, and tell them, when they were checked for leaving their business undone, that they had been occupied either in reading god's word, or in hearing some sermon. . . . After the same sort did children order their parents, wives their husbands, and subjects their magistrates: So that the feet ruled the head, and the cart was set before the horse', and the end is 'Government turned upside down'.[4] The lament for headstrong youth, of course, recurs interminably!

Far more serious was the uneasy discussion of the alleged increase in hatred of 'gentlemen' by the lower orders. Cheke derided the pretended concern for the commonwealth of the 'rabble of Norfolk rebels' in 1549: 'How amend ye it? By killing of gentlemen, by spoiling of gentlemen, by imprisoning of gentlemen? Why should ye thus hate them?'[5] Cranmer's sermon on 'Time of Rebellion' warned that this unreasoning hatred of gentlemen would ruin the whole realm,[6] while Protector Somerset himself expressed the fear that 'a number would rule another

---

[1] *A new book of spirituall Physik*, fol. 3.b.
[2] J. O. W. Haweis, *Sketches of the Reformation*, 138.   [3] 7 and 17.
[4] *An exhortation*, pp. T.i–T.vi.
[5] *The hurt of sedition*, in Holinshed, iii, 989.
[6] T. Cranmer, *Miscellaneous Writings and Letters*, ii, 194–6.

while, and direct things as gentlemen have done; and indeed all have conceived a wonderful hate against gentlemen, and taketh them all as their enemies'.[1]

An unusual and intriguing treatment of this theme of the alleged deterioration of relationships between nobility and gentry on the one hand and commons on the other is found in John Heywood's allegory *The Spider and the Flie* (1556). Although this contains religious allusions its main theme is clearly social and economic. The plot centres on discussion of the fate of a Fly caught in a Spider's web. This widens into a general debate as to the respective rights of each in the Window in which the incident occurs, and the true nature of relationships between them. The Fly accuses the Spider of spreading his webs over far too much of the Window:

> When you in the tops and sides there kept your estate,
> And we in the holes, as stood with our degree,

then relations were amicable, but this has been ruined by the Spiders' greed. After angry charges of pride and cupidity on either side a reckless Fly spokesman bursts out in query of the assumption that Flies owe obeisance to Spiders—

> Wise flies cannot brook it, for they find in book
> This demand written, When Adam dolve and Eve span,
> Who was, in those golden days, a gentleman?—

and asserts that yeomen Flies might rule as well as Spiders gentlemen.[2]

An equally aggressive Spider sneers that now 'every knave will be a lord', points to the disastrous effects of the Flies' rebelliousness, and ends by asking sarcastically

> Shall Jack sauce rule now, fly?
> Shall we not find a knave fly, not worth two straws,
> Look more proudly than the best lord in a shire?

The attack of the Fly army on the Spiders' fortress is now repulsed with heavy losses, but before the captive Fly can be executed the Maid of the house intervenes. She condemns the behaviour of both sides, but that of the Spiders in particular, in

---

[1] Letter to Sir P. Hoby, in T. Cranmer, op. cit., ii, 195n.
[2] 195 and 199.

> usurping to excel
> In governance, out of your place natural;
> Which for few years past brought and kept flies so thrall,
> That you (well nigh) brought flies to grant to agree
> You as head governor general be.

The Maid now executes the Spider and gives a final warning that

> We may live in love all, each in his degree.
> Each in his degree (I say) mark that point well.[1]

It is true that much of this material, and the fear and hatred to which it refers, must be set against the background of the particularly unfortunate economic circumstances existing at the mid-century. But a phrase of Gilpin's—'never so many gentlemen and so little gentleness'[2]—points not only to the bitterness generated by desperate distress but also to the criticism that gentlemen were failing in their traditional duties. In the literature of the time acceptance of the essential part which the gentry should play in a well-ordered commonwealth remained unquestioned, and most contemporary discussion of the topic may be related to the two favourite issues of the origin and the behaviour of true gentility.

It was agreed that gentry or nobility—for the two were often equated—did not spring solely or automatically from ancestry. Any who might boast of the accident of birth were reminded that without virtuous conduct they were as counterfeit nobles (a play on words with the coin then current) or as Aesop's crow, decked in other birds' feathers. William Baldwin summed up

> ... that true gentry standeth in the trade
> Of virtuous life, not in the fleshly line:
> For blood is Brute, but Gentry is divine.
> How would we mock the burden bearing mule
> If he would brag he were an horse's son,
> To press his pride (might nothing else him rule,)
> His boast to prove, no more but bid him run.[3]

In Rastell's *Gentleness and Nobility*, a dialogue between merchant, knight and ploughman, the last-named makes a Shylock-like outburst:

[1] Ibid., 195–6, 200, and 412–15. The allusion to the oppressive regime of Northumberland and his execution in the following reign seems clear.
[2] *Sermon . . . before King Edward VI*, 45.
[3] *A Myrroure For Magistrates*, p. F.ii.a.

> Ye came of one first stock and progeny
> Both of adam and eve ye will not deny
> The beggar and thou were both doubtless
> Conceived and born in filth and uncleanness
> Thy blood and the beggar's of one colour be
> Thou art as apt to take sickness as he
> If thou be in the body wounded
> Thy flesh is as ill as his to be healed.[1]

In regard to the behaviour expected of true gentility the concept of measure was perhaps as important as that of hierarchy to
the composition of society. In the use of one's wealth liberality
without ostentation was the ideal. Hales implied approval of
those who had not abandoned this standard when he hoped that if
prices could only be lowered then those gentlemen who had not
raised their rents or behaved as graziers and sheepmasters would
once more be able to show traditional hospitality.[2] Nowhere was
this ideal more nostalgically extolled than in the *Institucion of a
Gentleman* (1555):

to be good housekeepers, to relieve their neighbours with meat and
drink, to feed many and be themselves fed of few, to seek London
seldom, and at their own houses often to be sought, to have their
smoky kitchens replenished with victual, their stables with Horses,
their Wardrobes rather with harness than silk Garments, their Halls
with men, their chambers with plenty of Fuel and few perfumes. . . . In
the ancient time when curious building fed not the eyes of the wayfaring man, then might he be fed and have good repast at a gentleman's
place so called. Then stood the buttery door without a hatch, yeomen
had then no cause to curse small dishes, Flanders Cooks had then no
wages for their devices, nor square Tables were not used. . . .[3]

The implied criticism, that now the well-to-do were guilty of
ostentation and extravagance without true liberality, was often
related to excess in apparel, 'curious building' and gluttony. The
first not only encouraged gentry and nobility to waste their
substance, but also tended to blur the traditional, and desired,
distinction between the social orders. Bishop John Longland, in
his *Sermonde made before the Kynge*, in 1538, found it 'for the most
part outrageously, excessively, and exceedingly out of order. In

---

[1] ll. 527–34.   [2] 'Charges', in Strype, ii (Part II), 363.   [3] Anon., 100–1.

especial mean men, serving men, bestowing upon one pair of hoses, in manner as much as his half year's wages. . . .'[1] Ostentatious building, attempting 'to bring paradise into earth',[2] was almost as often condemned, being compared by Becon 'to the web of Penelope. For that one setteth up, another, after the disbursing of many pounds, destroyeth, and buildeth it up again with double expences.'[3] Frith remarked mordantly that whereas Christ had resisted the Devil's temptation to turn stone into bread '(which might have succoured the poor) . . . these builders turn the bread into stones. For they bestow the good which should be given to the poor for their sustenance, upon an heap of stones.'[4]

Denounced also was inordinate appetite of a more literal kind. Elyot devoted a chapter to 'Sobriete in Diete',[5] and the second *Book of Homilies* included a sermon 'Against Gluttony and Drunkenness'.[6] A memorial drawn up in 1539, apparently by Morison, pleaded for a more abstemious approach to 'belly cheer' in such anxious times: 'When 10 dishes were, may not five serve in time of war? The superfluities of our tables would maintain a great host.'[7] Hugh Rhodes combined measure and manners in his instruction:

> With much flesh and little bread
> Fill not thy mouth like a barge.[8]

Together with unmeasured indulgence of its appetites, excessive care of the body itself was deprecated, as leading to neglect of the soul.

Such moralizing—and particularly that pertaining to apparel— was by no means new in the sixteenth century,[9] and it illustrates the continued attachment to measure as the universal touchstone of conduct. It applied to all aspects of personal behaviour, to sleep and exercise, even to laughter and swearing, and to one's relationships with others, particularly inferiors and servants. In Starkey's *Dialogue* Lupset reminds Pole that 'you know well there is in all

---

[1] P. D.iii.   [2] B. Gilpin, op. cit., 41.   [3] *Jewel of Joy*, 430.
[4] *Works*, iii, 273–4.   [5] *The Governour*, Book III, Chapter xxii.
[6] Op. cit., ed. J. Griffiths, 306.
[7] *L. and P. Henry VIII*, xiv (Part 1), No. 869, 405–7.
[8] *Boke of Nurture*, 20.
[9] See G. R. Owst, *Literature and Pulpit in Medieval England*, 369 and 409–11, for fourteenth- and fifteenth-century attacks upon sartorial extravagance.

things a measure and mean',[1] while Cheke defined the whole 'drift of policy' in a commonwealth as directed to prevent 'any excess of unmeasurableness, either of the one side, or of the other'.[2]

Interwoven with this ideal were such concepts as stewardship, liberality, and competence, which again testify to the continuity of medieval social values. Ponet related the first of these to the whole realm in describing its ruler as 'but God's minister or steward . . . to see the people do their duty to their lord God, that the goods of this world be not abused but spent to God's glory. . . .'[3] Frith was typical in warning that 'if God have given thee riches, thou mayest not think that he hath committed them unto thee for thine own use only, but that he hath made thee a steward over them . . . to see whether thou wilt be faithful in distributing this wicked mammon, according to his commandments'.[4] Frith's fellow-martyr, Tyndale, in *The Parable of the Wicked Mammon* (1528), defined '*mammon*' as 'an Hebrew word [which] signifies riches or temporal goods, and namely, all superfluity, and all that is above necessity. . . . God hath given one man riches to help another at need.'[5]

But in avoiding the pitfall of avarice one must beware also of that of reckless spending. Measure in spending made up the whole theme of the anonymous *Spare your good* (*c.* 1555), while Simon Fish described everything spent unnecessarily as robbed from the poor.[6] Neither was true liberality compatible with indiscriminate charity,[7] although it was usually discussed in the context of one's charitable duties as well as in that of the virtues of the happy mean. In the *Institution of a Christian Man* (1537) the concepts of stewardship, degree and charity were linked: 'And to them, to whom thou dost vouchsafe to give more than their own portion necessary for their vocation and degree, give thy grace, that they may be thy diligent and true dispensators and stewards, to distribute that they have (over and above that is necessary, considering their estate and degree) to them that have need of it.'[8]

---

[1] 97.   [2] *The hurt of sedition*, in Holinshed, iii, 1003.
[3] *Politike power*, p. F.viii.   [4] *Works*, iii, 271.   [5] *Works*, i, 106 and 118.
[6] *The Summe of the holy scrypture* (*c.* 1529), fol. lx.
[7] See Sir T. Elyot, *The Governour*, i, 114, and John Larke, *The boke of wisdome*, p. k.ii.a.
[8] Printed in *Formularies of Faith put forth by Authority during the Reign of Henry VIII*, ed. C. Lloyd, 188.

Others agreed with Frith's view of riches as a challenge compounded of opportunity and temptation. Lupset stressed, with an interesting variation of phrase, that 'as hard a thing it is to pluck through the small needle's eye a great cable rope, as to bring a rich man in at heaven's wicket',[1] and Latimer that 'riches must be had *cum tremore*, with fear' because they made difficult the way to heaven.[2] Thus the medieval notion that it is 'competence', acquired and used in measure, which constitutes true wealth, recurs, as in Becon and the *Institution of a Christian Man:* 'give me neither poverty nor riches: only grant me a necessary living; lest if I be too full, I deny thee . . . and lest I, being constrained through poverty, fall into stealing'.[3] The unknown author of *An enterlude of welth, and helth* (1558) declares that 'when a man has a competent living . . . then he is wealthy'.[4]

Acceptance of a competent living implies a belief in measure not only in the disposal but also in the acquisition of worldly wealth. This was often discussed in relation to the concept of vocation or calling. These words may remind us of the yet unfinished debate on the Weber thesis as to the social implications of Calvinism, especially in regard to personal economic advancement. Yet it was Luther who first revolutionized thought in this field, rejecting the traditional Catholic distinctions, 'making the callings common to all men and . . . placing them in the world'.[5] Luther taught that 'there is, at bottom, really no other difference between laymen, priests, princes, bishops . . . between religious and secular, than that of office or occupation, and not that of Christian status. All have spiritual status. . . .'[6] But at the same time, 'everyone should take care, that he remains in his estate . . . realizes his calling, and in it serves God'.[7]

It is contended that the Calvinist idea of the calling went further. As defined by Ernst Troeltsch, it 'raised the ordinary work of one's profession (within one's vocation) and the ardour with which secular work was prosecuted to the level of a religious duty

---

[1] *The way of Dyenge well*, 35.   [2] *Sermons*, 477.
[3] *Jewel of Joy*, 159; *Institution*, in C. Lloyd, op. cit., 190.
[4] In *'Lost' Tudor Plays*, ed. J. S. Farmer, 278.
[5] F. E. Cranz, *An Essay on the Development of Luther's Thought on Justice, Law, and Society*, 153–9.
[6] *An Appeal to the Ruling Class of German Nationality*, in Woolf, i, 115.
[7] See F. E. Cranz, op. cit., 157.

in itself', so that Christian morality was exercised not merely *in vocationem* but *per vocationem*.[1] The crux of Max Weber's interpretation is perhaps to be found in his statement that 'even a change of calling is by no means regarded as objectionable, if it is not thoughtless, and is made for the purpose of pursuing a calling more pleasing to God, which means, on general principles, one more useful'.[2]

Apart from the question whether any change which took place may confidently be ascribed to Calvinist theology, the sources studied do not encourage dogmatic generalization as to the nature and degree of modification of traditional values which occurred in mid-Tudor England. Certainly we find that abandonment of one's vocation and rejection of one's calling are universally condemned, but several different shades of meaning of the words may be broadly, though not always clearly, distinguished.

The first *Book of Homilies* linked 'degree, state, and vocation'.[3] Those who 'ran out of' their true degree neglected their vocation. Crowley, in *The Voyce of the laste trumpet* (1550) 'calling all estates of men to the right path of their vocation', advises the Merchant to 'content thy self with a living', and not strive to climb the social ladder:

> Let it suffice thee to marry
> Thy daughter to one of thy trade:
> Why shouldst thou make her a lady,
> Or buy for her a noble ward?

Eternal damnation will follow from 'walking inordinately' and 'forsaking thy vocation'.[4] In *The Way to Wealth* (1551) Crowley repeats the advice to remain content 'with that estate wherein your fathers left you, and strive not to set your children above the same'.[5] Belief in vocation in this sense—condemning inflated social pretensions—is clearly just an aspect of that ingrained belief in due degree which we examined earlier; but Crowley, we may note, provides evidence for the continuity of these traditional beliefs in mid-century in one who has been described as 'a Puritan of the narrowest school'.[6]

---

[1] E. Troeltsch, *The Social Teaching of the Christian Churches*, i, 609–10.
[2] *The Protestant Ethic and the Spirit of Capitalism*, 162.
[3] Ed. J. Griffiths, 4.   [4] *Works*, 87–90.   [5] *Works*, 147.
[6] J. M. Cowper, Introduction to R. Crowley, *Works*, p. xi.

Acceptance of the need of diverse vocations or occupations in respect of their functional purpose in society is again completely traditional, and frequently expressed. So, too, is forthright criticism of those who desert their own proper function to usurp another's, as when Hooper takes the novel case of Jonas to illustrate the danger when a man 'transgresseth his vocation'. For if the commonwealth be likened to a ship, then upon whom should fall responsibility for its present distress? 'Upon Jonas; that is to say, upon every man that neglecteth his vocation, and doeth not as he is bid . . . how many Jonases should there be found in England?'[1]

The Institucion of a gentleman finds it particularly regrettable that 'it hath appeared of late days how cunning gentlemen have been in other men's occupations, and how lightly they have regarded the preservation of their own states . . . like Storks devourers of their own kind, in running out of their profession they destroy themselves . . . they are not esteemed as gentlemen but merchants'.[2] Turner derides 'the crowish start ups . . . from the dunghill', and suggests that a proclamation 'that sir Mathew muckfork, had taken any lands or goods away from any poor man, or from any commonalty' should be issued wherever their greedy acquisitions become known. But he is equally disturbed that 'some gentlemen, yea some knights and lords do now in England not be ashamed to sell oxen, sheep, beer, corn, meal, malt, coals & things much viler than these be'.[3] William Forrest is another who stresses the social stigma involved in such conduct:

> For lords and men of high nobility,
> or other endowed with possessions great,
> to use th'office of inferior degree,
> to chop and change, advantages to get,
> as Market men doth,

is quite degrading.[4] To stoop beneath oneself for greed is as bad as to climb above oneself for pride.

Hales and Becon, reminding the nobility and gentry of their

---

[1] *Early Writings*, 456 and 459–60.   [2] Anon., 103–4.
[3] *A new book of spirituall Physik*, fols. 50.b, 52, and 85.b.
[4] *Pleasaunt Poesye of Princelie Practise*, ll. 603–7.

moral obligations towards their inferiors, regret that many of them have so far neglected their vocations as to become graziers, sheepmasters and clothiers, pulling down villages and ejecting husbandmen; such caterpillars of the commonweal, who have so wrung the poor people that the silly souls are like dried haddocks, abuse the very name of gentleman and bring it into disrepute among the commons.[1] A striking instance of this strain of criticism occurs in Henry VIII's message to James V of Scotland in 1540. For 'the second thing which the King wishes to inform James is that it is bruited by some that he gathers into his hands "numbers of sheep and other such vile and mean things in respect of his estate, being the livings of the poor men, therewith to advance his revenue"'. Henry thinks that, though it may be profitable, this kind of profit 'cannot stand well with the honour of James' estate, but might cause his subjects to mutter and mutiny, conceiving that their livings might be taken from them by other great personages after the King's example'. James should therefore rather follow Henry's example and confiscate monastic estates— a project on which the English king will be happy to advise him— so as to be able to live like a king 'and yet not meddle with sheep and mean things, which should occupy the meanest of his people'.[2]

Becon's prayer that he might 'diligently walk in my vocation, unto the glory of thy blessed name, and the commodity of my neighbour',[3] suggests two aspects of this concept. Acceptance, in principle, of the second of these seems to be clear-cut; to abandon one's own vocation and meddle with another's distorted and weakened the body politic. But the question of vocation or calling in its relationship to God is far more complex. Few would have quarrelled with Latimer's definition of the duty to 'labour in thy vocation', to which one is 'called' by God, and the corollary that 'when we leave our vocation whereunto God hath appointed us, no doubt we do naught and damnably'.[4] His message that 'God doth consecrate every man's vocation', and that as good Christians 'we may be content to live in our calling, and not to

---

[1] J. Hales, 'Bill on Decay of Tillage', printed in *Discourse*, p. xlvi; T. Becon, *Fortress of the Faithful*, 598–600.
[2] *L. and P. Henry VIII*, xv, No. 136, 43–4.
[3] *Early Works*, 403.   [4] *Sermons*, 215 and 516.

gape further',[1] seems equally clear, as does Edward VI's counsel of acceptance of 'our calling . . . without any disorder or debate'.[2] Of course, only those occupations which were socially and morally acceptable, and followed from the right motives, were thus sanctified. This comes out clearly in Crowley's story of the Usurer; when the Prophet reproaches his exorbitant gains he pleads that 'it is my living', only to receive the crushing reply: 'Yea . . . but it is not your calling.'[3]

But we cannot ignore the fact that, in several of the Protestant writers of these decades, the duty of following one's vocation, in the sense of obeying the calling of God, is not necessarily incompatible with a change in one's occupation or status, or with economic and social advancement. Crowley does indeed give the advice:

> First walk in thy vocation,
> And do not seek thy lot to change;
> For through wicked ambition,
> Many men's fortunes hath been strange.

But it is as part of 'The Beggars Lesson', teaching acceptance of the will of God if He has 'made thee low in all men's sight', and a few pages later we find the 'Servant' promised that as a reward of faithful labour in his vocation God shall make him 'Master of a great multitude' as in the case of Jacob.[4]

Tyndale and Gilpin certainly envisage worldly advancement as part of the will of God: the former explicitly, when he advises that if a man 'be of low degree let him patiently therein abide, till God promote him, and exalt him higher',[5] the latter by implication in condemning the type of man who 'exalteth himself, and tarrieth not the calling of God', and those who 'climb by their own might, uncalled'.[6] Even Latimer's warning that one may leave one's vocation only if called by God to another implies that this may occur.[7] The suggestion that there is nothing necessarily wrong in watchful concern for one's economic interests is to be found, set in a matrix of traditional medieval ideas on measure,

---

[1] *Sermons and Remains*, 35 and 122.
[2] *Primer*, in *Writings of Edward VI*, 92.   [3] *Works*, 50.
[4] *Works*, 57–60. See H. M. Robertson, *The Rise of Economic Individualism*, 7.
[5] *Works*, i, 137.   [6] *Sermon . . . before King Edward VI*, 31–2.
[7] *Sermons and Remains*, 122.

degree and charity, in Hugh Rhodes's *Boke of Nurture*, which urges the reader:

> When occasion comes, thy profit take,
> time lasteth not for ever:
> Time flits away, thy wealth augments
> as pleaseth God the giver.[1]

Thus the touchstone of conduct in this context is faithful service in the path to which one is called; that path may be one of poverty, or it may lead to social and economic preferment—the essential thing is to follow it gladly in furtherance of the will of God. In this respect a passage in *The Summe of the holy scrypture*, by Simon Fish, is significant. The servant is exhorted to work faithfully: 'Therefore thou shalt in all things have god all ways before thine eyes, and not the men whom thou servest outwardly. . . . Be not sorry that thy master doth not suffer thee to go to the church to hear mass. For thou mayst please god as well in doing thy work.'[2] This might be interpreted as foreshadowing what C. H. and K. George suggest as a Protestant reversal of the medieval moral hierarchy of vocations in favour of the economic and productive callings[3]—which incidentally, in so far as it is true, would contribute to an increasing tendency among radical Protestant idealists to define the duties and functions of the commonwealth in socio-economic terms.

It seems evident that the concept of the calling or vocation at this time has more than one aspect. It reflects, first, the essentially medieval ideal of a fixed station in life, ordained by God, within which one should labour to help others—and herein the ingrained dislike of the upstart and the meddler in other men's occupations easily finds its place. But alongside this, a more dynamic interpretation sees the calling of God as a command to do faithful service indeed, but with the added incentive of possible improvement in worldly status. Consideration of the sources, of their dates of composition, and of the fact that—as in Crowley—the notion may assume different aspects in the same writer, suggests that for mid-Tudor England any rigid sociological pattern has little relevance. It has long been accepted that the evolution of

[1] 42.　　　　　[2] Fol. lxxv.
[3] *The Protestant Mind of the English Reformation*, 143 and 169–70.

Church attitudes towards the question of resistance to established political authority owed perhaps as much to environment and expediency as to theology. May not the same concession be made in regard to economic and social issues? In this time of economic and social flux, we should do well not to look for too much precision of definition and of pattern in the views of men subject to conflicting and changing pressures.

An element of uncertainty may be found in the approach to social mobility in general, despite the almost universal lip-service to the hierarchical ideal. The latter, indeed, was reflected not only in the spate of protests at the failure to observe the proper distinctions in apparel which gave it tangible expression, but also in statutory form in the sumptuary legislation—although fear of the vitiating effects of luxury-loving extravagance, and economic arguments against foreign imports, have also been suggested here as contributory factors.[1]

The reign of Henry VIII saw several attempts at more stringent regulation,[2] though Wolsey's efforts in this respect understandably increased his unpopularity. The king himself was apparently the instigator of an act of 1533 which stated explicitly that 'Excess in Apparel' led to 'the subversion of good and politic order in knowledge and distinction of people according to their estates preeminences dignities and degrees',[3] but later proclamations complained of infractions of such legislation 'to the great hurt of the common weal'.[4] Edward VI drew up a Bill which proposed limitations in apparel for each rank of nobility, with no one below the rank of gentleman to 'wear any fur save lamb's fur', or 'velvet in his cap', or silk points.[5] Amendments of existing law designed more strictly to control 'the meaner sort' were enacted in 1554,[6] but the problem of enforcement remained intractable, although further strenuous efforts were made in the reign of Elizabeth I.[7]

[1] See F. E. Baldwin, *Sumptuary Legislation and Personal Regulation in England*, 10 and 131; also M. Beer, *Early British Economics*, 71.
[2] 1 Hen. VIII, c.14; 6 Hen. VIII, c.1; 7 Hen. VIII, c.6.
[3] 24 Hen. VIII, c.13.
[4] See *Proclamations*, No. 163, 239–40; F. E. Baldwin, op. cit., 156–7; W. Hooper, 'The Tudor Sumptuary Laws', 433–6; and T. F. Plucknett, 'Some Proposed Legislation of Henry VIII', 124.
[5] *Literary Remains of King Edward the Sixth*, 495–8.
[6] 1 & 2 P. and M., c.2.
[7] See W. Hooper, op. cit., 436–7.

Edward VI's wish to preserve sartorial distinctions as indicative of established status combined with differentiation of function within the social hierarchy[1] may fairly be taken as expressing a traditional objective of royal policy. The agreed task of good government was to maintain 'them all, from the highest degree to the lowest, in a good concord and unity among themselves'.[2] But a danger to the whole concept perhaps more insidious and fundamental than mere excess of apparel is implicit in the discussion of whether social mobility was in fact permissible.

The unknown author of *The Institucion of a gentleman*, after voicing his regret that in these days 'an inordinate disdain among most sorts of persons hath risen, in that one sort of men can not stand content with the state and degree of an other',[3] attempts to define social categories. First is the 'gentle gentle', joining noble birth with gentle conduct; then the 'gentle ungentle', of noble parentage but corrupt and ungentle manners; third, and of particular interest, the 'Ungentle gentle': 'Ungentle Gentle is he which is born of a low degree, of a poor stock . . . which man taking his beginning of a poor kindred, by his virtue, wit, policy, industry knowledge in laws, valiancy in arms', rises to wealth and high office and establishes his line as gentlemen. There are now many such in England, and only those 'kelles [cauls?] of ignorance' who ignore the reality of rising through merit call them upstarts.[4] But there are also those who have risen not through merit but through 'a little dunghill forecast to get lands . . . purchased by certain dark augmentation practices. . . .' After this allusion it is not surprising to learn 'that such intruders, such unworthy worshipful men, have chiefly flourished since the putting down of Abbeys. . . .' These are 'the right upstarts, and not those which climb to honour by worthiness'.[5]

The point is fairly taken that the author is perhaps being rather idealistic about the 'ungentle gentle' and the way in which his rise was actually achieved. Moreover, it has been urged that much of the insistence on virtue in discussion of this topic was intended primarily to admonish the well-born, rather than to advocate that quality as the sole criterion of social advancement. Such

[1] 'Discourse on the Reformation of Abuses', in *Literary Remains*, 478–86.
[2] E. Dudley, *The Tree of Common Wealth*, 103.
[3] 1–2.   [4] 39–42.   [5] 51–4.

conventional moralizing as the statements that 'of no better clay
. . . is a gentlemen made than a carter',[1] and that 'both rich and
poor be engendered of earth',[2] may be found in the pages of a
conservative like Elyot or of the far from radical Paynell. In
general, contemporaries were scathing about both motives and
methods of those newly claiming to be of the gentry, and sneered
at gentlemen being made 'good cheap' in England. Edward VI's
comment in parenthesis, when writing of 'true gentlemen', that
'I mean not these farming gentlemen, nor clerking knights',[3]
and the proverb that it 'is better to be the head of the yeomanry
than the tail of the gentry',[4] were typical.

Nonetheless, the possibility of rising from humble origins to
gentility was much debated in Tudor England. A striking
exposition of the case for merited promotion occurs in Cranmer's
account of a discussion concerning selection of pupils for the
grammar school in Canterbury in 1539. Certain of the commissioners would have excluded husbandmen's children, as fit
only for the plough or to be artificers, only gentlemen's children
being 'meet to have the knowledge of government and rule in
the commonwealth'. To this Cranmer replied, acidly, that 'I
myself have seen no small number of them very dull and without
all manner of capacity', and went on to argue 'that none of us all
here, being gentlemen born, (as I think), but had our beginning
that way from a low and base parentage; and through the benefit
of learning and other civil knowledge, for the most part, all
gentles ascend to their estate'. The stock answer being made,
'that the most part of the nobility came up by feat of arms and
martial acts', Cranmer countered, using a term normally employed by the opponents of his case, that the Scriptures themselves
taught 'that Almighty God raiseth up from the dunghill and
setteth . . . in high authority'.[5]

Ten years later Cheke held out the prospect of social better-
ment as an argument against egalitarianism, in exhorting the
Norfolk rebels: 'If there should be such equality, then ye take
away all hope from yours to come to any better estate than you

[1] *The Governour*, ii, 205.
[2] *The preceptes teachyng a prynce or a noble estate his duetie*, p. a.v.
[3] *Literary Remains*, 482.
[4] Cited in M. Campbell, *The English Yeoman*, 21.
[5] *Miscellaneous Writings and Letters*, ii, 398–9.

now leave them. And as many mean men's children do come honestly up, and are great succour to all their stock: so should none be hereafter helped by you, but because ye seek equality, whereby all cannot be rich. . . .'[1] Thus the fact of social mobility seems to have been clearly recognized, the criterion of judgement in each case being the circumstances and method of advancement.

It has been suggested that the Cromwellian group of propagandists, in particular, voiced the principle of social equality in a purely secular context, partly in self-defence against the gibes of the Pilgrims of Grace at their own preferment.[2] This contention is supremely well illustrated in Morison's *A Remedy for Sedition*, in which two potentially contradictory themes are interwoven. On the one hand Morison defends traditional views as to acceptance of the established social order, obedience to legitimate authority, and avoidance of egalitarianism of the 'Anabaptist' type with its threat to property; on the other he advocates the principle of careers open to talent, and attacks the outmoded type of rigid social stratification which would make this impossible. The two are brought into rather uneasy reconciliation by relating them both to the criterion of loyal and efficient service of Crown and commonwealth combined with the inducement of self-advancement whose fruits are made safe only by respect for the law. 'The worser sort' are advised 'to be content, that the wiser rule and govern them'. But these are next defined as 'those that nature hath endowed with singular virtues, and fortune without breach of law, set in high dignity'. Morison scorns the complaints of the Pilgrims of Grace against low-born councillors, and their resentment 'that virtue should be rewarded, when she cometh to men that had no lords to their fathers', and credits Henry VIII with wishing 'all his subjects to contend, who may obtain most qualities, most wit, most virtue: and this only to be the way to promotion, and here nobility to consist'.[3] He twice states explicitly that every man must be content with his degree and to have 'that he lawfully may come by'.[4]

---

[1] *The hurt of sedition*, in Holinshed, iii, 990.
[2] See W. G. Zeeveld, *Foundations of Tudor Policy*, 191, 196, and 211; also W. G. Zeeveld in E. M. Nugent, *The Thought and Culture of the English Renaissance*, 163–5.
[3] *Remedy*, pp. A.ii.b and B.i.b.
[4] Pp. A.iiii and B.iv. See also *Lamentation*, p. A.iiii, and above, 57–8.

Estimates of the significance of Morison, and of the sincerity with which he held this utilitarian concept of degree, have varied. Sir Thomas Smith also commended the prince's power to 'honour virtue' and to 'make knights and create barons or higher degrees'. Gentlemen indeed 'be made good cheap in England', but even that 'is not amiss'.[1] Certainly the idea that careers should be open to talent irrespective of social origins was supported by others. But in aggregate such opinions were outweighed by the more traditional emphasis upon acceptance of status and function as a requisite of social stability, by fear of those who would have all in common, and by resentment—at both ends of the social scale— of upstarts.

We may discern a certain ambivalence on this issue in men whose stand on other matters of policy has led to their inclusion in the Commonwealth tradition. The humanist reverence for ability and 'virtue' would discard previous social rigidities where these barred the way to the exercise of abilities for the common good. But the harsh truth that many who rose in the social scale did so by methods which were despised as exploiting the economic needs of the less fortunate, and were then accused of rejecting the essential social obligations of the power and wealth thus gained, caused a nostalgic revulsion in favour of gentility by birth. It may nonetheless be conceded that if there were to be more equality of opportunity, a greater chance to climb the social ladder, and yet fear of class hatred as leading potentially to revolution and social dissolution were to be allayed, then the significance of the State as guarantor of law and order would increase, as reverence for a divinely-sanctioned rigid social hierarchy diminished.

But for the present the generally accepted task of government was to maintain the stability of the existing social order, subject always to the guiding principle of equity. For whereas almost any concept of equality was subject to grave suspicion—equality of opportunity at best a subject of debate, equality of possessions rejected as an 'Anabaptist' nightmare, and political equality in any modern sense simply not discussed—that of equity stood out as a principal aim of government. We have already noted Hales's passionate avowal of social justice as a major objective of policy,[2]

---

[1] *De Republica Anglorum*, 39–40.   [2] Above, 35.

and it is worth recalling Edward VI's definition of the 'temporal regiment' as consisting 'in well ordering, enriching, and defending the whole body politic of the commonwealth, and every part of the whole, so one hurt not th'other'. Just as 'no member in a well fashioned and whole body is too big for the proportion of the body' so, in a well-ordered commonwealth, proportions of wealth must be limited according to rank and occupation. Due degree, measure and equity are thus combined within the familiar corporeal analogy.[1]

It has been observed that the young king's ideas, if unoriginal, are all the more truly representative.[2] Starkey diagnosed a lack of common justice and equity as a principal cause of disease in the body politic, in that one part had too much and another too little; the duty of government was 'chiefly to see that all such things may be distributed with a certain equality', having regard to the dignity of all citizens.[3] The measure of good policy was not the form of government but whether it sought to promote the public good, for the true commonwealth stood in the prosperity not of any part but of the whole. Therefore a prince should not claim the power to abrogate and dispense with good laws, for the favour shown to special interests injured the common good.[4] Forrest agreed that a king's honour lay in the well-being of the whole, so that he should ensure 'that one clubbed cobbe should not so encroach an hundred men's livings', that the strong did not eat up the weak 'as the great fowl the small', for as the Lord's elect he was bound to implement God's intention of the sharing of His gifts.[5] In respect of the problem of excessive rents, the king should appoint discreet and incorruptible men of his Council to force 'Private Commodity' to give way to 'Commonwealth' so that 'Equity may rule bear'.[6] Equity was the yardstick by which the Crown should measure its duty in regard to those economic problems of the commonwealth which will concern us in the following chapters.

---

[1] *Literary Remains*, 480–1. [2] L. Einstein, *Tudor Ideals*, 78.
[3] T. Starkey, *Dialogue*, 157–8. [4] Ibid., 51–8, and 102.
[5] *Princelie Practise*, pp. lxxxviii–lxxxix. [6] Ibid., pp. xcvii–xcviii.

CHAPTER SEVEN

The Social and Economic Problems of the Commonwealth

II. 'POVERTY ... AND HIS COUSIN NECESSITY'

IN 1526 the duke of Norfolk, in parley with a rebellious force of unemployed cloth-workers of East Anglia, asked for their captain and received this reply: 'Since you ask who is our captain, for sooth his name is Poverty, for he and his cousin Necessity, hath brought us to this doing.'[1] The incident points to several of the reasons for mid-Tudor preoccupation with the problem of poor relief. Recent interpretations suggest that what took place was an increase not so much in poverty itself as in public sensitivity on this issue, whether attributable to a growth of social conscience or to the emergence of circumstances in which the poverty-stricken became a danger to public order. But there is no doubt that contemporaries believed poverty itself to be increasing.

In this chapter we shall examine the way in which the inherited medieval attitude to poverty became tempered by the realization that certain of its assumptions were no longer valid; the reasons for the growing significance of the problem; and finally the evolution of a more discriminating approach in ideas of appropriate treatment. The recognition and elaboration of the responsibility of society and its ruler not only for the punishment of the idle and the vicious but also for the relief of the victims of misfortune and, where possible, the removal of the causes of distress, form a most important aspect of the emergence of a heightened conception of the economic and social duties of the commonwealth.

[1] E. Hall, *Chronicle*, 699–700.

Certainly we must not antedate the disappearance of medieval attitudes. The shift in emphasis from the idea of almsgiving as a personal testimony of religious faith, to that of provision for the poor and the attempted elimination of causes of poverty as functions of an efficiently governed commonwealth, was gradual. Edward VI reiterated the traditional belief that 'as riches, so likewise poverty is thy gift, O Lord; and as thou hast made some rich to despise the worldly goods, so hast thou appointed some to be poor, that they may receive thy benefits at the rich man's hands'.[1] The poverty-stricken were the poor lively images of Christ, the poor members of Christ; their poverty came of God, to evoke Christian resignation and Christian charity.

The idea that poverty was at once a blessing, a challenge and a chastisement runs through such works as William Hughe's *The Troubled Mans Medicine . . . wherein they may learne pacyently to suffer all kyndes of adversitie* (1546), or the anonymous *A Newe Interlude of Impacyente pouerte* (*c.* 1549). The cross of poverty was a frequent figure of speech, and Lazarus and Job the favourite exemplars: the poor man should 'rather starve and die for hunger, as poor Lazar did, than to trouble a commonweal . . . rather take that cross patiently';[2] he should 'let Job's trouble be thy cheer'; indeed,

> . . . though thou shouldest perish for food,
> Yet bear thou thy cross patiently;
> For the end shall turn thee to good,
> Though thou lie in the streets & die.[3]

To the rich man, also, poverty presented an opportunity and a challenge; for 'Christ so straitly commandeth alms deeds . . . for the rich man's sake.'[4] The 'Homily of Almsdeeds and Mercifulness Toward the Poor and Needy' reminded him that 'the poor man . . . is the way to heaven', and pressed into service the analogy of the hated practice of usury: 'he which sheweth mercy to the poor doth lay his money in bank to the Lord for a large interest and gain; the gain being chiefly the possession of the life everlasting'. It is, however, carefully explained that 'almsdeeds do wash away our sins, because God doth vouchsafe then to repute us

[1] *Writings*, 90–1. [2] T. Becon, *Fortress of the Faithful*, 601.
[3] R. Crowley, *Works*, 58. [4] T. Lupset, *The way of Dyenge well*, 33.b.

clean and pure, when we do them for his sake, and not because they deserve or merit our purging, or that they have any such strength or virtue in themselves'.[1]

A distinction was often made between genuine and assumed or 'wilful' poverty. Starkey implied it in explaining that to the true Christian 'all worldly adversity which cometh not to him by his own negligence and fault, is to him turned into joy and plain felicity'.[2] Latimer condemned 'the friar's poverty, the same wilful poverty . . . [for only] when I come to poverty by chance, so that God sendeth poverty unto me, then I am blessed'.[3] Frith attacked begging friars who 'leave nothing behind for the very poor, which are sick, lame, crippled, blind, and maimed',[4] and William Marshall described professional beggars as tempting God.[5] Despite this, there remains the purely medieval idea that charity will bless the giver regardless of any just claim to alms on the part of the recipient. In Robert Copland's *The Highway to the Spital-House* (1535–6) the Porter explains that

> Where any giveth alms with good intent
> The reward cannot be no wise misspent.[6]

After exposing the stratagems of counterfeiting beggars Crowley can still advise his readers to

> . . . cease not to give to all,
> Without any regard;
> Though the beggars be wicked,
> Thou shalt have thy reward.[7]

But this evidence of the survival of medieval attitudes to poverty is shot through and through with expressions of regret that in reality 'poverty was never so abundant, and charity never so scant',[8] that the rich were quite unmindful of the duty of steward-ship. Gilpin, preaching before Edward VI, lamented that 'the images of your ancestors graven in gold, and yours also, contrary to your mind, are worshipped as gods; while the poor lively

---

[1] *The Two Books of Homilies*, 385, 387, and 392.
[2] *An Exhortation*, 13.(ii). [3] *Sermons*, 478. [4] *Works*, iii, 275.
[5] W. Marshall, Preface to *Forma Subventionis Pauperum*, in F. R. Salter, *Some Early Tracts on Poor Relief*, 45–6.
[6] In A. V. Judges, *The Elizabethan Underworld*, 5. [7] *Works*, 14–16.
[8] J. Hales, 'Defence', in *Discourse*, p. lxvi.

images of Christ perish in the streets through hunger and cold'.[1] The charge of charity grown cold was often related to that of misuse of church wealth, which found angry, and even scurrilous, expression in *A Supplicacyon for the Beggers*, by Simon Fish, and in Barlow's *The Burial of the Mass*.[2] The latter was particularly savage at the expense of Wolsey, while the former provoked a spirited counter-attack by More in *The supplicacion of soules*. Tyndale, in turn, replying to More, condemned misallocation of gifts, so that 'they which be most wont to offer to images and to shew them, be so cold in offering to the poor, that they will scarce give them the scraps which must else be given dogs, or their old shoes, if they may have new brooms for them'.[3]

Latimer, preaching before Convocation in June 1536, ridiculed the belief that dead images

not only ought to be covered with gold, but also ought . . . (yea, in this scarceness and penury of all things,) to be clad with silk garments . . . laden with precious gems and jewels; . . . to be lighted with wax candles . . . at noon days; as who shall say, here no cost can be too great; whereas in the mean time we see Christ's faithful and lively images, bought with no less price than with his most precious blood . . . to be an hungred, a-thirst, a-cold, and to lie in darkness . . . till death take away their miseries.[4]

Two months later, Cromwell's 'Injunctions to the Clergy' ordered them to persuade their parishioners 'that it doth conduce more toward their souls' health if they do give that to the poor and needy that they thought to bestow upon the said images or relics'.[5]

Tyndale contrasted the priesthood with the deacons who ministered alms in the Early Church where 'love maketh every man's gift and goods common unto the necessity of his neighbour'.[6] Frith likened bishops and abbots who defrauded the poor by wasting charitable bequests on sumptuous living to thieves and murderers,[7] and Latimer preached that they 'should not have

---

[1] *Sermon . . . before King Edward VI*, 46.

[2] In his very different *Dialogue On the Lutheran Factions* (1531), written after his recantation, Barlow was still to concede approvingly that the Anabaptists were 'ready to help their needy brethren, using their goods in common', 57.

[3] *An Answer unto Sir Thomas More's Dialogue*, in *Works*, ii, 65.

[4] *Sermons* (Everyman), 33.   [5] *Life and Letters*, ii, 27.

[6] *Practice of Prelates*, in *Works*, i, 401.   [7] *Works*, iii, 273.

so many servants or so many dishes, but go to their first foundation and feed the needy'.[1] Armstrong warned the spiritualty not
to 'strive with rigorous means to rule the commonalty, having
need to be ware of their malice and enmity', and bluntly put
forward self-preservation as an inducement to a more charitable
disposal of church wealth.[2]

But the hopes raised by the break from Rome and the secular-
ization of much church property—hopes given statutory backing
by the promise of support of preaching and education, and of
establishment of 'Alms-houses for poor folk to be sustained in',
with 'daily Alms to be ministered'[3]—were dashed, and the attacks
of the early radical reformers upon the work of monastic institutions were sometimes replaced by regretful expressions of
nostalgia. As late as 1544, in his *Supplication to . . . Henry the
Eyght*, Brinklow was still hopeful that the lands and wealth taken
from religious houses would be used for poor relief and schools.[4]
But in his *Supplication of the Poore Commons* (1546) disillusioned
reproach is clear: the king should 'call to remembrance that
dreadful day, when your Highness shall stand before the judgement seat of God in no more reputation than one of those miserable creatures which do now daily die in the streets for lack of
their due portion . . . which they trusted to have received, when
they saw your Highness turn out the other sturdy beggars'. In
fact, their position is now worse, for 'although the sturdy beggars
got all the devotion of the good charitable people from them, yet
had the poor impotent creatures some relief of their scraps, where
as now they have nothing. Then had they hospitals, and alms-
houses to be lodged in, but now they lie and starve in the streets.'[5]
Crowley also deplored the wasted opportunity of applying the
confiscated abbey wealth to charitable purposes,[6] while Brinklow
was even prepared to advocate confiscation of the riches of bishops
to this end.[7]

Criticism was not confined to the works of radical pamphleteers. Cranmer confessed the fault of the Church in neglecting its
charitable duties, 'because the goods of the church are called the
goods of the poor, and at these days nothing is less seen than the

---

[1] *L. and P. Henry VIII*, x, No. 462, 189–90. [2] *Treatise*, in *T.E.D.*, iii, 112–13.
[3] 31 Hen. VIII, c.9. [4] 44. [5] 77–9. [6] *Works*, 7.
[7] *Lamentacyon of a Christen*, 115–16.

poor to be sustained with the same'.[1] But often, as Lever pointed out, the income of the clergy was insufficient to enable them to relieve the poor,[2] although Bradford apparently set a notable personal example in that 'after that God touched his heart with that holy and effectual calling, he sold his chains, rings, brooches, and jewels of gold . . . and did bestow the price of this his former vanity in the necessary relief of Christ's poor members . . . lying sick or pining in poverty'.[3]

The contemporary assertion that individual almsgiving, which had traditionally supplemented the charitable efforts of Church and monasteries, was declining is supported by the evidence of Professor Jordan that amounts of charitable benefactions fell sharply if temporarily during the fourth and fifth decades of the century.[4] Lever regretted the passing of such communal arrangements as the practice of keeping a stock of six or twelve cattle and selling the milk to aid the poor.[5] The citizens of London were scathingly attacked for lavishing expenditure upon idolatry or upon feasts for 'aldermen and other rich commoners, which have as great need of your feasts as hath the sea at the highest of the spring tide, of the pissing of the wren; and the poor forgotten, except it be with a few scraps & bones, sent to Newgate for a face!'[6] The London authorities came in for more rough treatment in *The prayse and commendacion of such as sought comenwelthes*, whose author wished that 'men would be as careful for their poor brethren, as they are for their dogs. We see the City of London can of the Chamber's cost provide a house to keep 20 or 30 dogs in . . . but they will not allow 10 pence by year . . . towards the finding of the poor.'[7] *The Ordre of the Hospital of S. Bartholomewes* (1552) indignantly rebutted such unjustified slanders by busybodies and preachers, pointing out that the city had to relieve its own poor and those from elsewhere: in the past five years 800 had been healed and 92 had died, who would have stunk in the noses of the city 'for all these charity-tenderers, if this place had not

---

[1] *Miscellaneous Writings and Letters*, ii, 500.　　　　　　[2] *Sermons*, 108.
[3] T. Sampson, Introduction to J. Bradford, Writings, 30.
[4] *Philanthropy in England, 1480–1660*, 243 and 367. The criticism that Professor Jordan's calculations take no account of the fall in the real value of money may actually strengthen this point.
[5] *Sermons*, 79–80.　　　　　　[6] *Lamentacyon of a Christen*, 90–1, also 79–80.
[7] Pp. A.iv. (b)–A.v.

vouchedsafe to become a pump alone, to ease a common abhor-ring'.[1] But a few years later Cardinal Pole made a fierce attack upon London's lack of charity, drawing unfavourable compari-sons with Italy.[2]

The implied failure of surviving medieval concepts of poverty and of charity to match contemporary realities may be ascribed largely to changing economic and social circumstances. What was new was not poverty itself but the background to poverty. In the medieval economy, where poverty was the norm and its crises the result of specific catastrophes such as plague or harvest failure, the acceptance of the poor as part of the natural order, indeed as fulfilling a God-ordained function, is easily compre-hensible. But with the increasing complexity of society's eco-nomic mechanism poverty was seen as attributable to identifiable economic causes—the enclosure of land, the increase in wage-labour at the mercy of the market, the price inflation—rather than to natural catastrophes, in short, to human agencies rather than to inscrutable providence. There thus ensued an uneasy tension between the idea of 'the poor by the will of God' and that of poverty as a result of the economic malfunctionings of society. The traditional ideal of Christian charity persisted, but a more analytical approach to the causes of poverty, and the realization that the burden of relief must fall upon the organized resources of society as a whole, led to condemnation of wilful or avoidable poverty.

The extent to which enclosures caused unemployment is diffi-cult to assess, but they must surely rank as a major contributory cause of distress.[3] Elimination of the waste, with improved land utilization, might also mean elimination of the inefficient and the loss of those safeguards for the lame dog which existed in the open-field system and the institution of the common. Contempor-ary fears of depopulation as a result of agrarian developments are given an ironic twist by the present view that a major cause of poverty was the steep increase in population.[4] More rational use —whether for sheep or arable—of existing land, together with

---

[1] Printed in T. Vicary, *The Anatomie of the Bodie of Man*, ed. F. J. and P. Furni-vall (E.E.T.S., London, n.d.), 291–3.

[2] 'Speech to the citizens of London, in behalf of religious houses', in Strype, iii (Part II), 482–4 and 506–7.

[3] Below, 157–9.   [4] Below, 138.

the demographic trend suggested, must inevitably have created problems of unemployment and underemployment. Put briefly, it is argued that on the whole agriculture was unable to expand, either intensively or extensively, at sufficient pace to raise either its labour force or its product proportionately to the rise in population. Indeed, concern about depopulating enclosure on the one hand, and excess of unemployed population on the other, was expressed by Starkey.[1]

The surplus labour sought wage-employment, often in industry. But in the craft or industrial sector of the economy a similar deterioration in the individual's security took place. Although the ideal of the medieval gild was not always attained many of the town workers had, under gild regulations, enjoyed a fair degree of security in employment and a not inconsiderable form of social insurance. But the individual craftsman running a small trade or business on his own account was now increasingly replaced by the wage-earner who relied wholly or in part upon a larger-scale employer for his livelihood. Domestic industrial work became for many the major occupation, rather than something ancillary to agriculture, at the very time when the difficulties of communications and fluctuations in demand of an expanding market caused irregularities of work to become more marked. The influence of slumps and booms upon employment was accentuated by the absence, under the domestic or 'putting-out' system, of very heavy overhead costs, making it easy for the employer to check or cease production. Such factors explain

the opinions of many great wise men; which think it better that all our wool were sold over the sea unwrought, than any clothiers should be set awork within the Realm . . . [For] all these Insurrections do stir by occasion of all these clothiers; for when our clothiers lack vent over sea, there is great multitude of these clothiers idle . . . then they assemble in companies, and murmur for lack of living.[2]

Unemployment and poverty stand in starker relief against the background of contemporary price movements.[3] It is established that from about 1510 onwards rising prices helped cause a downward trend in the wage-workers' standard of living, and that the fall in their real earnings was probably most rapid during the

[1] *Dialogue*, 72, 75–80, and 146 ff.   [2] *Discourse*, 88.   [3] Below, Chapter 8.

'forties and 'fifties. The view of J. E. T. Rogers and Sir John Clapham that the gains of the fifteenth century—which rising wages and falling prices had made 'the golden age of the English labourer'[1]—were more than wiped out in the sixteenth is confirmed by recent statistical investigations which describe what occurred as 'catastrophic . . . there is nothing like it anywhere else in wage-history'.[2] The 1540s and 1550s in particular inflicted 'a traumatic experience' upon the wage-earner.[3] The conclusion that 'the proportion of meat to bread [in a representative basket of consumables] must surely have fallen'[4] is borne out by People's complaint in *Respublica* that

> . . . their great grazing hath made fleshe so dere, I wotte,
> that poore volke att shambles cannot bestowe their grotte,[5]

and by Ponet's allusion to 'the people driven of hunger to grind acorns for bread meal, and to drink water in stead of ale'.[6]

Fears were expressed for the Englishman's traditionally high standard of eating. An attack upon the import of the products of cheap foreign labour explains that 'the very poor Labourers here in england have always heretofore been accustomed to be fed with Flesh and white meats, whereas the common people in other realms live only with roots and herbs'; thus comparative wage-costs explain why 'all other Nations, can afford to make and send hither all those kind of wares . . . at a lower price than they can be made here'. Indeed the English beggar has always eaten better than the French labourer or artificer,[7] a contention which receives some support from a statutory reference to 'beef mutton pork & veal which is the common feeding of the mean & poor persons'.[8]

The contrast with the foreigner was a favourite theme. Despite the deterioration around the mid-century, John Aylmer in 1559 could still pity 'the peasants of France, how they are scraped to

---

[1] J. E. T. Rogers, *Six Centuries of Work and Wages*, 326; also Sir J. Clapham, *A Concise Economic History of Britain to 1750*, 211–13.

[2] E. H. Phelps Brown and S. V. Hopkins, 'Wage-rates and Prices: Evidence for Population Pressure in the Sixteenth Century', 289, also 291–4 and 299.

[3] J. D. Gould, 'The Price Revolution Reconsidered', 265, also 251.

[4] E. H. Phelps Brown and S. V. Hopkins, 'Seven Centuries of the Price of Consumables', 363.

[5] Anon., 36. [6] *Politike power*, K.viii. [7] *Policies*, T.E.D., iii, 328–9.

[8] 24 Hen. VIII, c.3.

the bones', while as to the Italians, they do not get 'Beef or Mutton, Veal or sea fish, as you do: but a quart of oil to make salads of herbs, wherewith he liveth all the week following. And in Germany . . . yet eat they more roots than flesh. For what cheer so ever they have beside, they are sure of roots and stinking herbs, which they call crowte. . . . God defend us from the feeling of their misery.'[1] Forrest urged that

> Our English nature cannot live by Roots,
> by water, herbs or such beggary baggage,
> that may well serve for vile outlandish Coots.

The position of the labourer, caught between low wages and high prices, was therefore impossible:

> To Thresh all day for penny half-penny,
> and delve in ditches up to the hard knees
> for like value, how can he live thereby?[2]

The allusion to beggary points to that aspect of poverty which probably aroused most concern in Tudor England: the wandering beggars. The origins of this class have been related to the increased mobility of labour which dated from the fourteenth century but must now be set against the unfavourable demographic background, agricultural displacement, and the drift from country to town, with people sometimes of good stock being driven by desperation to vagabondage. The great increase in numbers which made them appear a social menace probably took place from about 1520, but it has been contended both that these numbers have been greatly exaggerated and that there is little proof that they included a sizeable proportion of unemployed genuinely seeking work.[3] The view that a problem of the first magnitude did in fact exist[4] is nonetheless supported by the weight of discussion in the source-material and the evidence of governmental concern.[5]

---

[1] *An Harborowe For Faithfull and Trewe Subiectes*, pp. P.3–P.3.b.
[2] *Princelie Practise*, ll. 393–5 and 659–61.
[3] On these issues see F. Aydelotte, *Elizabethan Rogues and Vagabonds*, 17; W. K. Jordan, *Philanthropy in England*, 62 and 78; E. M. Leonard, *The Early History of English Poor Relief*, 3–4 and 11–13; S. and B. Webb, *English Local Government. Poor Law History. Part I*, 27; and G. R. Elton, *England Under the Tudors*, 260.
[4] See A. V. Judges, *The Elizabethan Underworld*, p. xv. [5] Below, 126 ff.

The significance of the dissolution of the monasteries for the problem of poor relief has also been questioned. In particular, it is urged that such monastic charity as still existed was ill-ordered and indiscriminate, doing as much harm as good, that its volume had in any case diminished, and that few of the monastic inmates actually became paupers, since they received pensions or became secular priests; even the indirect effect of the dissolution upon poverty through the nature of exploitation of monastic estates by their new owners is questioned.[1] The detailed investigations of Dr Savine do not encourage extreme statements. His conclusion that obligatory monastic alms, the 'allowances' of the Valor Ecclesiasticus, composed less than 2·5 per cent of gross monastic income, while the number of mouths fed by the monasteries, including officers and working men who were receiving employment rather than charity, was about 35,000, justifies scepticism as to the great charitable influence of monasticism in England.[2] Most importance seems to have been attached to doles and hospitality, sporadically given, sometimes on the monks' own initiative: gifts of money, food and clothing to the poor on appointed days, and overnight lodging granted to wayfarers of varying social status. The picture which emerges is one of relatively insignificant total monastic charity within which must be included the possibility of greater importance in individual or regional instances and the traditional belief in sporadic relief, particularly for the wayfaring destitute.[3]

This is confirmed by much contemporary comment. A ballad composed at the time of the Pilgrimage of Grace described the poor as finding 'good bate, At church men gate',[4] a clear allusion to outdoor relief. Robert Aske pleaded that suppression of the abbeys deprived the North not only of alms but of essential hospitality 'in the mountains and desert places'.[5] Even Sir Francis Bigod conceded grudgingly of the monasteries that 'though they

[1] See A. G. Dickens, *The English Reformation*, 139–66; S. and B. Webb, op. cit., 17–18; W. K. Jordan, op. cit., 58–60; E. M. Leonard, op. cit., 18 and 63; and G. R. Elton, *England Under the Tudors*, 187–8.

[2] For a blindly enthusiastic Elizabethan encomium see M. Sherbrook, *The Fall of Religious Houses*, in A. G. Dickens, *Tudor Treatises*.

[3] A. Savine, *English Monasteries on the Eve of Dissolution*, 227, 239, 241 and 263–5.

[4] M. Bateson, *The Pilgrimage of Grace. Aske's Narrative*, 345.

[5] 'Aske's Examination', in *L. and P. Henry VIII*, xii (Part i), No. 901, 405–6. See also M. Bateson, op. cit., 336.

preach not, yet they keep some hospitality'.[1] Several appeals by
the commissioners themselves show that good work was sometimes done: that in favour of St. James's Abbey, Northampton,
explains that its alms relieve 'three or four score folks of the town
and the country adjoining, daily. . . . There are many poor in
Northampton, and they are greatly relieved by this house.'[2] The
abuses of indiscriminate relief, and the fact that many of the poor
'be not poor at heart',[3] were clearly grasped, yet belief in the
reality of monastic charity in the North was strong enough to
be one cause of the Pilgrimage of Grace, while the London City
authorities petitioned Henry VIII as to the effect of dissolution
upon over a dozen hospitals. Monastic charity cannot be entirely
discounted.[4]

It seems probable that the problem of poverty vexed men's
minds so much at this time because in fact the problem itself was
of greater magnitude. On the one hand, accelerating changes in
the economic organization of society led to an increase in poverty
which was either rootless or not attributable to natural catastrophe—both characteristics which were potentially dangerous to
peace and order. On the other hand, men saw those institutions
which—with all their defects—had traditionally been responsible
for the relief of destitution in the past now crumble between the
pincers of decay from within and attack from without. The problem assumed its peculiar urgency because the circumstances
accentuating the cumulative causes of poverty brought its incidence to a spate at the very time when the former channels for
its relief broke up or were swept away.

Contemporary discussion shows a growing appreciation of two
points of fundamental importance: first, of the need for more
discrimination in assessment of the causes of poverty, leading to
differentiation between its types and the appropriate modes of
treatment; secondly, of the fact that the assumption of the past,
that relief could be left to individual alms-giving and corporate

[1] *Treatise Concernynge Impropriations of Benefices*, in A. G. Dickens, *Tudor
Treatises*, 51.

[2] *L. and P. Henry VIII*, x, No. 916, 384; see also No. 917, 385; No. 563, 221;
No. 716, 301; No. 858, 354; and xiii (Part II), No. 306, 120.

[3] R. Copland, *The Highway to the Spital-House*, in A. V. Judges, *The Elizabethan
Underworld*, 2.

[4] W. K. Jordan, op. cit., 59.

institutions, was no longer valid, and that organization of poor relief was now essential.

The distinction between the genuinely needy and the sturdy beggar had been explicitly made at least as far back as the Ordinance of Labourers of 1349, but within an essentially repressive framework.[1] The sixteenth century saw a more positive approach to the problem of classification and treatment. The existence of the poor by vocation or by the will of God, and the corollary of almsgiving as an act of piety, these notions were still accepted, but they were increasingly balanced by a 'causative' classification of pauperism, by a rational assessment of the status and motives of the recipient of alms, and by the belief that since poverty was partly caused by specific economic or social malfunctionings, its cure was the responsibility of society. Quite apart from the duty of Christian charity, the institution of systematic and ubiquitous provision for the poor as a measure of civil administration had now become essential in the public interest, in view of the failure of the Church and of the charitably-inclined to cope with the need.

That this was a problem common to Western Europe at this time is evidenced by the foreign origin of some of its most interesting and influential discussions. The main thesis of *De Subventione Pauperum*, by the enlightened and humanist Spaniard, Juan Luis Vives, who visited England and was acquainted with the More circle, is the duty of the community to provide for the poor, for 'in a State, the poorer members cannot be neglected without danger to the powerful ones'. Beggars should be reformed rather than punished,[2] a trade taught to those who needed it, and orphans educated. There should be special places for the sick so that 'as in nature and in shipbuilding . . . the foulness will all be restricted to one place, and the rest of the body not infected', while the insane receive psychological treatment. Vives would rely on voluntary alms-giving and believes that since the poor will always be present they should 'learn not to have provision for a long time in advance [and] trust, not in man, but in God'.[3] His

---

[1] See E. M. Leonard, op. cit., 4–5, and S. and B. Webb, op. cit., 23–9.

[2] The ideas of Vives were attacked by the Spanish mendicant orders who defended begging as a fundamental human right. See J. H. Elliott, *Imperial Spain, 1469–1716* (London, 1963), 181.

[3] Trans. F. R. Salter, in *Some Early Tracts on Poor Relief*, 6, 9, 13, 15, 16–18, and 24–5.

work thus combines recognition of the need for classification and control of the poor with surviving medieval values.

The *Forma Subventionis Pauperum* of Ypres, translated in 1535 by Cromwell's protégé William Marshall, concurs in the doctrine of corporate responsibility: 'It appertaineth no doubt to all rulers both of the ecclesiastical and of the political or civil sort to care and provide for poor folks . . . whose maintenance Christ's law comitteth indifferently to all men.' Therefore prefects and over-seers of the poor are appointed, begging is prohibited and the lazy are made to work. The costs of the scheme will be met out of the response to the clergy's appeals in their sermons. Not only are the poor thus protected, but 'rich men fear not now lest they should feed with their benefits idle belly guts', while suspicion and dis-order diminish in a city which 'like a common parent handleth so her members'.[1] Both these works had some influence in England: Starkey explicitly mentions that of Marshall,[2] while Vives's classification of the destitute foreshadows that later adopted.[3]

Another work of particular interest is *A Treatise How By The Worde of God, Christian mens Almose ought to Be distributed*, by Martin Bucer. Bucer had been the leader of religion in Strassburg, the greatest centre of relief for Protestant refugees in Europe, but he wrote with full knowledge of the problem of poverty in England where he spent the last years of his life. The work is a fascinating blend of the medieval religious and the modern utilitarian approach to the problem, of continuing belief in Chris-tian motivation and appeal to State regulation. The idea that no shame necessarily attaches to poverty as such is accompanied by a remarkably shrewd and clear-headed analysis of the motives and attitudes of both givers and takers of charity. For if individual, indiscriminate alms-giving is practised it is usually vitiated by the dishonest and professional beggar's ability to solicit aid more skilfully; this type 'were not to be suffered in A common wealth' and should be forced to labour. Those who indulge in open almsgiving from an unworthy motive of ostentation, and use 'painted Charity . . . to get A little vain glory', in reality

[1] In F. R. Salter, op. cit., 41, 42–6, 51–4, 56–7, 60–1, 63–5, 66–8 and 69–71.
[2] *Dialogue*, 176.
[3] See S. and B. Webb, *Poor Law History*, 35–9.

'purchase themselves at length, by maintaining the Lewd, ever-lasting damnation'.[1]

Bucer therefore appeals to 'all Magistrates, and Governors . . . to Restore in the Church the right kind of giving, and distribution of Alms, and Provision for the poor'. Income from voluntary contributions to the 'Common Chest, or Box of the Church, to the use of the poor' may be supplemented by taxes on 'rich spiritual Promotions'. Deacons should search out the poor in each congregation and ascertain the nature and causes of their poverty. Alms are to be distributed to the genuine poor, and an account rendered to the ministers and elders, for 'the poor that have not yet learned, by the spirit of Christ, to be contented, whether they have plenty, or do suffer need, be very suspicious, and full of complaints'. If need be, poor people may be sent to other congregations which can afford relief. The idle must be made to work. Finally, those skilled in any craft should be helped with loans or gifts to become 'profitable members of the common wealth'.[2] Bucer's suggestions illustrate admirably the growing recognition, first, of the need for reappraisal of traditional attitudes towards alms-giving in the light of mid-sixteenth-century reality, and second, of the fact that enforcement of the standards laid down relied in the last resort upon compulsory organization by the civil authority.

The three works cited typify a general tendency to define certain categories and attitudes. First, 'the poor by physical affliction or weakness'—the young, the sick or maimed, the aged; the treatment thought appropriate was to maintain, where cause of destitution was permanent, and to aid where temporary. Secondly, 'the poor by economic circumstances'—here a distinction was sometimes made between poor in the sense of 'not well-off' and poor in the sense of 'destitute'; in both cases patience was expected of the individual concerned, but there was a growing conviction that for the latter it was the duty of society to take action to provide relief or work, and to remove the causes of poverty. Thirdly, 'the poor by their own idleness'; whether alms should be given to such became, as we have seen, a moot point,

[1] A translation in 1557(?) of a section of his *De Regno Christi*, title-page, and 3–4, 6–7, 16–17 and 20.

[2] Pp. 7, 9–14, 16–18, and 24.

but certainly society as a whole should punish and endeavour to reform.

Projects suggested in order to relieve the afflicted of the first category, so that they should be spared the shame of open begging,[1] have sometimes a modern-sounding ring. Cranmer relates how 'certain bishops . . . of the new learning' displeased Henry VIII by urging that at least some of the abbey spoils should be devoted to education and to 'the founding of hospitals, where poor and impotent people should have been sufficiently provided for with physicians and surgeons which should have ministered physic and surgery freely, not only to them but also to all other poor folk within this realm'.[2] Brinklow pleaded for use of confiscated church wealth so that

certain houses be maintained to lodge and keep poor men in, such as be not able to labour, sick, sore, blind, and lame. And every one of them to have wherewith to live, and to have poor whole women to minister unto them. . . . Let physicians and surgeons be found in every such town or city, where such houses be, to look upon the poor . . .; and they to live upon their stipend only, without taking any penny of their poor, upon pain of losing both his ears and his stipend also.[3]

Simon Fish suggested that 'we should also buy houses for the poor to dwell in, as are the hospitals situate in a fair pleasant and large (*sic*) out of the town', and that the poor should be given a sermon each day to comfort them in their poverty.[4] The more conservative Elyot produced an early statement of the 'less eligibility principle', urging that the quantity of meat provided in such institutions must be below the requirement of a fit working man: for 'such miserable nature remaineth in some men, that to live idly and voluptuously, they will choose rather to be sick, than to be healed'.[5]

Concern was not limited to relief of the sick or impotent on the one hand, and punishment of the work-shy and the lawless on the other; for it was agreed that many of the poor were

[1] As by S. Fish, *Summe of the holy scrypture*, fol. lvi.(b), and N. Ridley, *Works*, 60.
[2] *Miscellaneous Writings and Letters*, ii, 16.
[3] *The Complaynt of Roderyck Mors*, 52–3.
[4] Op. cit., fol. lxxi.(b).
[5] *The Image of Governance*, 44.b and 45.

unemployed through no fault of their own. Crowley stated explicitly that

> ... there are poor people,
> Well-most innumerable,
> That are driven to beg,
> And yet to work they are able,
> If they might have all things
> Provided aright.
> Alas! is not this
> A great over sight?[1]

Forrest advocated the further treatment of wool within the country so as to provide work, and urged also that labour should be fairly paid,

> else will they loiter ever now and then,
> counting as good to be idle unwrought
> as sore to travail and profit right nought.[2]

Starkey would establish officers in each town to see that there was not only full but also useful employment,[3] and Latimer thought it 'the king's honour that . . . the commodities of this realm [be] so employed, as it may be to the setting of his subjects on work, and keeping them from idleness'.[4]

The reciprocal duties of society and the individual—the one to provide and the other to perform work—were often stressed in a religious context,[5] and the latter's shortcomings were condemned at least as often as the former's neglect. Economic historians may ascribe underemployment to seasonal fluctuations in agriculture, precarious demand in industry, difficulties and dislocations in regard to transport and markets, and 'partly to the high leisure preference which the inhabitants of poor countries so often possess'.[6] Tudor commentators expressed the last point frequently, forcefully, and less elegantly as 'that most damnable vice of idleness, chief subverter and confounder of commonweals . . . mother and root of all vices'.[7]

---

[1] Works, 10.   [2] Princelie Practise, ll. 330–3 and 670–2.
[3] Dialogue, 153–5.   [4] Sermons, 99.
[5] S. Fish, op. cit., fols. lxxi–lxxi(b); W. Tyndale, Works, i, 135.
[6] F. J. Fisher, 'The Sixteenth and Seventeenth Centuries', 6; also 17.
[7] Proclamations, No. 128 (June 1530), 191–3; the latter phrase occurs also in 3 & 4 Edw. VI, c.16.

Henry VIII, in his 'Corrections' to the *Institution of a Christian Man*, or 'Bishops' Book' (1537), was at pains to include a clarification of the statement that 'good Lord, thou dost provide for thy poor people that have nothing, by them which have of thy gift sufficient to relieve themselves and other', lest it be construed to mean that the idle might expect charity as a right. For 'there be many folk which had liefer live by the craft of begging slothfully than either work or labour for their living'; such should be compelled to labour, not indulged with alms.[1] In his will a bequest of 1,000 marks in alms to the poor contains the proviso: 'common beggars, as much as may be, avoided'.[2] The 'Homily Against Idleness', prepared in the early 1560s, asked bluntly: 'what shall we need to stand much about the proving of this, that poverty followeth idleness? . . . For a great part of the beggary that is among the poor can be imputed to nothing so much as idleness.' It was the clear duty of all with authority 'to labour to redress this great enormity of all such as live idly and unprofitably in the commonweal'.[3]

This was not merely the voice of conservatism. Fish and Hooper, Frith and Bradford, Latimer and Becon, deplore the numbers of able-bodied, deliberate idlers, whose begging of alms which should go to the genuine poor makes them thieves before God. Morison and Starkey agree in an estimate that 'you shall find . . . the third part of our people living in idleness . . . much like unto the drone bees in a hive'.[4] The large number of beggars they attribute not to inevitable poverty but to 'much idleness and ill policy; for it is their own cause and negligence that they so beg'.[5] Particularly significant is the growing tendency to regard begging as symptomatic of a defect in the functioning of society rather than as an opportunity for the exercise of individual Christian charity. Becon's regret that society, 'seeing the number of beggars increasing daily more and more, do not only not provide any means to exile and banish this absurdity out of the commonweal, but also suffer them to live comfortless, yea, and

---

[1] In T. Cranmer, op. cit., ii, 108.
[2] *L. and P. Henry VIII*, xxi (Part II), No. 634, 320–2.
[3] *Two Books of Homilies*, 516–24.
[4] T. Starkey, *Dialogue*, 70; also Sir R. Morison, *Remedy*, p. E.iv.
[5] T. Starkey, *Dialogue*, 90.

many to die . . .',[1] typifies an increasingly logical and empirical approach.

Opinion was especially sensitive to the problem of the beggar by choice, the hardened professional vagrant. In *The Highway to the Spital-House* Copland chides the Porter with encouraging 'people of such iniquity' and exposes their deceits: some counterfeit leprosy, while others 'put soap in their mouth to make it scum' and fall down as with epilepsy.[2] Turner relates how, when he was physician to Somerset, beggars who sought alms spurned his offer to heal their diseases, 'for they had much liever be sick still with ease and idleness, than to be whole, & with great pain and labour, to earn honestly their living'.[3] But probably the best and most systematic account of Tudor vagabondage is *A Caveat for Common Cursitors* by Thomas Harman, a country magistrate, which appeared in 1566. By this time the rogues have a special language which has existed for about thirty years, and are organized under 'upright men' who conduct installation ceremonies, anointing with 'a gage of bouse, which is a quart pot of drink'. Harman outlines the various crafts of the rogues, including Anglers (who hook clothing through open windows), Dummerers, and Counterfeit Cranks (who practise the device described by Copland), and the surprisingly large amounts which some claim to make. Yet amid all this we are still told that charity blesses the giver regardless of the merit of its object![4]

A declaration addressed to the Privy Council by the citizens of London in 1552 observes shrewdly 'that the greatest number of beggars fallen into misery by lewd and idle service, by wars, by sickness, or other adverse fortune, have so utterly lost their credit, that though they would show themselves willing to labour, yet are they so suspected and feared of all men, that few or none dare, or will receive them to work'. The solution lies in 'making some general provision of work, wherewith the willing poor may be exercised; and whereby the froward, strong and sturdy vagabond may be compelled to live profitably to the commonwealth'.[5] This clear recognition of the difficulty of distinguishing between

---

[1] *Early Works*, 40. [2] In A. V. Judges, *The Elizabethan Underworld*, 4–7.
[3] W. Turner, *A new book of spirituall Physik*, fols. 1.b–2.
[4] In A. V. Judges, op. cit., 64–5, 72, 85, 87, 91.
[5] 'The Citizens of London to the Privy Council', in *T.E.D.*, ii, 302 and 307–9.

the workless and the work-shy, and the proposal of what would be at once a common remedy and a test, found expression in the establishment, between 1555 and 1557, of the famous Bridewell institution which was to become the model of many other 'Houses of Correction'.[1]

Such recognition of the need for a systematic and discriminatory approach to the problem of pauperism and its relief led inevitably to the crucial question of responsibility for financing and implementing the necessary measures. Contemporaries agreed that individual alms-giving was diminishing and provided no solution. Certainly the charitable impulse was still thought of in a religious context; but circumstances demanded more effective organization in the application of its fruits. This, and the realization that dependence upon this impulse alone was no longer practicable, were among the factors which led to increasing emphasis upon the belief that 'the prince's watch ought to defend the poor man's house',[2] that 'the palace of a prince, or a magistrate, should be the refuge and sanctuary of the poor'.[3] In discussing the principle of equity, Forrest had singled out the care of the poor as the king's especial 'dole', for

> So that the Poor be ever seen unto,
> the Rich him self will sure save harmless.[4]

Very prominent among the pressures making for a growing assessment of governmental responsibilities in this sphere was the fear of unrelieved poverty grown desperate. Becon, while deploring tumult and sedition, recognized the force of 'the common proverbs: "The belly hath no ears:" "Hunger is sharper than thorn." '[5] Expressions of concern were not always so sympathetic, describing poverty as an excuse for, rather than a cause of, trouble; Cheke, addressing the rebels of 1549, alleged that their camp 'like a boil in a body, nay like a sink in a town, have gathered together all the nasty vagabonds and idle loiterers'.[6] Crowley compared 'Commotioners' to corrupted humours in a body, but

---

[1] E. M. Leonard, *Early History of English Poor Relief*, 33–7; S. and B. Webb, *English Local Government*, 50.
[2] J. Ponet, *Politike power*, p. F.viii.   [3] J. Hooper, *Early Writings*, 366.
[4] *Princelie Practise*, pp. xcviii*–xcix*.
[5] *Fortress of the Faithful*, 583; also 601.
[6] *The hurt of sedition*, in Holinshed, iii, 992–3.

went on to say that forceful purgation was far from being a sufficient remedy; positive steps conducive to the health of the body politic were essential.[1] Thus motives of expediency as well as the promptings of Christian charity and general grounds of equity were urged as reasons for an enlightened and methodical policy for relief of poverty.

In short, men saw that former charitable methods and assumptions were no longer adequate or applicable and that the only body capable of tackling the problem for society as a whole was the State. Hence, in the legislation of the period, the gradual shift in the concept of the functioning of the institutions needed from an ecclesiastical to a civil context, and from reliance on voluntary gifts to compulsory poor rate assessment, although the continued use of the parish as the administrative unit symbolizes the gradual transition of responsibility from Church to State. In a sense, the effect of the Reformation in England was at once to necessitate and to facilitate this transition. For the head of society in its political aspect had now also become its head in the field of religious organization. The Christian charitable impulse was still appealed to and the unit of ecclesiastical administration employed, but the duty of clarifying principles and enacting methods of treatment of the various aspects of poverty fell more and more upon secular authority.

The change was not sudden or complete. Indeed, in the development of methods or machinery of relief three threads interlace: the religious, the municipal, and the national. The belief that relief of the poor was a Christian obligation, and the idea of the parish as the area of relief, tended to merge into the new arrangements. The London hospitals reorganized by the municipal authorities carried on essentially the same work as they had done for centuries. Meanwhile municipal experiment was often a precursor of legislation on a national scale. In this such cities as Norwich and Bristol played an important part, but the most striking advances were made in London during the period 1544 to 1557. A combination of religious leadership—notably that of Nicholas Ridley, who became bishop of London in 1550 and secured the interest and support of Edward VI—and municipal enterprise produced a scheme for classification of the poor into

[1] *Works*, 21-3.

'three degrees' ('the poor by impotency; poor by casualty', and 'thriftless poor') with appropriate treatment and institutions for each, financed in part by what has been described as the first assessed compulsory poor rate in Britain.[1]

But ultimately the evolution of machinery on a national scale was essential, and in the statutes and proclamations of the mid-Tudor decades almost all the essential principles of the later Elizabethan Poor Law were hammered out. In them we may trace the continued reliance on the parish as the administrative unit, the persistent attempts to exhort Christian charity and the progressive recourse to compulsion, and the gradual realization that provision of work was needed as well as punishment of the idle and 'sturdy'.

Statute and proclamation alike of the early Tudor period[2] order the punishment and subsequent return to their native district of 'beggars able to work' and those who 'delight to live in idleness, untruly feigning themselves to be sick and diseased'. But a proclamation of June 1530[3] complains that vagabonds and beggars 'have of long time increased and daily do increase in great and excessive numbers . . . whereby have insurged and sprung . . . continual thefts, murders' and so forth. Justices of the Peace are therefore to set aside 'all vain pity', to whip and send them home with a 'schedule or billet' to prevent a second dose of punishment on the way! This clearly foreshadows a major statute of 1531[4] which distinguished between impotent poor and sturdy beggars: J.P.s were to grant the former licences to beg in their own area, and to punish those who broke this ruling, but all vagrants outside their home district were to be whipped, given a 'punishment certificate', and sent home to work.

In striking contrast with this limited type of approach is a draft poor law of about 1535, probably composed by William Marshall.[5] This is of the very greatest interest as indicating an early grasp of the need for systematic and large-scale State action, and also as an illustration of the relationship between Commonwealth thought of the type we have been considering and legislative

[1] See N. Ridley, *Works*, 410–12; R. Holinshed, *Chronicles*, iii, 1060–2; *T.E.D.*, ii, 305–6 and 312; S. and B. Webb, op. cit., 47–8.

[2] 11 Hen. VII, c.2; *Proclamations*, No. 30 (18 Feb. 1493), 32–4; No. 63 (5 July 1511), 85–93.

[3] *Proclamations*, No. 128, 191–3.   [4] 22 Hen. VIII, c.12.   [5] Above, 30.

projects. The draft, which Professor Elton believes to have been of great influence on later legislation,[1] laid down all the principles of the future: 'the responsibility of the lay power, the need to provide work, the prohibition of begging, the parish organization. Its general levy foreshadowed the later poor rate.' Of special interest is the proposal to tackle unemployment by a scheme of public works, including harbours, roads, fortresses and watercourses. The projects were to be supervised by a 'Council to avoid vagabonds' with powers of delegated legislation, and financed through royal benevolence, church collections, and an 'annual levy or graduated income tax'.[2] (This scheme is perhaps echoed in a note in Wriothesley's hand on disposal of the Crown revenues, in 1538, which mentions that the king 'may assign yearly for repair of highways or other good deeds, whereby valiant beggars may be set to work, 5,000 marks'.[3]) The proposal 'that if any such vagabond and idle persons be sick, which of likelihood might well labour if they were whole, that then the said deputies shall assign certain Physicians and Surgeons to look unto and remedy their diseases',[4] is reminiscent of several of the suggestions of the idealists at which we looked earlier.[5] The need for enforcement of legislation was recognized: justices and mayors were to appoint two 'Censors or Overseers of poverty and Correctors of Idleness' for each parish, and these in turn would appoint 'beadles of the poverty' to collect alms for the poor.[6]

The measure which actually became law in 1536[7] was much more limited in scope. Local officers and churchwardens were to collect voluntary alms for the impotent poor, and preachers were to exhort charitable bequests. Vagrants were to be forced to work, and punished by whipping and the loss of part of one ear for a second offence. Orphan or vagrant children of between 5 and 14 were to be put to masters, and whipped if they deserted or idled when over 12. This act is described by Professor Elton as 'an enfeebled version of part of Marshall's draft', but even as such it 'represents the one positive achievement of the commonwealth movement in the 1530s', and 'still embodied the essential ideas

---

[1] G. R. Elton, 'An Early Tudor Poor Law'.   [2] Ibid., 58–9 and 63.
[3] *L. and P. Henry VIII*, xiii (Part II), No. 1, 1.
[4] G. R. Elton, op. cit., 59.   [5] Above, 123.
[6] G. R. Elton, op. cit., 60–1.   [7] 27 Hen. VIII, c.24.

on which the later poor law was to rest' in making the parish responsible for collecting alms, relieving the needy and employing the fit.[1]

A proclamation of 1545 ordered vagabonds to the galleys,[2] but was followed two years later by a much more draconian measure.[3] The act of 1547 is both notorious and puzzling; notorious for the extreme harshness of its clauses, and puzzling in its enactment under the otherwise benevolently paternal regime of Somerset. It decreed branding with the letters V and S for sturdy vagrants, with forced labour and finally slavery as the indicated penalties for repeated offences. Enforced apprenticeship was enacted for the needy young—up to 24 years of age. Charitable collections for the impotent were to be made on Sundays.

To what must we attribute the near-savagery of this measure, in which repression bulks so much larger than relief? Professor Elton has suggested that it reflected the temper of the house of commons itself,[4] while Dr. C. S. L. Davies conjectures that the act might have resulted from a panic for no clearly discernible reason unless it be the increased incidence of enclosures or the return of a force of 48,000 from Boulogne.[5] Davies relates the resort to slavery to Sir Thomas Smith in particular, and to the influence of the Commonwealth Party, 'of men inclined to reason *a priori* . . . with little conception of what was realistically possible', in general.[6] This seems rather sweeping; Commonwealth suggestions for poor relief were usually too comprehensive rather than too limited, and erred on the side of humanity rather than of repression; the Commonwealth tradition is surely more faithfully reflected in the draft of 1535.

Be that as it may, the double weakness of the failure to provide machinery for enforcement of its provisions, and the impracticable ferocity of those provisions themselves, made the act a dead letter. This was attested by an act of 1549[7] which, alluding to previous legislation, stated that 'the extremity of some whereof have been occasion that they have not been put in use', and repealed the statute so obviously referred to. An act passed two years later[8]

[1] G. R. Elton, *England under the Tudors*, 188–90.
[2] *Proclamations*, No. 250, 352. [3] 1 Edw. VI, c.3.
[4] G. R. Elton, op. cit., 207.
[5] 'Slavery and Protector Somerset; the Vagrancy Act of 1547', 537–8.
[6] Ibid., 541–5. [7] 3 & 4 Edw. VI, c.16. [8] 5 & 6 Edw. VI, c.2.

gave more consideration to the relief of poverty. Collectors of alms in church were to be appointed by mayors, householders and clergy. A book of the needy was to be compiled and alms distributed by the collectors. The clergy, and the bishop if need be, were to admonish reluctant contributors. A broadly similar measure in 1555[1] enacted weekly collection and distribution of alms within each parish, the establishment of a register of impotent needy, and provision of employment for some of the poor, but was still forced to concede that if their number were too great J.P.s might license some to wear badges and beg.

Thus far it might well be urged that certain municipal schemes were ahead of any parliamentary enactment in regard to the positive provision of work for those who—whatever the reason —were unemployed. But the transference to the civil power of organized and compulsory charity, the recognition that the responsibilities of government go far beyond the mere repression of menaces to property and order, these stand out clearly enough, even though few of the more idealistic schemes of the Commonwealth writers and preachers are reflected in the statute book.

[1] 2 & 3 P. and M., c.5.

The Social and Economic Problems of the Commonwealth

III. 'THE NAUGHTINESS OF THE SILVER'

IN the last chapter we met with more than one allusion to the problem of rising prices. This is of fundamental importance, for if an increase in the part played by money payments is accepted as a primary characteristic of the transition from a medieval to a modern economy, then anything affecting the stability of this monetary link will obviously have increasingly significant repercussions. This is precisely what happened in the sixteenth century. Successive manipulations of the English coinage took place in 1526, 1542-4, 1545, 1546, 1549 and 1551, and despite later restoration prices continued to rise. This was doubtless due in part to the prolonged effect of the influx of precious metals from America—'in part' because we cannot ignore the effect of real (as distinct from monetary) causes, upon which recent research lays increasing emphasis. Finally, we shall find that in contemporary discussion the middleman was blamed probably as often as the coin in which he dealt. The responsibility of government to maintain a true and stable coinage as the essential basis of just prices, and its duty to control the actions of the suspect middleman, were generally accepted, but we shall find the record in regard to the second perhaps more impressive than that in respect of the first.

The exchange value of money was intrinsic and depended on its precious metal content. The level of prices would therefore be determined, largely, by the interaction of the following variables: volume of goods and transactions, quantity of silver in the country, amount of coinage in the country, and proportion of silver per coin. To this must be added the complicating factor of overseas transactions, involving movement of precious metal into or out of England, exchange rates with foreign currencies, import or export of goods, and royal borrowings abroad. This last point raises an issue which is the key to the first phase of the price inflation in England: the immense and direct influence of the monarch. Through control of the mint he decided the proportion of precious metal in the coinage and the quantity of coinage in the country, while his political or military activities might lead to foreign expenditure or borrowings with consequent effects upon the exchanges.

It is generally acknowledged that after the downward trend of the late fourteenth and early fifteenth centuries prices had remained stable, partly because of short supply of the precious metals. This was now changed by the influx of gold and silver from the New World in an ever-thickening stream, particularly after the discovery of the Potosi mines in 1545. Meanwhile, the reason given for Henry VIII's first debasement, in 1526, was the alleged export of English coin caused by its high precious metal content and consequently enhanced value overseas.[1] The suggestion that war expenditure abroad had turned the exchanges against England, forcing Henry to accept depreciation of the pound,[2] gains some support from Sir Thomas Gresham's later analysis of the reasons for the fall of the exchange,[3] but more recent research indicates that the official explanation was in fact basically true.[4]

This was followed in the next decade by the coining of the silver plate from the monasteries, a step which, *ceteris paribus*, can only have had inflationary effects. But the Great Debasement came in the 1540s, under direct pressure of royal monetary needs, above all for the wars which cost over £2,000,000 in that decade. Indeed a proclamation in 1551 was to recall frankly how 'the late King of most famous memory . . . considering at the beginning of his last wars that great and notable sums of money were requisite . . . for

[1] *Proclamations*, No. 111 (22 Aug. 1526), 156–8; No. 112 (5 Nov. 1526) 158–63. Also C. Armstrong, *Treatise*, in *T.E.D.*, iii, 110.

[2] A. E. Feavearyear, *The Pound Sterling*, 48–9.

[3] In *T.E.D.*, ii, 146–7.

[4] For this point I am indebted to Dr C. E. Challis, whose views have now been published in *Econ. Hist. Rev.*, 2nd Ser., xx (1967), 441–66.

the maintenance . . . of the same, did therefore devise to abase and diminish the goodness of the coin. . . .'[1] In 1542–4 commenced a pattern which was repeated in 1545 and 1546: the Crown debased the coinage and thereby made a large profit, the higher price of precious metals being both pretext for and inevitable result of this step, which, in turn, led to higher prices for all commodities, as well as precious metals, and to the need to offer a higher price for bullion and make it into money at yet a lower grade of fineness in order to make a profit on the next round.

Estimated figures vary, but it seems that on coinage issued between 1542 and Michaelmas 1551 the Crown made a net profit of £1,285,000[2] as a result of its powers of timing and control. It is difficult to avoid the impression of a deliberate and gigantic fraud.[3] What is really surprising is the fact that apparently king and ministers thought that the foreigner would accept the bad coins at their face value.[4] Actually the Netherlands merchants had discovered their baseness within two months, and their exchange value inevitably slumped. Thus Henry VIII's extravagance and search for military glory more than outdid the effects of raids on church property,[5] and he bequeathed to his successor a debased currency, a lowered foreign exchange rate, and a large debt, much of it contracted abroad at rates of interest that were ruinously high.

Already the fall in the value of the pound was something over 25 per cent. But worse was to follow, for the problem left by Henry proved beyond the abilities of at least his immediate successors, beset as they were by difficulties other than economic. The size of the debt, the heavy interest burden, the expenses of war with Scotland and France, and the incompetence and rapacity of ministers, go far to explain the record 'of good resolutions, of vain attempts to put the coinage to rights, and of backslidings into the old vice of debasement'.[6] Debased coinage had been minted almost continuously since 1544, but in 1549 it was decided to increase the standard of fineness but make smaller coins. An increase

---

[1] *Proclamations*, No. 372 (30 April 1551), 518–19.
[2] Information from Dr C. E. Challis.
[3] See the calculations in *L. and P. Henry VIII*, xix (Part I), No. 513(5), 319; also No. 272(2), 144.   [4] A. E. Feavearyear, op. cit., 54.
[5] See W. C. Richardson, 'Some Financial Expedients of Henry VIII', *Econ. Hist. Rev.*, 2nd Ser., vii (1954), 47–8.   [6] A. E. Feavearyear, op. cit., 61.

in fineness from 4 oz. to 8 oz. in February of that year produced the coin alluded to in Latimer's sermon of March 8: 'we now have a pretty little shilling indeed, a very pretty one. . . . I had put it away almost for an old groat.'[1] But the larger issue later in the year was reduced to 6 oz. fine,[2] and as a result of the minting of about £1,000,000 of this money on into 1550 prices rose and the exchange rate fell away. Northumberland now produced a plan for one last coup which would net enough profit to pay off the royal debts and leave over a stock of bullion sufficient to carry out a recoinage. Coins were to be made of only 3 oz. fineness (the mint making a profit of 11s. 8d. on every £1 of money), and then the coinage was to be called down in value. The announcement of the scheme in advance[3] and the appearance of the new coins accelerated the rise in prices and fall of the exchange; a flight from the pound ensued.

The value of the pound had now reached its nadir, its internal purchasing power and external exchange value having fallen to about half of pre-debasement level. But issue of the new coinage was checked and the money called down, the shilling to 9d. in July and to 6d. in August 1551.[4] Other aspects of a deflationary policy were an economy campaign in state expenditure, including a lower level of royal hospitality, and an attempt to call in some of the coins. Meanwhile Gresham undertook manipulation of the exchanges in order to force up the valuation of English coinage and pay off the king's debts.[5] These efforts were not unsuccessful, but their effects upon cloth exports were disastrous: the consequent raising of cloth prices in terms of foreign money was a major reason for the slump of some 15 per cent in 1551 and of a further 20 per cent in 1552. Mary Tudor's hands, compared with those of her predecessors, were clean of monetary debasement, and the comparative stability achieved by the end of her reign was consolidated by the restoration of the coinage by Elizabeth I.

The course of debasement sketched would obviously raise prices for internal purchasers (in monetary terms), and impose hardship

---

[1] *Sermons* (Everyman), 81.   [2] Information from Dr C. E. Challis.
[3] *Proclamations*, No. 372 (30 April 1551), 518–19.
[4] Ibid., Nos. 376 (8 July 1551), 525, and 379 (16 Aug. 1551), 529–30.
[5] See Gresham's account of this, printed in *T.E.D.*, ii, 147–8.

upon the poor and strain upon those in receipt of fixed incomes. But the foreign exchange value of English currency reflected not only the assessment abroad of the value of its precious metal content but also the supply and demand position of currencies themselves. Assuming a mint par exchange (valuation strictly according to metallic content) then debasement would of itself depreciate English currency. But this must now be related to the extremely significant fact of the influx of precious metals from the New World to other parts of Europe—Spain, France and the Netherlands—before this phenomenon affected England.[1] Thus, for a while, a rise in prices took place in England and in Western Europe simultaneously but for somewhat different reasons; in the latter, because there was more silver in circulation, in the former, because there was an increased supply of money but less silver in the coinage. English goods, in terms of precious metal content of our coinage, were therefore cheap for Western European importers, while continental commodities were dear for English importers. The connection of these facts with the boom in export of English cloth obviously occurs, but so too in terms of modern analysis does the suspicion of unfavourable terms of trade—grasped, though not in that terminology, by some contemporary critics—and the question of the balance of payments.

A third determinant of the exchanges was the supply and demand (as distinct from the mint par exchange) relationship between any two currencies emerging from the balance of trade in goods and, of particular importance to England at this time, interest payments on foreign debts. This in turn was complicated by a fourth consideration: dealings in, and sometimes deliberate manipulation of, the exchanges by specialists whose business was to profit by such variations. The highly organized and complex international exchange mechanism which all this assumes did indeed exist, and both contemporary and later commentators seem agreed that within this financial arena England got the worst of the exchanges. Adverse real terms of trade, the consequent

[1] See Y. S. Brenner, 'The Inflation of Prices in Early Sixteenth Century England', 228–9 and 231; J. U. Nef, 'Prices and Industrial Capitalism in France and England, 1540–1640', 114, n. 25 and 134; E. V. Morgan, *The Study of Prices and the Value of Money*, 21; J. M. Keynes, *A Treatise on Money*, ii, 152–4; M. Beer, *Early British Economics*, 119–20.

unfavourable balance of trade, and the necessity of delivering large quantities of English coin to the professional exchanger, provided every opportunity for undervaluation. It has been argued that this, not intrinsic or extrinsic value, was the factor 'that priced and tariffed money', leading in mid-century to a 30 per cent under-valuation of sterling by exchange, driving up prices of imports, and affording every incentive to smuggling abroad of specie.[1] The suspicion that at every step the Englishman was outwitted by the foreigner is understandable.

Before looking more closely at contemporary criticism and interpretation of this inflationary movement we must consider its real, as distinct from its monetary, causes. These would include any upsurge in demand and relative shortage in supply. Certainly the rise in population from about 3 million to about 4 million during the sixteenth century might be expected to increase aggregate demand; but the position is complicated by the fact that prices rose unevenly—more quickly for grain than for manu-factures, and fastest of all for firewood.[2]

Recent research has attributed to population expansion an in-creasingly important part in the inflation of prices.[3] Now a growing population might increase the need for goods, but un-less it was matched by expansion of productive employment would raise neither output on the one hand nor effective demand on the other. It must therefore be seen in relation to the low level of both productivity and elasticity of the dominant agricultural sector of the economy. From the failure of agriculture to expand, either in area or in productivity, sufficiently rapidly to keep pace with population growth there followed land hunger, higher grain prices, surplus labour, lower real wages and movement from countryside to town.[4] Meanwhile, whereas for agriculture and basic industries 'the difficulty lay in raising output rather than in

[1] M. Beer, op. cit., 103, 109, 113.

[2] On these points see J. U. Nef, op. cit., 130, and E. H. Phelps Brown and S. V. Hopkins, 'Wage-rates and Prices', 296–8.

[3] See Y. S. Brenner, op. cit., also his 'The Inflation of Prices in England, 1551–1650'; also E. H. Phelps Brown and S. V. Hopkins, op. cit.

[4] See P. J. Bowden, 'Agricultural Prices, Farm Profits, and Rents', in J. Thirsk, (ed.), *The Agrarian History of England and Wales*, IV, *1500–1640*, 593–695. In this context, the conclusion of a recent study that 'the agricultural revolution cannot be said to have commenced until about 1560-3' is of interest: E. Kerridge, *The Agricultural Revolution*, 347.

disposing of it',[1] for secondary industries the reverse applied and they were therefore more elastic in regard both to supply and demand. The preponderance of agriculture in the economy was matched by that of foodstuffs in consumer expenditure, so that demand for industrial products would tend to vary inversely with food prices. Hence the divergence of prices between the relatively elastic and inelastic sectors of the economy.

The extension of the market—another symptom of the transition from a medieval to a modern economy—meant more specialization, increased importance of transport of goods, and a lengthening of the link between demand and supply, in terms both of space and of time. All this inevitably enhanced, and indeed made crucial, the function of the middleman—a function which was both indispensable and highly suspect, the charge of deliberate extortion being a facile contemporary explanation of rising prices. The importance of the evolution of the market in relation to problems of supply and price may be seen in a sphere to which public opinion was particularly sensitive: that of food supply. The population of London rose from about 60,000 to about 225,000 during the century. Other towns were dwarfed by this growth, but in itself it constituted an increase in urbanization which sharpened problems of food supply and marketing. Under the stimulus of expanding population corn production rose, even, apparently, at the time when the enclosure movement was causing most outcry. But prices in London rose more rapidly than elsewhere, the disparity increasing in the 1540s and 1550s; the real shortages reflected might be expected to make the sharpest impact upon contemporary discussion, while the fact that the onus of suffering would fall on the poorer inhabitants posed problems of public security as well as of public conscience. London was only an extreme instance of a general trend. Prices for the country as a whole rose during the mid-Tudor era, with a frightening upsurge in the decade or so before 1560 which must be related not only to currency developments but to bad harvests.[2]

In most spheres output seems to have increased in response to

[1] F. J. Fisher, 'Tawney's Century', in *Essays in the Economic and Social History of Tudor and Stuart England*, 3–6.

[2] See N. S. B. Gras. *Evolution of the English Corn Market*, and A. Everitt, 'The Marketing of Agricultural Produce', in J. Thirsk, (ed.), *Agrarian History*, 466–592, on the issues raised in this paragraph.

demand.[1] But the debasement of the coinage, the greater length of the link between producer and consumer, and such catastrophes as bad harvests or unemployment, explain the very real fear of high prices and shortage of supply in Tudor England. We have noted[2] the conclusion that, against this background, the wage-workers' living-standard declined, from the second decade of the century until at least the 'sixties, the fall in their real earnings probably becoming most rapid during the 'forties and 'fifties.

Contemporary explanations of high prices may thus be related to three major issues: the 'naughtiness of the coin'; the responsibility of the foreign exchanges and of the thoughtlessness or greed of merchants trading abroad; and the behaviour of the middleman. In regard to the first, the 'general sentence, or curse' printed in 1532 censured 'all those that make false money . . . and all those that good money clip or shear',[3] but in the following decades the Crown itself was to be the prime offender. Ponet, attacking its record, alluded to

evil governors and rulers [that] walk in nets, and think no man doth see them. . . . Those that contrary to all laws . . . counterfeit the coin that is ordained to run between man and man, turning the substance from gold to copper, from silver to worse than pewter, and advancing and diminishing the price at their pleasure, For in coins all laws command, and equity will, that these four things be observed and straightly kept. First, the pureness of the matter. . . . Second, that it have the just weight. Thirdly, that it be not clipped. The last, that it be not at the prince's will sometime priced at a more value, and sometime at a less.[4]

The late 'forties and the 'fifties saw a spate of denunciation, in pulpit, pamphlet and doggerel verse. John Heywood's couplet:

These Testons look red: how like you the same?
Tis a token of grace: they blush for shame,[5]

is of particular interest. As more copper was added to silver the colour of the resultant amalgam passed from white to red, so before leaving the mint the debased coins were blanched with acids to leave a thin surface film of silver. But this soon wore off

---

[1] See J. U. Nef, op. cit., 123-4.   [2] Above, 115-16.
[3] In T. Cranmer, *Miscellaneous Writings and Letters*, ii, 281-2.
[4] *Politike power*, pp. F.ii-F.iii.   [5] *Epigrammes*, in *T.E.D.*, ii, 179.

the highest reliefs of the coin and left the king, presented full face, with a red nose.[1] Latimer's allusion in 1549 to the new 'pretty little shilling' apparently provoked the comment that he was seditious. But a fortnight later he returned to the charge and quoted Esau as his fellow in sedition and in grasping 'that it tended to the hurt of the poor people: for the naughtiness of the silver was the occasion of dearth of all things in the realm'.[2]

The anonymous *Respublica* (1553) contains an attempt to express in dialect form the reaction of the simple and unlearned. People, when informed that 'the coin eke is changed', replies:

> . . . yea from silver to drosse,
> (twas told vs) vor the beste; but pore wee bare the losse!
> whan chad with swette of browes got vp a fewe smale crummes,
> at paiing of my debtes ich coulde not make my sommes.
> my landlord vor my corne paide me zuche sommes & zuche;
> whan he should hate vor rent, yt was but haulfe zo muche.
> zix pence in eche shilling was I-strike quite awaie,
> zo vor one piece iche tooke, che was vaine to paie him twaie.
> one woulde thinke twer brasse, &. zorowe have I els,
> But, ichwin, mooste parte ont was made of our olde bells.[3]

The allusions to the calling down of the coinage by Northumberland, and to confiscations of church bells, seem clear.

Probably the most detailed and methodical contemporary analysis of the effects of debasement and rising prices is to be found in the debate of the Knight, the Capper, the Merchant and the Husbandman in *A Discourse of the Common Weal of this Realm of England* (1549). While it is asserted that 'this alteration of the coin is the chiefest and principal cause of this universal dearth . . . being the original of all',[4] the cumulative nature of what is happening is clearly grasped. For 'as many of them as have wares to sell, do enhance as much in the price of things that they sell as was enhanced before in the price of things that they must buy'. It follows that those most injured are 'such as have their Livings and stipends rated at a certainty; as common labourers at 6*d*. the day, journey men of all occupations, serving man (at) 40*s*. the year', and gentlemen whose lands are on long let. In short, 'all those that

---

[1] Sir John Craig, *The Mint*, 113; see also A. E. Feavearyear, *The Pound Sterling*, 59.
[2] *Sermons* (Everyman), 117.   [3] 35–6.   [4] *Discourse*, 104.

live by buying and selling' do not lose by the price inflation as do those with fixed incomes.[1]

Several aspects of the matter are considered. With regard to employment, it is pointed out that the master craftsman who has to pay higher wages as a result of the rise in price of victuals cannot employ so many.[2] As to the wisdom of royal monetary policy, while the Knight has indeed 'heard wise men say, that the king's father did win inestimable great sums by the alteration of the coin', the Doctor explains that this was only temporary, 'as if a man would take his wood up by the roots . . . or to pull the wool off his sheep by the root', and that we cannot make foreigners accept our base coin.[3] The Knight queries whether, since 'the coin is but a token to go from man to man . . . stricken with the king's seal to be current', it matters 'what metal it be of, yea though it be but leather or paper?' But the Doctor replies 'that the substance and the quantity is esteemed in coin and not the name', so that 'loss comes of loss of credence' when the coin is tampered with. For 'we may not set the price of things at our pleasure, but follow the price of the universal market of all the world'.[4]

The cumulative effects of the rise in prices, and the tendency of each section of the community to blame another, are also discussed in Heywood's *The Spider and the Flie*. The Spider alleges that many Flies are now rich

> In occupying in windows under us,
> By price of things raised there in foul overplus.

To this the Fly answers that rising prices are the inevitable result of the exorbitant fines, incomes and rents exacted by Spider landlords. This the Spider denies, for

> Five foot to two in windows of this room
> Ye flies hold yet in lease at unraised rent;
> All holders whereof sell their wares as extreme
> As though their farms at the most raised rent went.

The Fly defends such behaviour as a precautionary measure

---

[1] Ibid., 33 and 80–1.   [2] Ibid., 15, 18 and 32.
[3] Ibid., 87–8, also 44.   [4] Ibid., 69–71, 77 and 87.

against the time when leases fall, but goes on to trace the effect of all this on other sections of the community:

> Th'one letting farms high, th'other selling victuals dear;
> And of all ware sellers each shifteth from harms
> By raising his ware, as other wares appear.
> But all that on their pension (or pence) live mere
> In windows, without land to let or ware to sell,
> Wherever they dwell may think they dwell in hell.

He accuses 'high head spiders' of conspiring to hold prices high and keep farms in their own hands, but the Spider replies that if rents are doubled, then prices of wares—and often worse wares at that—are trebled, so that the Flies, while pleading beggary, are still able to purchase the farms they occupy.[1]

Before examining discussion of the foreign exchanges we may repeat that there were, in effect, three reasons for the higher price of imports: first, the debasement of the coinage which of itself drove up English internal monetary prices, lowered its own exchange rate with foreign currency, and raised the prices (again in English monetary terms) of imports; secondly, the increasing quantity of silver in Western Europe, which resulted in higher prices in terms of silver itself; thirdly, undervaluation of our coinage by the exchangers as the result of an unfavourable supply and demand position for that currency and sometimes of deliberate manipulation of the exchange rate. The first would not of itself lower our real terms of trade; the second and third would do so.

These three factors were not grasped with equal clarity by contemporary analysts. Many were well aware of the connection between the debasement of the coinage and its lower exchange value. But some believed also that lack of social conscience and business acumen on the part of Englishmen who dealt in foreign trade and exchanges, together with trickery on the part of the foreigner, resulted in the exchange mechanism itself acting as an internal price-raising factor. Sir Thomas Chamberlayne, in a letter to the Council in 1551, expressed the view that 'the exchange is but merchants' practice; with how little they regard the common weal, for the advancement of their private lucre,

[1] *Spider and Flie*, 196–8.

I think the world doth see',[1] while a memorandum prepared for the Royal Commission on the Exchanges in 1564 described in detail 'the Rising and falling of the Exchange by Cunning handling' by 'the Conspiracy of the great Bankers'.[2] Indeed the anonymous author of *Policies to reduce this realme of England vnto a prosperus wealthe and estate*, in 1549, went further: seeking for 'certain general causes' for the rise in prices, he found it 'easy to be perceived that all things is not now risen according to the Baseness of our coin: But the most things be risen of price according unto the falling of the exchange'.[3]

The remark of the Doctor in the *Discourse* that it were not expedient to sell our wares cheaply to foreigners whilst paying dearly for theirs, 'for they should have much treasure for theirs, and have our commodities from us for a very little',[4] evinces a clear appreciation of the idea of terms of trade. But although he knows that 'every thing brought beyond the sea is commonly dearer by the third part than it was', his belief that 'setting our coin apart . . . we shall have as much silk, wines or oils from beyond the seas, for our tod of wool now as we might have had before the alteration of this coin'[5] seems to indicate that he has not grasped the fact that real terms of trade had turned against the English.

Two particularly interesting treatments of this aspect of the rise in prices were written by William Lane and William Cholmeley respectively, both merchants of London. The first, addressed to Cecil in 1551, observes of the proposed new coins that 'although the silver were fine yet was it too dear and the money naughty'. Indeed, the very news of the coinage experiments has caused a fall in the exchange of 'about 7 in 100' within a week or so and led to export of bullion. Continued coinage of base money will cause 'a greater fall of the exchange, which is the father of all dearth. . . . It is well known that the exchange between our Realm and other foreign Realms is the very Rule that setteth the price good cheap or dear of almost all things where of is no scarcity, as well of the commodities and merchandise of this Realm as of other foreign commodities brought hither.' Thus the fall of the exchange causes 'to be bought cloths at £56 the pack, which before would not

---

[1] Printed in Tytler, i, 380.
[2] Printed in *T.E.D.*, iii, 352.
[3] In *T.E.D.*, iii, 315–16.
[4] *Discourse*, 40.
[5] Ibid., 80.

have been bought for £52 the pack': the exchange engenders dear cloth, dear cloth means dear wool, dear wool dear sheep, dear sheep much pasture and decay of tillage, whence spring 'scarcity of corn and the people unwrought, and consequently the dearth of all things'.[1]

In *The Request and Suite of a True-Hearted Englishman* (1553) William Cholmeley, a 'grocer and one that selleth spices',[2] reaches similar conclusions as to the dangers of the position, but seizes points missing in Lane and the *Discourse*. He urges that what our merchants sell abroad will not balance our imports, 'for our cloth is sold to the strangers at his old price;[3] but the merchandise that cometh in is doubled'. Therefore 'money must needs be disbursed and conveyed hence'.[4] Many foreign wares are bought at 'an excessive price, by reason that we seek them so greedily'. Nor is it the whole explanation to say that 'the exchange . . . is the cause, by the means of the basing of our coin. Indeed the exchange doth hurt somewhat; as to say in every hundred £30, but the exalting of merchandise of foreign countries was in every hundred 200 and 300; which robbeth the realm of all our gold and silver' and plagues all men with dear prices. But he lays some of the blame for the disastrously adverse real terms of trade upon the merchants of Antwerp, who are 'confederated and bent against the English nation' and take advantage of the folly of our merchants, making us pay dearly for 'their pins, their painted papers, head cloths for women . . . glasses, hobby horses, babies [baubees?] for our children' and a thousand like things we could do without.[5]

The belief that at least part of England's foreign exchange difficulty must be attributed to the folly or greed of her merchants exemplifies contemporary suspicion of middlemen in general. For despite the inevitably increased significance of the middleman in an economy which was becoming more complex and commercialized, his activities still seemed dubious *per se*. The following practices were especially shameful. 'Engrossing', a term of fairly wide application, could mean dealing in many types of commodity instead of only one, or monopolizing the supply of any one

---

[1] In *T.E.D.*, ii, 182–6.
[2] Ed. W. J. Thoms, *Camden Miscellany*, ii, 17.
[3] He is writing after the calling down of the coinage.
[4] Op. cit., 11–12.   [5] Ibid., 17–18.

commodity by forestalling or by regrating. A 'forestaller of the market' went outside a borough or market town in order to intercept and buy up goods, thus undermining the public and open market and raising prices. To 'regrate' was to purchase goods for sale in the same or a nearby market. Such actions had attracted notice, and legal prohibition, from the thirteenth century on, and the taint of exploitation or even creation of scarcity attaching to them is in obvious contravention of the traditional idea of legitimate trading. With regard to the regrater, the modern concept of arbitrage through time would receive scant sympathy, being quite outweighed by the apparent lack of utility of his actions (since he did not necessarily transport goods) and the moral objection to speculation upon dearth.[1]

Professor Fisher's statement that 'under the Tudors the villain most frequently consigned to eternal damnation was "that caterpillar which cometh between the bark and the tree"—the middleman in primary produce',[2] must be related in particular to fear of food shortage, but the dealer in other commodities, including manufactures, was often judged guilty of sacrificing the interests of the commonweal to his own advantage. In the woollen industry the engrossing activities of middlemen often broke the law; they were accused of driving up prices and of adulteration of wools, and their competition angered the larger clothiers. But they were not parasitic; their ubiquity witnessed their necessity. The brogger's selection and distribution of the finer wools was an essential function. In particular, the middleman made possible the survival of the small manufacturer in face of the larger capitalist. Dr Ramsay concludes that the general rise in wool prices should probably be attributed to middlemen's manœuvres only in a very small degree. Nonetheless, he cites the case of one John Stephens of Bourton-on-the-Hill, accused, while acting under a licence which he had bribed Northumberland to grant, of having doubled the price of Cotswold wool.[3]

At the root of the Tudor hatred of the middleman was the fear of a 'monstrous and portentous dearth'[4] contrived by those who

[1] 5 & 6 Edw. VI, c.14 contains full definitions of terms; see also N. S. B. Gras, op. cit., 130–1, 161, 180–2, and 201, on these points.

[2] F. J. Fisher, 'The Sixteenth and Seventeenth Centuries', 8.

[3] G. D. Ramsay, *The Wiltshire Woollen Industry in the Sixteenth and Seventeenth Centuries*, 7–13 and 30.　　　　[4] H. Latimer, *Sermons*, 99.

'study how of plenty to make scarcity, for their singular weal to destroy the common weal',[1] 'forestallers of the market [who] have gotten all things so into their hands'.[2] Hales declared that 'the cause of the dearth is, that those have it that may choose whether they will sell it or no; and will not sell it but at their own prices',[3] while Latimer attacked such as 'bought corn in the markets to lay it up in store, and then sell it again', together with burgesses and farmers who had become regraters and aldermen who profiteered in wood and coals.[4] Lever condemned hoarders of corn whom 'neither God by blessing and cursing, neither the king by proclamation and commission, neither the poor by praying and paying' could move, and pointed to the discrepancy between the price wrung from the consumer and that received by the husbandman who tilled the ground and paid the rent.[5]

The continuity of thought with the medieval suspicion of men who bought to sell again runs right through the literature. The common factor in such sins as engrossing and regrating is the crime of taking too much, of occupying more than one man's living, dealing in too many commodities, creating too many steps between producer and consumer, taking too large a profit. And it is evident that the wider market gave the opportunity to do these things, that, paradoxically, the replacement of a limited local market, in which a regulated and corporately controlled monopoly existed, by a national and even international market, led to attempts at a private and unregulated monopoly taking advantage of the wider gap, in terms both of space and of time, between producer and consumer in order to exploit one or both.

In these circumstances unsupported local attempts at control of the market and of prices were no longer adequate, and the Crown was expected to take action. The belief that this was indeed a clear duty of government appears in a passionate appeal addressed to Cecil by Bishop Hooper in 1551:

For the love and tender mercy of God, persuade and cause some order to be taken upon the price of things, or else the ire of God will shortly punish. All things be here so dear, that the most part of people lacketh,

---

[1] C. Armstrong, *Reforme*, in *T.E.D.*, iii, 117.
[2] T. Becon, *Jewel of Joy*, 434.   [3] 'Charges', in Strype, ii (Part II), 359.
[4] *Sermons*, 279.   [5] *Sermons*, 128–9.

and yet more will lack necessary food. .... Master Secretary, for the passion of Christ take the fear of God and a bold stomach to speak herein for a redress, and that the goods of every shire be not thus wrested, and taken into few men's hands.[1]

The case for governmental intervention rested not only on the grounds of humanity and equity but also on that of the stark connection between hunger and revolt.

Indeed, the constant concern of government with the problem of prices and with the behaviour of middlemen is revealed in scores of royal proclamations as well as in the statutes. This appears in marked contrast with its irresponsible record of coinage debasement almost throughout the mid-Tudor era, since that record of course contributed largely to this problem. Apart from the basic concern with grain, meat and other victual,[2] commodities subject to sale and price control included wood and coal,[3] wines,[4] harness and armour,[5] and sugar. A proclamation in respect of the last of these has an interesting reference to food adulteration: 'sundry persons after they have bought such sugar at first hand do new-cast again the same in mounds, mixing therewith other things perilous and unwholesome for man's body'.[6] Many proclamations, a dozen of them between 1547 and 1550, controlled or prohibited the export of certain commodities, usually victual of all types.[7]

[1] In Tytler, i, 365–6.
[2] For grain see *Proclamations*, Nos. 118 (Nov. 1527); 121 (Dec. 1528); 125 (Aug. 1529); 127 (Oct. 1529); 151 (Nov. 1534); 242 (Nov. 1544); 280 (May 1547); 365 (Sept. 1550); 366 (Oct. 1550); and 377 (July 1551). For meat, Nos. 139 (July 1533); 142 (Jan. 1534); 144 (Mar. 1534); 148 (Oct. 1534); 154 (Mar. 1535); 159 (July 1535); 162 (Feb. 1536); 164 (Apr. 1536); 193 (Mar. 1540); 196 (Oct. 1540); 231 (May 1544); 232 (May 1544); and 336 (July 1549); also 24 Hen. VIII, c.3; 27 Hen. VIII, c.9; and 31 Hen. VIII, c.8. For measures pricing victual in general see *Proclamations*, Nos. 336 (July 1549); 366 (Oct. 1550); and 380 (Sept. 1551).
[3] Ibid., Nos. 226 (Feb. 1544), and 373 (May 1551); also 34 & 35 Hen. VIII, c.3, and 7 Edw. VI, c.7.
[4] *Proclamations*, Nos. 149 (Nov. 1534); 170 (Jan. 1537); 206 (Dec. 1541); 230 (May 1544); 260 (Dec. 1545); 267 (June 1546); and 383 (Feb. 1552).
[5] Ibid., Nos. 213 (Aug. 1542), and 235 (Aug. 1544).
[6] Ibid., No. 218 (May 1543), 318–19.
[7] Ibid., Nos. 134 (Sept. 1531); 225 (Jan. 1544); 241 (Nov. 1544); 258 (Dec. 1545); 262 (Jan. 1546); 269 (June 1546); 280 (May 1547); 285 (July 1547); 295 (Dec. 1547); 301 (Mar. 1548); 304 (Apr. 1548); 306 (May 1548); 310 (June 1548); 315 (Oct. 1548); 319 (Jan. 1549); 357 (May 1550); 361 (July 1550); 365 (Sept. 1550).

The popular belief in the responsibility of middlemen for high prices was shared by many in authority. A proclamation of November 1534 ascribes a sudden rise in corn prices directly to 'the subtle invention and craft of divers covetous persons' who have plenty but wish to contrive a dearth.[1] Two edicts issued in 1551 allude to 'the devilish malice and slight of ... naughty people injurious to the whole commonwealth ... especially such as make their gain by buying and selling'.[2] The Assise of Fuel, in 1553, attributed high prices to the fact that 'by the greedy appetite and covetousness of divers persons, Fuel Coals and Wood runneth many times through four or five several hands or more before it cometh to the hands of them that for their necessity do burn or retail the same'.[3]

While the possible utility of middlemen was recognized, in general the tone was unmistakably hostile. Proclamations of September and October 1550 permitted 'broggers and common carriers of grain' to buy in order to sell again, subject to certain provisos as to open marketing and the quantities involved, but related the 'great scarcity and unreasonable prices' of victuals to 'frequent unlawful exportation', to 'many detestable frauds and covins', and to 'unlawful engrossing, forestalling and regrating of the same'.[4] The references to engrossing, forestalling, regrating and hoarding recur constantly.[5] An edict of July 1551 ruled that 'no forestaller shall be suffered to dwell in any town'; he was to be 'grievously amerced', pilloried, imprisoned and fined, and finally banished from the town for successive offences.[6] J.P.s were repeatedly granted, and exhorted to use, powers of search and of forcible marketing.[7] Not only dealers in foodstuffs were suspect. An act of 1530 attacked 'broggers regraters and gatherers of Wools' as raising prices and causing unemployment, and attempted

---

[1] *Proclamations*, No. 151 (11 Nov. 1534), 221–2.
[2] Ibid., Nos. 373 (11 May 1551), 520–2; and 379 (16 Aug. 1551), 529–30.
[3] 7 Edw. VI, c.7.
[4] *Proclamations*, Nos. 365 (24 Sept. 1550), 499–503; and 366 (20 Oct. 1550), 504–9.
[5] Ibid., Nos. 118 (Nov. 1527); 121 (Dec. 1528); 125 (Aug. 1529); 127 (Oct. 1529); 151 (Nov. 1534); 242 (Nov. 1544); 365 (Sept. 1550); 366 (Oct. 1550); 373 (May 1551); 377 (July 1551); and 380 (Sept. 1551).
[6] Ibid., No. 377 (24 July 1551), 526–7.
[7] Ibid., Nos. 118 (Nov. 1527); 151 (Nov. 1534); 242 (Nov. 1544); 365 (Sept. 1550); and 366 (Oct. 1550).

to restrict their activities in certain counties.[1] The charge and enactment were repeated in 1545,[2] and the scope of the latter extended in a statute of 1552 which forbade the sale of wool save to authentic staplers or cloth manufacturers.[3]

Since fear of disorder was one motive for such intervention, any sign of a critical shortage occasioned a spasm of activity. This happened between 1527 and 1529,[4] but above all in the late 'forties and the 'fifties. A proclamation pricing victual in July 1549 warned people to seek redress for any breach of its terms 'only by order of his majesty's laws, without force, riot' or other disturbance.[5] By May 1551 public resentment again rose to such a pitch that an order then published against 'unreasonable and fraudulent engrossing' of all types warned 'the lower sort of people' not to be 'like to those sick madmen' who 'have presumptuously taken upon them the office of his majesty, both in reprehending their superiors and attempting redress of things after their own fantasies'.[6] A proclamation of September 1551 was particularly indignant; for the king has 'of late to his own great loss, abated and decayed the valuation of his coin . . . thinking thereby the excessive prices of all things . . . should consequently fall and abate as by natural reason and equity' it should. But 'divers insatiable and greedy persons in whose hands a great part of the victual of this realm by regrating resteth' still maintain excessive prices. Nonetheless, the prohibition of any attempts at redress outside the law is repeated.[7] The bad harvests in the middle of the reign of Queen Mary evoked a new spurt of action: a statute of 1555 prohibited any unauthorized export,[8] and in October 1556 justices of the peace were given powers of search and forcible marketing—the provision that those who owned a farm themselves were to be subject to 'view and order . . . of their corn by the rest of the Justices' indicating that the professional dealer was not alone in his hoarding and profiteering.[9]

What was the reaction of merchants and middlemen to these attempts to control them? One cynical estimate of the efficacy of

[1] 22 Hen. VIII, c.1.   [2] 37 Hen. VIII, c. 15.   [3] 5 & 6 Edw. VI, c.7.
[4] See R. Holinshed, *Chronicles*, iii, 722, and E. Hall, *Chronicle*, 736, on the dearth caused by poor harvests.
[5] *Proclamations*, No. 336, 464–9.   [6] Ibid., No. 373, 520–2.
[7] Ibid., No. 380, 530–3.   [8] 1 & 2 P. and M, c.5.
[9] See N. S. B. Gras, *Evolution of the English Corn Market*, 448–9.

such regulation is expressed in a letter of Sir John Mason to Secretary Cecil in December 1550:

I hear here [in France] a great bruit of the discontentation of our people upon a late proclamation touching cheese and butter. . . . I have seen so many experiences of such ordinances; and ever the end is dearth, and lack of the thing that we seek to make good cheap. Nature will have her course, etiam si furca expellatur; and never shall you drive her to consent that a penny-worth of new shall be sold for a farthing. . . . For who will keep a cow that may not sell the milk for as much as the merchant and he can agree upon?[1]

He would presumably have been pleased at the cancellation of the edict two days later,[2] and also, possibly, with the very apposite case of the repeal of 'An Act for the true making of Pynnes'[3] within a session of its enactment, because of great 'scarcity of Pins within this Realm'.[4]

Another critic, in 1549, agreed that 'long experience have so well declared that the foresaid setting of prices of victual, do nothing at all bring down the high price thereof. . . . Surely it is not the setting of low prices that will any thing amend the matter. But it must be the taking away of the occasion of the high prices.'[5] Thus by mid-century governmental regulation of middlemen was already subject to the charge that it failed in its avowed objectives;[6] we shall return to the significance of this criticism on the grounds of economic expediency later. We must note, also, the contention of a recent study that the language of public welfare often served as a cover for private interest and that, in particular, legislation against the wool middleman resulted partly from the influence of pressure groups.[7] Nonetheless, there is no doubt that public opinion in general wholeheartedly supported the avowed aim of governmental efforts to control the middleman.

There remains one aspect of prices that aroused bitter feeling: the pricing of money itself, in the form of interest or usury. Although of crucial importance it is only from about mid-century on that this appears to have been extensively debated,

---

[1] In Tytler, i, 341.
[2] See Calendar of State Papers, Domestic . . . 1547–1580, 311.
[3] 34 & 35 Hen. VIII, c.6.   [4] 35 Hen. VIII, c.13.
[5] Anon., Policies, T.E.D., iii, 340.
[6] See E. F. Heckscher, Mercantilism, i, 267; ii, 105.
[7] P. J. Bowden, The Wool Trade in Tudor and Stuart England, 112–17.

possibly because it was conducted in so clandestine a fashion. It is tempting to suggest a frame of mind which combined moral rejection, to a degree which rendered it something just not discussed, with an uneasy suspicion that—as the tone of the references suggests—to charge for the use of money had become normal.

Rigid prohibition of any payment for the loan of money had indeed been relaxed by the late-medieval Schoolmen.[1] But in England public opinion remained conservative. Medieval hatred of the usurer had sprung from the fact that most loans were thought to be made either for 'ostentatious consumption' or to a poor man in economic distress, whose misfortune was often ruthlessly exploited. It has been urged that in mid-Tudor England the money-lending which concerned nine-tenths of the population—such as the peasant or the small master driven to have recourse to it—remained this casual, irregular credit, and that it was transactions of this type, rather than the activities of large-scale, often international, trade and finance, that the usury laws were designed to control.[2]

After the comprehensive act of 1487 'agaynst Usury and unlawfull Bargaynes',[3] the law remained virtually unchanged until 1545. The measure then enacted, probably connected with the financial straits of the Crown and its difficulties in raising loans,[4] sanctioned interest of up to 10 per cent,[5] and provoked a great outburst of criticism. Crowley attributed it to the need to restrain 'the insatiable desire of the usurers', but rejected the concession made. In a significant passage he referred to Christ's teaching on the duty to lend without hope of gain: 'I am not ignorant what glosses have been made upon this place, and how men have wrested & made it no precept but a counsel of our Saviour; & therefore not to infer necessity to Christians, but to leave them at liberty either to do it or leave it undone. Oh merciful Lord, what manner of religion is that these men profess?'[6]

Brinklow echoed this, and criticized the clergy for ceasing to preach against usury now that the law no longer forbade interest

---

[1] Above, 10, n. 1.
[2] R. H. Tawney, Introduction to T. Wilson's *A Discourse upon Usury*, 21–2, 30 and 130.　　　　[3] 3 Hen. VII, c.6.
[4] H. M. Robertson, *The Rise of Economic Individualism*, 120.
[5] 37 Hen. VIII, c.19.　　　　[6] *Works*, 172–4.

below 10 per cent.[1] Lever, at least, was not guilty of this dereliction: in a sermon at St Paul's in 1550 he not only condemned usury but deplored the fact that it 'is now made so lawful that an officer if he would, can not punish, to make men to leave it'.[2] The effectiveness of the upper limit was itself called in question by Latimer, who declared that 'I hear there be usurers in England, that will take forty in the hundred; but I hear of no promoters to put them up.'[3]

While the extent to which the discussions and decisions of legists and theologians alike had any influence upon the practical conduct of finance is thus doubtful, the effect of the united disapproval of almost all shades of religious thought in England at this time upon the official ruling on usury is clear. For an act 'against Usury' in 1552 protested, rather ambiguously, that the statute of 1545 'was not meant or intended for . . . allowance of Usury' but designed 'for the avoiding of a more ill and inconvenience that before that time was used and exercised: But Forasmuch as Usury is by the word of God utterly prohibited', that measure, which had been misinterpreted, was now repealed. Since all teachings and persuasions were ignored, the only way to avert God's vengeance on the realm 'for the great and open Usury therein daily used' was to enforce 'temporal punishment' by fines and imprisonment, with the inducement of rewards to promoters.[4]

But the tone seems that of a defiant declaration of faith in face of inevitable defeat; the colours were nailed to the mast but the ship was sinking. The first effect of the new act was to give fresh impetus to evasive or surreptitious practices.[5] Why this defeat of a principle of the old order on which, in terms of morality, nearly all commentators were agreed? That it should, in any positive way, be connected with Protestant doctrinal innovations is very doubtful. It is true that Bucer shocked his Cambridge contemporaries by his acceptance of *usura* as a rightful payment for the use of money, only quantitatively distinguishable from excessive, exploiting payment. His treatise *On Usury*, written in

---

[1] *Supplication of the Poore Commons*, 84.   [2] *Sermons*, 44.
[3] *Sermons*, 279. A 'promoter' was a type of informer-prosecutor.
[4] 5 & 6 Edw. VI, c.20.
[5] R. H. Tawney, Introduction to T. Wilson, op. cit., 142–3.

1550, expressed views almost identical with Calvin's. But though he perhaps sowed the seeds of opposition to the old ruling, and was to be cited by 'the Civilian' in Wilson's *Discourse* in support of 'moderate usury',[1] the 1552 act suggests that his immediate influence could not have been great.[2]

The reasons for what took place may be sought in the practical implications of the development of the economy rather than in ethical and legal discussion. For loan capital was increasingly required not for luxury expenditure or the relief of near-destitution but for what are now regarded as the normal processes of a commercialized economy. It has been observed that in the long run the rise of capitalism and the expansion of business activities were associated with lower, not higher, interest rates. One may perhaps, schematically, contrast the typical medieval loan, with its questionable circumstances, high risk factor, high interest rate, and consequent stigma of moral condemnation, with the later increasingly frequent business loan for productive use in trade or industry, subject to less risk and therefore a lower interest rate, and hence, with the greater consideration given to the purpose and terms of a loan, far less subject to ethical disapproval.

The divergence between inherited moral precept and common practice in mid-Tudor England is well brought out in *A Newe Interlude of Impacyente pouerte* (c. 1552). Abundance asks why should he 'lend without a profit?' and meets Conscience's condemnation of usury as 'contrary to God's laws' with the cold reply: 'It is used in our country.'[3] From mid-century onwards this erosion of the traditional position from without was helped by weakening from within such as Calvin's and Bucer's discussion of usury in a more discriminating manner, so that the permissive legislation of 1571 was largely the formalization of a victory already gained.

Contemporary reactions to this issue may well exemplify those to developments in money and prices in general: the dominant tone is one of bewilderment and anger, for what could be understood was not liked. The readiness of monarch, exchanger

---

[1] T. Wilson, op. cit., 351–2.

[2] See C. Hopf, *Martin Bucer and the English Reformation*, 32 and 122–5; also A. Hyma, in R. W. Green, ed., *Protestantism and Capitalism, The Weber Thesis and its Critics*, p. 98.

[3] Anon., printed in *'Lost' Tudor Plays*, ed. J. S. Farmer, 321–3.

and usurer to juggle with or profit from the loan of money, and the attempts deliberately to manipulate supply and demand so as to maximize personal gain, typify an increasingly amoral assessment of the pricing-mechanism which outraged the mid-Tudor ethical code. It was still the overwhelming consensus of opinion that government had the right and the duty to modify or control the pricing system in the interests of social justice and national security. But we have noted the occasional expression of dissent or cynicism as to the effect of such intervention, and we shall later meet with suggestions that government should in fact enlist that system as an ally in the achievement of its objectives, and substitute fiscal control, penalties and incentives for direct prohibition or moral exhortation.

The Social and Economic Problems of the Commonwealth

IV. 'MR AVARICE' AND 'LADY PUBLIC WEAL': AGRICULTURE, INDUSTRY AND COMMERCE

GOVERNMENT was expected not only to maintain equity between producer and consumer, in the form of the fair or just price, but also to secure social justice between employer and worker.[1] Its duty to preserve a correct relationship between the members of the body politic in respect of status was matched by a duty to ensure a healthy balance between sectional economic interests and those of society as a whole. But social justice, measure, and indeed all the inherited ideals we have considered, were alike incompatible with greed. Pursued *ad libitum* greed led to breaches not only of an accepted ethical code but also of the law of the realm, by men 'that neither have the fear of God before their eyes, nor yet of the laws, they be so drowned in covetousness, and this insatiable desire of the vile muck of this transitory world; not passing how they come by it, so they may have it'.[2]

Such adjectives as 'insatiable' and 'inordinate' recur in charges that the vice, or sin, of covetousness is endemic in the body politic. Sometimes it is a disease—'the great dropsy of avarice, always drinking, and ever athirst'[3]—and sometimes personified, as in Crowley's *Fable of Philargyrie. The Great Gigant* or as 'Mr. Avaryce' in the anonymous *Respublica*. The universality of covetousness, and of the fraud and deceit to which it often leads,

---

[1] See E. F. Heckscher, *Mercantilism*, i, 226–9.
[2] J. Hales, 'Charges', in Strype, ii (Part II), 355.
[3] B. Gilpin, *Sermon . . . before King Edward VI*, 40.

is remarked in Gilbert Walker's *Manifest Detection of ... Dice-Play* (1552) where the rogue expounds his philosophy of cheating: 'Suppose ye that offices would be so dearly bought, and the buyers so soon enriched, if they counted not pillage an honest point of purchase? Could merchants, without lies, false making their wares, and selling them by a crooked light, to deceive the chapman in the thread or colour, grow so soon rich and to a baron's possessions, and make all their posterity gentlemen?'[1]

We have noted[2] that such allegations were neither new nor peculiar to this age, and need not be taken entirely at face value in regard either to the novelty or to the extent of the subjects of complaint. But in commerce and industry as in agriculture, we hear the same basic criticisms of current trends: that they lead to a weakening of traditionally and communally enforced standards; that they undermine the security of the individual, and above all of the weaker member; that in their search for efficiency in terms of maximized profit they diminish efficiency in terms of individual and social welfare. The function of government in correcting these defects of the body politic—or perhaps, in this case, the body economic—is a major topic in discussion of the ideal of the Commonwealth.

Perhaps the greatest single cause of popular protest must be related to developments in agriculture.[3] Just as the large-scale estate corn-farming for the market of the high Middle Ages had been followed, as a result of falling population, depression and consequently contracting market, by more opportunities for prosperous peasant farming in the late fourteenth and early fifteenth centuries, so now, a century later, came the boom in demand for wool and the upsurge of population which formed the background to enclosures, rack-renting and evictions. The extent to which enclosure occurred, especially during the mid-Tudor decades, has been questioned. But there is no doubt as to the extent of the public outcry, and its reflection of the continued

[1] In A. V. Judges, *The Elizabethan Underworld*, 38.   [2] Above, 3, 94.
[3] On this subject see especially R. H. Tawney, *The Agrarian Problem in the Sixteenth Century*; J. Thirsk, (ed.), *The Agrarian History of England and Wales, IV, 1500–1640*; E. Kerridge, *The Agricultural Revolution*; E. A. Kosminsky, *Studies in the Agrarian History of England in the Thirteenth Century*; H. Nabholz, Chap. VIII in *Camb. Econ. Hist. Europe*, i; and A. R. Myers, *England in the Late Middle Ages (1307–1536)*, 40–51 and 132–7.

existence of at least the basic features of the traditional view of landlord-peasant relationships.

When all qualification has been made it remains broadly true that the medieval economy was based upon status and custom. But if one outstanding feature of the later Middle Ages was the emergence of personal freedom, another was that of freedom in the use of land as an economic asset untrammelled by communal restrictions and social obligations. Individual well-being would then depend largely upon such variables as the supply and demand positions for land and labour. The demographic catastrophe of the fourteenth century completely changed the latter's bargaining strength, and in general the position of the peasantry improved, until, from about the mid-fifteenth century, a reaction set in as shortage of labour started to disappear. Meanwhile, the consolidation of strips and the appearance of a ladder of prosperity reflect the increase of competition and the working of forces dissolvent of the old order among the peasants themselves.

How did rising prices and growing commercialization affect the landowner? He might decide to exploit the land himself, or to profit by the increased rent payable by an efficient farmer who developed to the full its commercial possibilities; in either event the decision would have serious effects where the land was at present still worked under the open-field strip system. For the method of increasing the yield which excited most interest was sheep-farming—attractive and profitable because of low labour costs on the one hand and the boom in wool and woollens on the other. In effect, increased concentration upon sheep-farming often meant enclosure, of the waste, commons, and finally of the open-field arable—each step a successive tightening of the screw upon the old-type peasant-farmer.[1] Hence the outcry against depopulating enclosure.

Divergence of statistics, definitions and interpretations counsel a cautious approach to the question of the extent and effects of enclosures.[2] But the general agreement that much of the enclosing of land took place in the open-field corn-growing heartland of

[1] See A. Everitt, 'Farm Labourers', in J. Thirsk, (ed.), *Agrarian History*, 396–465.

[2] See R. H. Tawney, op. cit.; E. F. Gay, 'Inclosures in England in the Sixteenth Century', 586–7; E. Kerridge, 'The Returns of the Inquisitions of Depopulation', 212 and 228; J. Thirsk, *Tudor Enclosures* and 'Enclosing and Engrossing', in *Agrarian History*, 200–255.

England, that 'engrossing'—amalgamation of two or more farms into one—might be just as harmful as enclosure, and the evidence of local and field investigations that there was a very real basis for talk of deserted villages, point to the dangers attached to a minimizing approach based upon the overall figures. The great era of depopulating enclosure appears to have been from about 1450 to about 1520, so that by the mid-Tudor period most of the damage had been done. Although Tudor legislation may have done something to limit new enclosures its weakness lay in the fact that its retrospective enactments went back no further than the early years of the reign of Henry VII. But the protest literature rose to a spate in the late 1540s and early 1550s—in works such as *Vox Populi Vox Dei*, *The Decaye of Englande only by the Great Multitude of Shepe*, and *Policies*, which asked rhetorically: 'Is there not exclamation made in every notable Sermon against the insatiable Sheep-pasturers?[1]—and it would be rash to dismiss it as without foundation, particularly since it was paralleled by governmental concern.

Modern criticism of alleged excessive concentration upon enclosures in the sermons and the pamphlet literature—'excessive' in relation to the supposed absence of any upsurge in the incidence of enclosure in mid-century—is rather unfair. For apart from the precarious nature of the statistical basis for this supposition Tudor commentators were very far from concentrating solely upon enclosure narrowly defined. Enclosure—depopulating or otherwise —is only one of a number of complaints, including extortionate entry fines, rack-renting, engrossing, and over-stocking of the commons, as to the effect of an increasingly commercialized attitude towards land, and in particular of the profitability of sheep-farming, against the background of population expansion and land-hunger.

The object of concern, by the mid-Tudor decades, may have been the shrunken village rather than the deserted village,[2] but the basis of concern remained the same. And, if the deserted village was a ghost, it remained a very frightening ghost to those who could still see the remains of ruined churches and ruined homes; a very real spectre of what could still occur, given the

---

[1] Anon., in *T.E.D.*, iii, 327.
[2] M. W. Beresford, *The Lost Villages of England*, 142.

conjunction of economic incentive, lack of social conscience, and absence of effective restraint. As late as 1550 Becon, although he gave no names, could recall that 'whereas in times past there were in some town an hundred households, there remain not now thirty; in some fifty, there are not now ten; yea . . . I know towns so wholly decayed, that there is neither stick nor stone standing.'[1]

Even such advocates of enclosure on the ground of economic efficiency as Fitzherbert and Tusser recognized that

> The poor at enclosing do grudge,
> because of abuses that fall,
> Lest some man should have but too much,
> and some again nothing at all.[2]

At the heart of the matter was a basic protest against the tendency to think of land solely as an economic asset, a tendency which cut across the traditional concept of the landlord's obligations. Tyndale, despite—or perhaps because of—his leanings towards radicalism in religion, expressed most conservative views on this. 'Let Christian landlords be content with their rent and old customs; not raising that rent or fines, and bringing up new customs to oppress their tenants: neither letting two or three tenantries to one man. Let them not take in their commons, neither make parks nor pastures of whole parishes. For God gave the earth to men to inhabit, and not unto sheep and wild deer. Be as fathers unto your tenants.'[3] The 'Prayer For Landlords' in the *Primer* of Edward VI endorsed these views, advising that 'they, remembering themselves to be thy tenants, may not rack, and stretch out the rents of their houses and lands; nor yet take unreasonable fines and incomes . . . and not join house to house, nor couple land to land'.[4] In this context the principle of stewardship is heard again and again.

Those who rejected it became, in Latimer's vivid phrase, as 'step-lords'.[5] In the sermons of divines and the works of radical pamphleteers the phraseology of condemnation recurs strikingly. Perhaps the favourite was that used by Becon in attacking 'these

[1] *Jewel of Joy*, 432–3.
[2] T. Tusser, extract from *Five Hundred Pointes of Good Husbandrie*, printed in T.E.D., iii, 68.
[3] *The Obedience of a Christian man*, in *Works*, i, 237.
[4] *Writings of Edward the Sixth*, 89.   [5] *Sermons*, 279.

caterpillars of the commonweal': ' "Wo and everlasting damnation be unto them that join house to house, and couple land to land so nigh together, that the poor man can get no more ground! Shall ye dwell alone in the midst of the earth?" '[1] But in assessing the justice of this denunciation of those gentry who failed in their duty to their tenants it must be remembered that it was often a choice between adjusting to the changing economic circumstances or going under. Rising prices, and the desire to achieve the potentialities of a higher standard of living, together with the obvious opportunities of increasing the income from the land, sometimes outweighed any traditional principles of social obligation. In fairness, too, it must be conceded that by now the original fixed monetary quit-rent might bear little relation to the land's economic worth.

Modern critics have justly characterized enclosure as a 'catch-all' description of several distinct practices; but contemporaries were in no doubt as to those which were harmful. Hales, instructing the Enclosure Commissioners of 1549, defined

what is meant by this word inclosure. It is not taken where a man doth inclose and hedge in his own proper ground, where no man hath commons. For such inclosure is very beneficial to the commonwealth; it is a cause of great increase of wood: but it is meant thereby, when any man hath taken away and enclosed any other men's commons, or hath pulled down houses of husbandry, and converted the lands from tillage to pasture. This is the meaning of this word, and so we pray you to remember it.[2]

With regard to the commons themselves the peasant was often in a cleft stick; for even if they remained open he was liable to be grazed off them by the flocks of the lord or large-scale farmer. But the angriest complaints were made at 'the great enclosing in every part of arable land',[3] with its alleged effects of unemployment and depopulation.

The methods used to squeeze more money out of the land, or to force existing tenants off it in order to do so, included rack-renting, large fines for in-going, legal chicanery, or plain intimidation. One John Bayker, in a letter addressed to Henry VIII himself in

---

[1] *Jewel of Joy*, 432–3.   [2] 'Charges', in Strype, ii (Part II), 361–2.
[3] T. Starkey, *Dialogue*, 96.

1538, relates in detail how a man might be driven off the land:
First the incoming fine is raised enormously, so that the poor man
must sell all in order to pay it; then, when the house itself inevitably falls into disrepair, the lord orders his now penniless
tenant to make good the damage or pay another fine; finally, the
man buckles under, the house comes down, and the land is used
for another purpose.[1] Forrest describes a variant procedure, the
trick of letting 'an old rotten house [with] a garden plot' instead
of the land belonging to it.[2] He points to the cumulative effects of
'these raging Rents' and exaction of a 'fourfold double' fine:

> must not the same great Dearth bring hither?
> for if the farmer pay fourfold double Rent,
> he must his ware needs sell after that stint.[3]

His conclusion that neither 'custom' nor 'Copy hold' provides
any real protection against a determined assault[4] suggests an issue
debated in Heywood's *The Spider and the Flie*. In answer to the
Fly's contention that custom entitles Spiders to build in tops and
sides of windows only, leaving the rest free for Flies, the Spider
points out that

> In every petty court of copyhold,
> All grants that pass, passing in their most might,
> Pass to hold at lord's will, and so enrolled.

The Fly agrees, indeed, that

> . . . copyholders of old
> Hold to them and theirs at will of the lord,
> As with custom of the manor doth accord.
> But this term custom standeth not here idle;
> Custom (in many cases) seemeth to me
> To tenants a buckler, to lords a bridle.[5]

But in this case, as in many others, the bridle proves too weak. In
the peace terms made after the failure of the Flies' attack upon him
the Spider concedes 'half the holes' in the window; but these

---

[1] Printed in F. Aydelotte, *Elizabethan Rogues and Vagabonds*, Appendix 3,
145-7.
[2] *Princelie Practise*, pp. xcvii-xcviii.　　　　[3] Ibid., ll, 369-71.
[4] Ibid., ll, 524-39.　　　　[5] Op. cit., 96-108.

occupy only one-sixth of the total space! The despairing Flies are rescued only by the symbolic intervention of the Maid of the house.[1]

Sometimes the sheepmasters' calculations were upset by a factor alluded to in *Utopia*: the 'vengeance God took of their inordinate and insatiable covetousness, sending among the sheep that pestiferous murrain which much more justly should have fallen on the sheepmasters' own heads',[2] while Armstrong advanced the theory that decay of tillage meant that the sheep might no longer 'feed of the inward layer of the earth' so that 'rank, foggy, wild grass' meant 'rank, wild hairy wool' in place of 'pure fine wool' as in time of 'works of husbandry'.[3] Starkey ascribed losses through 'scab and rots' to the fact that 'they are nourished in so fat pasture. For a sheep by his nature ... loveth a lean, barren, and dry ground. Wherefore, when they are so closed in rank pastures and butful ground, they are soon touched with the scab and the rot; and so, though we nourish over many by inclosure, yet over few of them ... come to the profit and use of man.'[4] A possibly more satisfying vengeance upon the biting beast become a devourer of men was that taken by Ket's men in their feasting on Mousehold Heath!

But usually sheep-farming was very profitable. Armstrong describes how commercial forces nurtured it: 'Then began the rank mischief and destruction of the whole realm to spring and spread out of London during this forty years past and more.' The activities of those 'called broggers' raised wool prices so high that 'farmers studied and devised how to destroy men's works of husbandry to increase more wool'. Comparison of the annual rent of, say, a village in which 'a 400 people had labours and living by works of husbandry' with what it would yield if put to pasture 'caused them for their own singular weal to break down all the houses ... putting the dwellers out from their labours and living'.[5]

The increasing tendency to regard land as a business asset like any other was certainly influenced by commercial and urban interests. But the extent to which such interests engaged in land

[1] Ibid., 327, 353 and 392.
[2] Sir T. More, 25.
[3] *Treatise*, in *T.E.D.*, iii, 101–2.
[4] T. Starkey, *Dialogue*, 98.
[5] *Treatise*, in *T.E.D.*, iii, 96–7.

speculation in the sense of deliberate purchase for resale is now questioned.[1] Contemporary moralists condemned those who, making merchandise of land, came between owner and cultivator and profited by driving up the price. Such 'leasemongers taking much of tenants and paying little unto the landlords, have both their livings, and doth the duties of neither',[2] and were 'sure to have hell by right inheritance'.[3] But land-hunger affected the peasant-farmer as well as the larger-scale capitalist. Lever himself urged that 'even you husbandmen which cry out upon the covetousness of gentlemen and officers, it is covetousness in you, that causeth, and engendereth covetousness in them. For, for to get your neighbour's farm, ye will offer and desire them to take bribes, fines, and rents more than they look for, or than you your selves be well able to pay.'[4] An 'Exhortation' relating to 'Perambulations' for boundary marks describes malpractices in the open fields by 'gleaners, gatherers, and incroachers upon other men's lands and possessions', those who 'plough and grate upon their neighbour's land' and encroach upon the common balks. In particular, 'it is a shame to behold the insatiableness of some covetous persons in their doings; that where their ancestors left of their land a broad and sufficient bier-balk to carry the corpse to the Christian sepulture, how men pinch at such bierbalks' and make them 'too strait for two to walk on'.[5]

Of the alleged effects of these developments upon the welfare of the body politic three in particular awakened fear: depopulation; diminished food supply; rebellion by the injured peasantry. Contemporaries believed the first to be true not only of particular regions but of the realm as a whole, and deplored the replacement of useful and productive inhabitants, good Christian people, by brute beasts, and of houses and churches to the glory of God by sheepcotes and stables to the ruin of man. Lack of people was consumption in the body politic.[6]

Special concern was expressed for 'the good yeoman', 'the body and stay' of the realm,[7] 'the major part' whose well-being

---

[1] H. J. Habbakuk, 'The Market for Monastic Property, 1539–1603', 363, 376–8, and 380.

[2] T. Lever, *Sermons*, 134–5.   [3] R. Crowley, *Works*, 41 and 88.

[4] *Sermons*, 37.   [5] *The Two Books of Homilies*, ed. J. Griffiths, 495.

[6] T. Starkey, *Dialogue*, 72–6, and H. Latimer, *Sermons*, 99.

[7] Anon., *Vox Populi Vox Dei* in *T.E.D.*, iii, 29–30.

should be the primary concern of all laws.[1] Queen Mary's chaplain, Christopherson, did not miss the opportunity of attributing the alleged decline of this class to doctrinal heresy. 'As for the yeomanry . . . wherein did consist a great part of the force of this realm, it hath so notably decayed since the time, that this pestilent doctrine began first within this realm. . . .'[2] The yeoman was usually equated with the archer, the traditional backbone of an English army. Now enclosure for pasture 'is great decay to artillery: for that do we reckon that shepherds be but ill archers',[3] and it ought to be considered that the mighty force of our enemies cannot be resisted with sheep be their wool never so fine.'[4]

The whole balance of the economy might be upset, if 'clothing' was allowed 'to destroy bodily living, [and] the less to destroy the more'.[5] For decay of tillage might lead not only to depopulation but also to inadequate food supply. Scory, bishop of Rochester, in 1551, found it 'lamentable . . . to behold that ground which, at this time of year . . . was wont to be richly adorned with corn, to be now, through God's curse, that is fallen upon us for our idleness and greedy avarice, replenished with mayweed, thistles, docks, and such like unprofitable weeds', and feared the effect of being compelled 'to seek relief of our scarcity and dearth of corn at the hands of strangers'.[6] The unknown author of *Policies* sketched the dangers when 'the most part of the . . . people live in extreme poverty, victual being always at so high price that in those years in which Corn doth mistake in any thing, or Cattle chance never so little through murrain or other incessions to Die, a great number of the people shall be in danger of famine'.[7]

There was all too much reason to fear the reaction of those of whom Christopherson remarks that, turned 'out of their farmholds and tenements . . . better had it been for them to have died in their cradles'.[8] Armstrong relates how 'the poor wretched beastly members of the body of the realm, ever meeting with other in company, complaineth of their sore grief of need and

[1] W. Forrest, *Princelie Practise*, ll. 510–14.
[2] *An exhortation* . . . , p. A.a.ii.
[3] Anon., *The decaye of England*. . ., in *T.E.D.*, iii, 55.
[4] Anon., *Policies*, in *T.E.D.*, iii, 314.
[5] C. Armstrong, *Treatise*, in *T.E.D.*, iii, 101.
[6] Letter to the King, in Strype, ii (Part II), 482.
[7] In *T.E.D.*, iii, 314.   [8] Op. cit., p. A.a.iii.b.

necessity of victuals, clothing and money. They sensibly feel scarcity, so living in misery. But they know not the cause thereof, which causeth them to murmur and grudge daily, ready to do any mischief, if they thought it might be any remedy.'[1]

Why such issues inevitably became the concern of government needs little elaboration. Few would cavil at Hales's description of husbandry and tillage as 'the very paunch of the commonwealth, that is, that nourisheth the whole body'.[2] Maintenance of food supply and of employment were the basic motives of opposition to enclosures. The suggestion that humanitarian feeling for any suffering of the weaker classes in society would not in itself suffice to cause action to be taken, but would certainly do so when the question at issue had repercussions in the spheres of order, defence or finance,[3] is also exemplified here.

Certainly the Crown was appealed to. Armstrong suggested commissions of inquiry and, on the basis of their information, the restoration of tillage to its former extent.[4] The interesting, and constructive, proposal was made in *Policies* that the 'distributing again of the Sheep-pastures into Divers men's hands' would be facilitated by means of a 'Subsidy upon Sheep': 'if all they which have above Two hundred might have payed for every sheep they have above the said number 4*d*. yearly during the king's wars . . . this Subsidy should have caused the Sheep with the Sheep pastures to be immediately distributed into divers men's hands'. If this did not suffice 'it may be enacted that no man be suffered to keep any Sheep or gelded beasts, except they keep for every eight sheep one acre of ground in tillage'. The abuse of over-stocking of the commons, to the detriment of the poor man's rights, might be corrected by limitation of the number of 'beasts and Sheep every man shall there upon keep, according to the quantity of their tenure, having never the less a special regard in the favour of the poorest cottagers'.[5]

Forrest proposed the investigation of 'Rents . . . that be out of the way', and their reassessment, and reduction where necessary, according to the fertility or barrenness of the soil. If this were done then farmers and their dependants would live no longer in 'thrall-

[1] *Treatise*, in *T.E.D.*, iii, 101.   [2] 'Charges', in Strype, ii (Part II), 352.
[3] R. H. Tawney, *The Agrarian Problem*, 314 and 341–2.
[4] *Reforme*, in *T.E.D.*, iii, 116.   [5] In *T.E.D.*, iii, 321, 327–8, and 338.

dom and pinching penury ... as drudges unto their landlords', but 'as yeomen becometh honestly'.[1] Thus government was urged not only to see that 'the statute of inclosure were put in execution, and all such pasture put to the use of the plough as before time hath been so used',[2] but also to take steps to control rents and protect the poorer classes in the countryside.

Between 1485 and 1559 seven statutes were passed which were principally concerned with prevention or even attempted reversal of the progress of enclosure and alleged depopulation.[3] A larger number of proclamations were issued in an effort to support or implement this legislation.[4] R. H. Tawney concedes that 'the activity of the Government in matters of land was not so incessant as it was in the regulation of prices and the administration of the Poor Laws', but one of the periods singled out as characterized by 'especially energetic' activity, from 1536 to 1549,[5] coincides with the upsurge of public protest. Wolsey, as well as Cromwell and Somerset, must be credited with interest in this problem. Apart from the Enclosure Commission which he appointed in 1571, five proclamations were devoted to this issue between 1526 and 1529, one of which specifically mentions Wolsey's 'diligence' therein.[6] We have noted Cromwell's commendation of a bill to control sheep-rearing,[7] and Somerset's efforts between 1548 and 1549 need only be mentioned.

The sentiments and fears of the moralizers are closely matched by the phraseology of statute and proclamation. Not only 'enclosers' but also 'engrossers' of farms who convert arable to pasture are described as 'enemies of the commonwealth'.[8] Their actions lead to idleness, disorder, 'the great decay of all manner of Victuals',[9] 'so that the realm thereby is brought to a marvellous desolation, houses decayed, parishes diminished, the force of the realm weakened, and Christian people, by the greedy covetousness of some men, eaten up and devoured of brute beasts and driven

---

[1] *Princelie Practise*, ll. 491–513.   [2] T. Starkey, *Dialogue*, 171.

[3] 4 Hen. VII, c.19; 6 Hen. VIII, c.5; 7 Hen. VIII, c.1; 25 Hen. VIII, c.13; 27 Hen. VIII, c.22; 5 & 6 Edw. VI, c.5; and 2 & 3 P. and M., c.2.

[4] *Proclamations*, Nos. 75 (?1514); 110 (1526); 113 (1526); 114 (1526); 119 (1528); 309 (1548); 327 (1549); 338 (1549).

[5] *The Agrarian Problem*, 358.

[6] *Proclamations*, No. 110 (14 July 1526), 154–6; also Nos. 113, 114, 119 and 123.

[7] Above, 28.   [8] *Proclamations*, No. 75 (?1514), 122–3.

[9] 27 Hen. VIII, c.22.

from their houses by sheep and bullocks'.[1] The remedial measures consisted usually of orders for reconversion to tillage, casting down of hedges, and rebuilding of decayed houses, while an act of 1534 established a limit of 2,400 sheep and two farms for any one person.[2] But, as we shall see,[3] the crucial problem was that of enforcement.

The principle of governmental intervention in the interests of equity, to safeguard the welfare of society as a whole and of the underdog in particular, was invoked also for trade and manufactures. Here, as in agriculture, the fundamental objection was to the type of conduct which rejected traditional restraints and communal obligations in favour of untrammelled self-interest. Specific charges included the making of excessive profits and the usurpation of other men's functions by manufacturers and merchants; the prevalence of dishonest practices, deteriorating standards of craftsmanship, and refusal to accept imposition or enforcement of standards; and the exploitation and 'swallowing up' of the craftsman by the capitalist employer.

The increased commercialization which lay at the root of so many causes of complaint is symbolized by the decline of the gilds. For these institutions were geared to a localized, limited or inelastic market, which itself created the possibility of control, and to small-scale enterprises which made feasible a community of interest between master and employee. This ideal, like that of community of interest between producer and consumer, had not always been attained, but betokened the acceptance of corporate restraint upon the selfish profit motive, and the objective of communal security for the individual. But by now the gilds had long entered a decline. It has been suggested that this was accelerated by such actions as the confiscation of certain gild property and funds in 1547, but governmental measures were usually designed to protect the gilds, and there is little doubt that the basic causes were economic and organizational.

The gilds' power to control manufacture or sale within a limited sphere implied the exclusion of the non-member or the 'stranger', the existence (technically and geographically) of an agreed demarcation line, and, most important, the loyalty of their

[1] *Proclamations*, No. 309 (1 June 1548), 427–9.
[2] 25 Hen. VIII, c.13.   [3] Below, 204–7.

own members. These assumptions broke down as the widening of the market and the increasing employment of capital tended to separate the functions of craftsman and trader and to undermine the former's independence. As trade and industry expanded, problems of regulation and enforcement inevitably became more complex. Both the greater degree of subdivision of labour, and the paramount necessity of elasticity and enterprise required to cater for a larger, and particularly an overseas, market, posed problems outside the normal scope and conceptions of the gilds. Differentiation within (the 'yeomanry' against the 'livery') and friction between the gilds had long developed. The amalgamation movement—attempts to close the ranks against the threat from without and to retain control of the local economy—itself showed clearly the loss of power and authority by the separate gilds. The real problem was the conflict between the opposing principles of restriction and freedom in trade and manufactures against the background of changing market conditions. In the long run freedom triumphed.

The decline of the gilds went side by side with that of some of the older corporate towns, as industry sought freer conditions and cheap part-time labour in the countryside. Indeed the frantic efforts of the gilds to retain their privileged position and tighten restrictions may well have accelerated this shift. It was often not in the interest of employers or merchants to support attempts to restrict the activity of the domestic labour of the suburbs or surrounding country which they exploited. In the van of this movement came the cloth industry, despite the reluctance of towns and gilds to lose control in so lucrative a sphere. Regional specialization already existed, and the organization of the industry varied, but by and large it was dominated by the capitalist clothier or 'putter-out'. Other industries expanded also, markedly from about 1540 onward, and gild and corporate control declined because many of these growing industries either had never been subject to it, or were new, or escaped from the town to the countryside.

While these developments inevitably enhanced the function of the middleman, we have already noted the suspicion aroused by his activities. Recognition of merchants as a necessary estate within the commonwealth was always conditional upon observance of a traditional code of conduct. Foreign trade was indeed essential, so that 'the abundance of one country help to satisfy that which lacketh in an other'.[1] On their voyage in 1553 Willoughby and Chancellor bore a polyglot document addressed by Edward VI to all rulers, urging that 'God . . . greatly providing for mankind, would not that all things should be found in one region, to the end that one should need of another; that by this means friendship and amity might be established among all men.'[2] The Merchant, in Rastell's *Gentleness and Nobility*, explained that he bought wares from foreigners 'good cheap', and imported things we could not produce ourselves, including spices, drugs and medicines.[3] In such a context, merchants might be 'good & trusty servants of the common wealth with moderate gains and profit of their wares without dissembling in maintaining their estate'.[4]

But the moralists despaired of contemporary observance of these ideals. Becon, Lever, Latimer and Hooper deplored the 'craft, deceit, subtility, and falsehood' with which merchants 'beguiled their Christian brother'.[5] 'Now buying and selling is not used as a provision for good cheap and great plenty, but made the most occasion of dearth and scarcity',[6] by 'compacts and agreements between the rich, that things may not be sold as they be worth, but as their avarice hath agreed upon . . . so that they cannot be sold as common goods of the civil wealth, but as the goods of one private person; the which monopoly or selling of one man is forbidden. . . .'[7]

Edward VI wrote scornfully of merchants who 'adventure not to bring in strange commodities, but loiter at home, send forth small hoys with 2 or 3 mariners, occupy exchange of money, buy and sell victual, steal out bullion, corn, victual, wood . . . out of the realm'.[8] When they did trade abroad, alleged Starkey, private profit led them to denude the realm of necessary commodities and to import luxuries and trifles: 'merchants carrying out things necessary for our own people, are over many; and yet they which should bring necessaries are too few'. In particular, the

---

[1] Anon., *The boke of Marchauntes*, p. A.iii.a.
[2] Cited in M. Beer, *Early British Economics*, 58.
[3] l. 257.   [4] Anon., *The boke of Marchauntes*, p. A.iii.b.
[5] T. Becon, *Early Works*, 253.   [6] T. Lever, *Sermons*, 98.
[7] J. Hooper, *Early Writings*, 391.
[8] 'Discourse on the Reformation of Abuses', in *Literary Remains*, 483.

import of articles which we could make ourselves injures English crafts, while that of luxuries such as silks and wines impoverishes all. Surely it is sheer folly to export raw materials—wool, lead and tin—and then buy them back as manufactures.[1] Some London merchants could not rest content with the wealth God gave in the pursuit of their 'honest vocation, and trade of merchandise', but took their riches 'abroad in the country to buy farms out of the hands of worshipful gentlemen honest yeomen, and poor labouring husbands',[2] so that 'a few men had in their hands a great many men's livings'.[3]

Sermon and statute condemn the sale of 'corrupt and naughty wares for good'[4] and the use of 'false beams, scales and weights'.[5] The complaint of reluctance to accept regulation, inspection or imposition of standards, whether in regard to buying and selling or to manufacture, is startlingly illustrated in Latimer's account of what befell 'a searcher in London which, executing his office, displeased a merchant-man. ... The merchant goes me home, and sharpens his wood-knife, and comes again and knocks him on the head, and kills him.'[6] Such an extreme expression of laissez-faire principles was probably rare, but at Chester, in 1557, 'the whole occupation' of the bakers stood together in refusing to produce bread according to the assize appointed to them by the mayor and city council.[7]

Edward VI asserted gloomily that 'the artificers work falsely, the clothiers use deceit in cloth, the masons in building, the clockmakers in their clocks ... to th'intent they would have men come oftener to them for amending their things'.[8] Latimer gave a detailed account of

a certain cunning come up in mixing of wares. ... If his cloth be seventeen yards long, he will set him on a rack, and stretch him out with ropes, and rack him till the sinews shrink again, while he hath brought him to eighteen yards. When they have brought him to that perfection, they have a pretty feat to thick him again. He makes me a powder for it, and plays the poticary; they call it flock-powder; they do so incorporate it to the cloth, that it is wonderful to consider.[9]

[1] *Dialogue*, 84, 93–5, 155 and 173.   [2] T. Lever, *Sermons*, 29.
[3] J. Hales, 'Defence', in *Discourse*, p. lxvi.
[4] T. Becon, *Catechism*, 108.   [5] 4 Hen. VIII, c.7.   [6] *Sermons*, 189.
[7] See *T.E.D.*, i, 124–5.   [8] *Literary Remains*, 482–3.   [9] *Sermons*, 138.

The author of *Respublica* alludes to this device when he makes
Avarice relate how he

> ... would have brought half Kent into Northumberland
> & Somerset shire should have wrought to Cumberland;
> Then would I have stretched the county of Warwick
> upon tenter hooks, & made it reach to Berwick.[1]

Hales cited a charge of 'the falsehood of Clothiers' who 'drew a
cloth from 18 yards to 27 or 28 yards'[2]—a feat which makes
Latimer's example seem venial!

Identical complaints occur in the statutes relating to cloth manufacture.[3] An act of Edward VI contains perhaps the fullest account
of the abuses prevalent in each particular process of cloth-making,[4]
while a statute of the first year of the reign of Elizabeth I describes 'deceitful Liquors mingled with Chalk and other like
Things, whereby the said Cloth is not only made to seem much
finer and thicker to the Eye than it is in deed, but also the Threads
thereof be so loosed and made weak, that after three or four
washings it will scarcely hold together'.[5] In regard to the abuse
mentioned by Latimer—the doctoring of over-tentered cloth by
the application of a concoction containing flocks, waste wool,
thrums, chalk and oatmeal—the very bad reputation of Yorkshire led to the appointment in 1533 of a commission to investigate
the West Riding industry.[6] But fraud was confined neither to this
area nor to this device; in Wiltshire the 'yarn badger' (a small-
scale dealer in thread) allegedly 'fummed the yarn with hot water
so as to make it weigh more', and was guilty of mixture and
adulteration of wools, while spinners embezzled wool put out to
them.[7]

Decline in standards was often attributed to the withdrawal of
industry from control by gilds and corporate towns. An act
concerning the 'making of Hats Dornyckes [a type of stout,
figured linen] and Coverlets at Norwich' is typical in its reference
to 'divers evil and covetous disposed' individuals, not fully

---

[1] Anon., 50.   [2] Loc. cit.,
[3] 3 Hen. VIII, c.6; 24 Hen. VIII, c.2; and 3 & 4 Edw. VI, c.2.
[4] 5 & 6 Edw. VI, c.6.   [5] 1 Eliz. I, c.12.
[6] H. Heaton, *The Yorkshire Woollen and Worsted Industries*, 131–5.
[7] G. D. Ramsay, *The Wiltshire Woollen Industry in the Sixteenth and Seventeenth
Centuries*, 14.

trained, withdrawing from the city to the countryside and there making their wares 'deceitfully & insufficiently without Control-ment', to the decay of both craft and city.[1] Professor Heaton cites the many complaints at the 'multitude of clothiers lately in-creased in the realm [since] every man that would had liberty to be a clothier', and the consequent plea for strict apprenticeship en-forcement. But the rules were sometimes broken within the town and the gild, as when a warden was detected mixing 'hair and wool together' and was fined and deposed.[2]

Abuses in the leather trade were often mentioned. Indeed the preamble to a statute of Henry VIII declared that by now very few of his subjects 'can go or ride dry either in shoes or boots',[3] while an enactment of Edward VI alleged that 'through the covetise of Tanners in over-hasting their work by divers subtle and crafty means, by negligence of the searchers and collusion of the curriers . . . the King's subjects are not only in their goods but also in the health of their bodies much damaged by occasion of ill Shoes and Boots made of evil Leather'.[4]

Particular concern as to the effect of the alleged deterioration of standards in cloth-manufacture upon the reputation of English ex-ports appears not only in moralizing pamphleteers[5] but in the statutes of the realm. 'An Act for true making of Woollen Cloths' states explicitly that 'great infamy and slander hath risen in late years in sundry outward parts beyond the Sea of the untrue making of Woollen Cloths within this Realm, to the great dero-gation of the Common weal of the same and to the no little hindrance of the sale of the said commodity'.[6] The Antwerp market was very discriminating, with licensed inspectors of cloths able to distinguish the quality and the area of provenance of English products. Apparently German buyers also were becoming more and more critical of shortcomings in size, weight or quality. Again, the blame must not be attached solely to inexperienced producers attracted by the boom in exports, for in 1546 cloths

[1] 5 & 6 Edw. VI, c. 24; see also 21 Hen. VIII., c.12, and 34 & 35 Hen. VIII, c.10.
[2] H. Heaton, op. cit., 58 and 102.
[3] 24 Hen. VIII, c.1.
[4] 2 & 3 Edw. VI, c.9; 2 & 3 Edw. VI, c.11 gives a very full account of the deceits used in tanning.
[5] As in W. Forrest, *Princelie Practise*, ll. 437–41.
[6] 27 Hen. VIII, c.12.

manufactured by the famous Stumpe of Malmesbury were declared faulty.[1]

The West Riding industry is perhaps atypical in that 'meaner clothiers' there predominated, for elsewhere we hear complaints not only of the decline in standards but also of the fact that the independent craftsman was being swallowed up by the capitalist employer of labour. Hooper attacked such as 'will occupy yet all crafts and trade of buying and selling, that the poor man shall have neither goods nor handicraft to help himself withal',[2] and Hales referred to 'certain complaints made by weavers of kent, that they having wives and children could get no living, for that the Clothiers were now become also weavers'.[3] The weavers of Suffolk and Essex complained in 1539 that 'by Reason that the Richmen the clothiers have their looms and weavers and also their fullers daily working within their own houses', they found themselves 'many times destitute of work'.[4] In London the device of demanding a very expensive masterpiece was used deliberately as a barrier against a flood of journeymen whom the masters wished to keep in the position of wage-earners.[5]

The treatment accorded by employers often caused discontent. 'The weavers being journeymen of worcester' alleged in effect exploitation of cheap apprentice labour, without adequate instruction in the skills of the craft; furthermore, they were often paid by the clothiers with 'soup, candles, rotten cloth, stinking Fish and such like baggage'.[6] Again, 'the Richmen the Clothiers be concluded and Agreed Among themselves to hold and pay one price for weaving of the said Cloths, which price is so little, that your said supplicants the weavers cannot with their Labour get wherewith to sustain and maintain their poor households, although they should work incessantly night and day, the holy-day and work day'.[7] Armstrong relates how the 'poor handy craft people' of London are injured by the emergence of the domestic system in order to supply 'a sort . . . called haberdashers, otherwise

---

[1] G. D. Ramsay, *English Overseas Trade During the Centuries of Emergence*, 19–21.
[2] *Early Writings*, 392.   [3] 'Defence', in *Discourse*, p. lxv.
[4] *T.E.D.*, i, 177–8.
[5] G. Unwin, *The Gilds and Companies of London*, 265–6; below, 175.
[6] J. Hales, 'Defence', pp. lxv–lxvi.
[7] *T.E.D.*, i, 177–8.

called hardware men': after working hard all week they are offered but little for their wares, and told that foreign goods are cheaper.[1]

Thus government was asked to take action to protect the consumer, to maintain both standards of craftsmanship and stability of manufactures, to uphold the good name of English products overseas, and to prevent exploitation of the worker by low wages and truck. These objectives resemble the declared aims of the gilds, which much of government policy was deliberately designed to protect, whilst recognizing the problem of their neglect of their own ideals. Legislation of 1531 and 1536 forbade the imposition of excessive entry fees by gild wardens,[2] and the binding of apprentices by an oath that they, after their term of years is expired, 'shall not set up, or open any shop, house nor cellar nor occupy as free men, without the assent and licence of the Master Wardens or Fellowships'[3]—a practice which in itself would tend to drive craftsmen into the countryside. An act of 1550 sought to prevent employers from hiring their journeymen by the week or for other short periods, and to enforce a one-to-three journeyman/apprentice ratio, and was clearly concerned with security of employment and maintenance of standards.[4]

A statute of the previous session had shown more concern with the interests of the consumer, being directed against victuallers who 'have conspired and covenanted together to sell their victuals at unreasonable price; and likewise Artificers handicraftmen and labourers [who] have made confederacies' not only not to meddle in another's work 'but also to constitute and appoint how much work they should do in a day and what hours and times they shall work'.[5] Together with recognition of the fact that abuses within the gilds called for intervention by the Crown went realization that changing conditions and the extension of the market had weakened the old system of regulation. Hence the implicit call to central government to integrate and enforce standards on a national scale, to control and to supplement the gilds as instruments of industrial supervision.[6]

---

[1] *Treatise*, in *T.E.D.*, iii, 111.   [2] 22 Hen. VIII, c.4.   [3] 28 Hen. VIII, c.5.
[4] 3 & 4 Edw. VI, c.22.   [5] 2 & 3 Edw. VI, c.15.
[6] On this issue see E. F. Heckscher, *Mercantilism*, i, 128–36, 224–31, and 234–5; J. D. Mackie, *The Earlier Tudors*, 466; and W. Cunningham, *Growth of English Industry and Commerce*, 513.

Concern with national interests is demonstrated in suggestions for enforcement of standards. Armstrong urged that if cloth-making were confined to market towns which should record satisfactory manufacture with their seals before forwarding the cloths for approval by the proposed 'king's staple of woollen cloth in London', then both deliberate export of 'false cloths' by unscrupulous merchants, and abuse and stretching 'upon tenters' of English cloth by middlemen in the Low Countries, would be prevented.[1] The *Discourse* regretted the fact that certain towns which had formerly enforced such a system of guarantee had lately abused it—to their own decay—and suggested its re-imposition.[2] Forrest also advocated supervision in the towns to ensure that cloth was well shrunk and dressed, while faulty products should be worn by 'our folks' rather than exported to damage our reputation.[3]

Certainly there is ample evidence of governmental interest in this problem. Over forty statutes wholly or partly concerned with maintenance of standards—ranging from the favourite subject of wool and cloth manufacture and finishing,[4] through the next most frequent topic of the leather trade,[5] to such matters as the making of barrels,[6] hats and caps,[7] cables,[8] pewter,[9] malt,[10] coverlets,[11] and 'the true stuffing of Featherbeds'[12]—were enacted between 1509 and 1559. In general enforcement of these measures was entrusted to the gilds and to such local authorities as the mayor or the J.P. We noted the special commission appointed in 1533 to investigate the West Riding cloth industry. Despite difficulty in getting information it eventually compiled a list of no less than 542 offenders, but apparently to little effect for a year later Cromwell was informed that despite the commission 'they do now the

---

[1] *Reforme*, in *T.E.D.*, iii, 118–19; also his *Treatise*, *T.E.D.*, iii, 114.
[2] 77–8.　　　[3] *Princelie Practise*, pp. xcvi–xcvi*.
[4] 3 Hen. VIII, c.6; 14 & 15 Hen. VIII, c.3; 23 Hen. VIII, c.17; 24 Hen. VIII, c.2; 25 Hen. VIII, c.18; 27 Hen. VIII, c.12; 3 & 4 Edw. VI, c.2; 5 & 6 Edw. VI, cc.6, 8; 2 & 3 P. and M., cc.11, 12; and 4 & 5 P. and M., c.5, for example.
[5] Including 3 Hen. VIII, c.10; 22 Hen. VIII, c.6; 24 Hen. VIII, c.1; 2 & 3 Edw. VI, cc.9, 11; and 1 Mary, c.8.
[6] 23 Hen. VIII, c.4; 35 Hen. VIII, c.8.
[7] 3 Hen. VIII, c.15; 5 & 6 Edw. VI, c.24; and 7 Edw. VI, c.8.
[8] 21 Hen. VIII, c.12.　　　[9] 4 Hen. VIII, c.7.　　　[10] 2 & 3 Edw. VI, c.10.
[11] 34 & 35 Hen. VIII, c.10; 5 & 6 Edw. VI, c.24.
[12] 5 & 6 Edw. VI, c.23.

same (flocking and false cloth making) much more and worse than ever they did'.[1]

The wish to arrest the shift of industry into the countryside and the consequent decay of some older corporate towns found expression in two very similar draft proposals of 1534(?) and 1538. They include the following: certain commodities, including grain, butcher's meat and cloth, to be retailed only in towns on market day; clothmakers' purchases of land in the countryside to be limited; no butcher to be also a grazier or a tallow-chandler; no clothmaker to be haberdasher, mercer or grocer; certain crafts to be practised only in cities and towns.[2] The double aim emerges fairly clearly as being protection of towns and prevention of 'engrossing' of occupations and of merchandise.

These rather sweeping proposals were probably of private origin rather than a responsible government plan,[3] but a fair number of measures aimed at protection of town industry actually became law. In 1534, in response to complaints, it was ordered that none were to make cloths in Worcestershire save residents of five specified towns,[4] while similar enactments concerned cable- and rope-making in Bridport (1529),[5] coverlet-manufacture in York,[6] and weaving in Bridgwater (1555).[7] The reigns of Edward VI and Mary saw quite a spate of legislation of this type, including a measure relating to hat- and coverlet-making in Norwich,[8] a statute inhibiting countrymen's retailing of goods in market towns,[9] the well-known 'Acte touching Weavers' of 1555,[10] and an act of similar intent two years later.[11]

One interesting account of the reaction to such regulation is given by Sir Thomas Audley, in a letter to Cromwell in 1537. He reports the complaint of certain clothmakers that 'if they are compelled to make cloth from Michaelmas forwards according to the King's Act, it will cause them to forbear clothmaking, for it is impossible to keep the breadth of the cloth limited by the Act', since they are too poor to provide the 'looms and slees'

---

[1] H. Heaton, *Yorkshire Woollen and Worsted Industries*, 132–5.

[2] *L. and P. Henry VIII*, vii (1534), No. 67, 27, and xiv, Part 1 (1538), No. 875, 409.

[3] G. R. Elton, 'Parliamentary Drafts, 1529–1540', 122.

[4] 25 Hen. VIII, c.18.   [5] 21 Hen. VIII, c.12.   [6] 34 & 35 Hen. VIII, c.10.

[7] 2 & 3 P. and M., c.12.   [8] 5 & 6 Edw. VI, c.24.   [9] 1 & 2 P. and M., c.7.

[10] 2 & 3 P. and M., c.11.   [11] 4 & 5 P. and M., c.6.

needed to observe the standards. Audley has made the significant reply that the act was passed because 'there was much slander in outward parts for false cloth-making'.[1] The clothmakers' lament (or threat?) that 'they would leave their trade for the time, for they could by no possible means make cloth according to the Act' has incurred a brusque warning to 'take heed and beware, for he thought that they might perform the Act if they had good will and zeal to the commonwealth, and if by obstinacy or wilfulness they left their cloth-making, any murmur or sedition among the people for want of work would be laid to their charge'.[2]

The act referred to,[3] enforcement of which was in fact postponed several times,[4] was one of a series of statutes and proclamations which tried to enforce standards in the woollen industry. Several were concerned with the quality of the raw material: a proclamation of 1550 referred to 'greedy and insatiable minds' who let sheep go three or four weeks unwashed before shearing so that 'by means of their sweating and ... other filth' they weighed more, and to those who 'deceitfully put into the said fleeces of wool, sand, stones, dust, pitch, tar, clay, iron, lead, double marks, shearlocks, dung, lamb's-wool, and other deceivable things ... to the great slander of this realm'; such were to be imprisoned for ten days and then pilloried with a fleece of wool hanging round the neck.[5]

But most were attempts to regulate the manufacturing processes. An early statute of Henry VIII prohibited over-stretching of cloth, and prescribed 'the pillory or the Cukkyngstole Man or Woman as the case shall require' for anyone adding 'oil bran moisture dust sand' or 'any Flock' to the 'Webbe'.[6] A later enactment was devoted to 'the true dyeing of Woollen Cloth' and forbade the use of 'Brasell & such like subtleties' allegedly introduced by aliens.[7] A proclamation of 1534 ordered aulnagers to 'be diligent and circumspect' in enforcing the 'sundry statutes and

[1] Above, 173.   [2] *L. and P. Henry VIII*, xii, Part II (1537), No. 737, 267.
[3] 27 Hen. VIII, c.12.
[4] *Proclamations*, Nos. 166 (1536); 175 (1537); 198 (1541); 202 (1541); 207 (1541).
[5] *Proclamations*, No. 359 (23 May 1550), 492–4; also 23 Hen. VIII, c.17, and *Proclamations*, No. 253 (17 June 1545), 354–5.
[6] 3 Hen. VIII, c.6; repeated largely by 6 Hen. VIII, c.9.
[7] 24 Hen. VIII, c.2.

acts ... concerning the true making of all sorts of woollen cloths, whereby a great multitude of ... subjects daily be set in work and preserved from idleness'.[1] The statute of 1535 which awakened so much protest specifically mentioned 'infamy and slander' abroad as the reason for its enactment. All clothiers were thereby ordered to weave their marks into all cloths, and to seal them with a record of their true length. New standard sizes were prescribed for broadcloths and kerseys.[2]

Several measures in the last two years of the reign of Henry VIII[3] were followed by a special burst of activity in that of his successor. A proclamation of April 1549 repeated concern about foreign reputation and again ordered the sealing of cloths 'declaring thereby the just lengths thereof to be tried by water'. It decreed permissible stretching and shrinkage tolerances, and prohibited flocking and the use of iron cards, and false colours and the use of 'brazil'. J.P.s and other local officers were to visit and enforce 'once every quarter of a year at the least'.[4] A proclamation in the following month recognized 'that wool is so necessary for the keeping of the multitude of his highness' subjects from idleness that it cannot be lacked' and charged middlemen with a rise in prices which might lead to unemployment and poor quality cloth at home, and ill-repute, burning and banishment of our products abroad.[5] The substance of the first of these proclamations was broadly repeated in a statute of 1550, which also directed J.P.s to appoint overseers of cloth to search and enforce standards, and enacted penalties for neglect or obstruction.[6] An act of 1552, the fullest of all, provided for the appointment of cloth searchers in every town, detailed the standards of a score of named types of cloth, specifically forbade the use of any tenters with 'wrench rope or ring' or of 'any other Engine unlawfully to strain or stretch any Cloth', prohibited export of any cloth not sealed by the aulnager and ordered that defective exports should be returned at the expense of the clothier involved.[7]

These Tudor measures were an intensification of a record of

[1] *Proclamations*, No. 152 (23 Nov. 1534), 223–4.
[2] 27 Hen. VIII, c.12.
[3] *Proclamations*, Nos. 253 (1545); 264 (1546); 278 (1547).
[4] *Proclamations*, No. 328 (17 April 1549), 453–5.
[5] *Proclamations*, No. 331 (18 May 1549), 457–8.
[6] 3 & 4 Edw. VI, c.2.   [7] 5 & 6 Edw. VI, c.6.

intervention by the Crown in the woollen industry which stretched back to the fourteenth century.[1] But the efficacy, degree of enforcement, and real motive of much of this type of legislation have been challenged.[2] Moreover, despite the wish to check the exodus of industry from towns to rural areas this was sometimes accepted as a *fait accompli*. An act of 1547 conceded that enforcement of anti-middleman restrictions would hamstring the small manufacturers of the Norfolk woollen industry and cause many poor spinners to be 'unset awork'; permission was therefore granted for any inhabitant of the county to buy Norfolk wool.[3] The reality of established country industry was just as clearly recognized and sanctioned by the grant of similar privileges in an 'Act for th'inhabitants of Halifax . . .',[4] the preamble of which contains the well-known exposition of the advantages which industry confers upon areas otherwise infertile and barren.

One might urge that the willingness to admit and to legislate for these exceptions is but another sign of the basic concern for the general welfare of its subjects that characterized Tudor paternalism. But other, and less admirable, motives have sometimes been discovered in the conflicts of opinion as to the nature and scope of restrictive legislation. Unwin pointed to the fact that each of five enactments concerning the leather trades between 1548 and 1558 legislated in the opposite sense to its immediate predecessor as illustrating the struggle of different vested interests rather than the policy of an omniscient paternal state.[5] Indeed, 1 Mary, c.8 avowedly repealed 5 & 6 Edw. VI, c.15 because 'the said former Act was procured for the singular commodity of a few rich Shoemakers and other Artificers that are now common Regraters and Engrossers of Leather'.[6] Dr Bowden suggests that the restrictionist policy which attempted to maintain the quality of English cloth and confine its manufacture to the towns, and to curtail the freedom of the middleman, coincided with the interests of the wool-exporting merchants, especially against the background of the shrinking foreign market after 1551.[7] Dr

[1] See the list given by P. L. Hughes and J. F. Larkin, *Proclamations*, 223, n.1.
[2] G. D. Ramsay, *Wiltshire Woollen Industry*, 17–19, 51, 54–6, and 58–9.
[3] 1 Edw. VI, c.6. [4] 2 & 3 P. and M., c.13.
[5] *Gilds and Companies of London*, 252–3.
[6] 1 Mary, c.8.
[7] *The Wool Trade in Tudor and Stuart England*, 112–17.

Ramsay stresses rather the complaints made to the Privy Council by shippers of cloth about the effect of deceits in manufacture upon would-be purchasers abroad as a prime cause of much of this legislation.[1] Such a motive, while not necessarily altruistic, was hardly detrimental to national interests. Contemporary discussion of the problem of resolving conflicts between sectional advantage and the general welfare will concern us later.

As far as the wage-workers' interests were concerned, historically the intervention of government had usually been designed to check any tendency towards excessive wages. But statutory prohibition of truck had indeed been enacted.[2] By an early act of Henry VIII clothiers were ordered to pay their employees 'for the same their labour and workmanship ready money of the king's coin' and not 'in wares or victuals'.[3] Efforts to keep down prices would clearly benefit the wage-earner, but above all the government sought to maintain stability of employment and to prevent idleness. Indeed, Heckscher attributes to mid-Tudor England the first great discussion of the idea of creating work at home and avoiding unemployment.[4]

Governmental concern sprang largely from the question of security. We have already met with the argument that because of the precarious nature of their employment textile workers were a potential threat to law and order.[5] This might suggest that any expansion of manufactures of this type should be discouraged. Cecil, in 1564(?), conceded the possibility 'that the diminution of clothing in this realm were profitable', not only because decay of tillage and consequent dependence on foreign corn would be checked, but because 'the people that depend upon making of cloth are of worse condition to be quietly governed than the husband men'.[6]

Alternatively, it might be thought the duty of government to take action to secure employment. This could consist of pressure on merchants or employers, the direct provision of work for the unemployed, including the idle vagabond, or the deliberate and systematic encouragement of native industry. An instance of the

[1] *Wiltshire Woollen Industry*, 54–6; *Overseas Trade*, 23.
[2] E. Lipson, *Economic History of England*, i, 481–2.
[3] 3 Hen. VIII, c.6.   [4] E. F. Heckscher, *Mercantilism*, ii, 121.   [5] Above, 115.
[6] Memorandum, printed in *T.E.D.*, ii, 45.

first of these occurred in 1529 when, as a result of political conflict with the Netherlands, so many unsold cloths accumulated at Blackwell Hall that Wolsey intervened and ordered the merchants to buy them up.[1] We have just observed Audley's warning to certain clothmakers against any needless or wilful dismissal of their work-people.[2] The second method, so frequently urged upon government, found expression in the public works projects alluded to, in the Bridewell scheme, and in the gradual acceptance in the Poor Law enactments of the existence of a category of unemployed genuinely seeking work.[3]

The third approach was often discussed in the context of foreign trade. Forrest pointed to the folly of permitting the foreigner to derive employment and profit from working our wool and selling us back the products, when its further treatment inside this country would prevent the existing unemployment.[4] William Cholmeley alleged that our broadcloth exports gave finishing work overseas to 'two hundred thousand persons and above'! Thus royal enforcement of his project for dyeing cloth in England would be 'a greater, and a more certain and durable foundation of relief for the poor, than many such hospitals can be, and shall be a greater deed of charity; for if it be charity to succour a thousand, it is greater charity to succour many thousands, even a hundred thousands or two'.[5] Armstrong proposed that the Crown should set up a staple in London, and centralize and control cloth-making in market towns, in order to 'cause great number of common people to have labours and living'—for 'the whole wealth of the body of the realm riseth out of the labours and works of the common people'.[6]

Most of those aspects of policy examined in this chapter reveal the State as intervening, on a national scale and with greater authority than could be commanded by local gilds or by the exhortations of the Church, to uphold a traditional code of economic conduct founded upon equity, and to control some members of the body politic in the interests of the whole. But

---

[1] G. D. Ramsay, *Wiltshire Woollen Industry*, 65.
[2] Above, 178.
[3] Above, Chapter 7.
[4] *Princelie Practise*, p. xciv.
[5] *The Request and Suite of a True-Hearted Englishman*, 17.
[6] *Reforme*, T.E.D., iii, 115.

these last suggestions seem to foreshadow more positive ideas of State action in the interest of the efficient working of the economy with regard to national employment, output and strength. It is with these developments that we shall be concerned in the next chapter.

CHAPTER TEN

'Private Liberties and . . . Public Wealth'

WE have met with charges of excessive governmental interference in social and economic affairs, whether on the ground of the socio-religious objections expressed by Gardiner,[1] or on that of the sheer economic inexpediency of such action as urged by Mason.[2] Yet as a rule such intervention was expected and commended. 'From the princes and rulers of the state', declared Starkey, 'cometh all laws, order and policy, all justice, virtue and honesty to the rest of this politic body.' Without such governance, abundance of material endowments is worthless, for 'they shall abuse all such commodities to their own destruction and ruin'. Indeed, 'the end of all politic rule is, to induce the multitude to virtuous living according to the dignity of the nature of man'.[3] Rastell defined the commonwealth as resting 'neither in increasing of riches, power, nor honour, but in the increasing of good manners and conditions of men whereby they may be reduced to know God . . . and to live in a continual love and tranquillity with their neighbours': the purpose of good laws is to bring this about, much as bridle and spur direct the horse.[4] Ponet described laws as the sinews of the body politic,[5] and Brinklow pointed to the ruler's duty 'for the common wealth to make and establish politic acts'.[6]

On the extent to which 'we know what policy was and can confidently ascribe it to Crown and government' Professor Elton sounds a note of caution, but suggests that as far as attempts at

---

[1] Above, 87.   [2] Above, 150–1.   [3] *Dialogue*, 48–54.
[4] *The Book of Assizes* (1513), see E. M. Nugent (ed.), *The Thought and Culture of the English Renaissance*, 171.
[5] *Politike power*, p. C.viii.   [6] *The Complaynt of Roderyck Mors*, 15.

control by statute are concerned the 1530s—dominated by Cromwell and his advisers—stand out, and that the 'penal' statutes were designed as a genuine body of economic and social controls rather than as a mechanism of revenue through sale of dispensations.[1] Professor Dickens points out that before its dissolution in 1536 the Reformation Parliament enacted about 70 social and economic statutes, and 37 reforming civil and criminal law.[2] Another recent assessment, while critical of some of Professor Elton's constitutional interpretations, comes to an identical conclusion in regard to the 'far greater dynamic', as well as scope, of State legislative action.[3]

It is of course true that one cannot construct a model of a coherent, integrated, completely consistent policy, logically pursued and valid for explanation of every action of government throughout this period. Certainly there is the clearest evidence of the pressure and satisfaction of partial and vested interests, and of contradictory legislation or actions. The attitude of government towards industrial expansion, for example, was equivocal: it welcomed the possibility that national wealth, prosperity, and military strength—as well as Crown revenue—might be enhanced; but it deplored the dislocation which change inevitably brought, and the strain which the insecurity and unemployment of the industrial worker imposed upon the machinery of poor relief and the maintenance of public order. Yet to describe such attitudes as contradictory is not to gainsay the validity of each of the two motives or the striving for a policy; and the attempt to reconcile potentially divergent though individually admirable objectives is no stranger to twentieth-century government. It would be unfair to dismiss the action of government during this era as a mixture of drift, prejudice and reflex actions. For the mid-Tudor decades there is ample evidence of the belief that government had the right and the duty to intervene in the social and economic spheres and of the fact that it did so intervene; discussion was concerned with the scope, purpose and type of action required.

[1] G. R. Elton, 'State Planning in Early Tudor England', 433–5, 437, and 439: see also his 'Parliamentary Drafts, 1529–1540', 118.

[2] *The English Reformation*, 43.

[3] Penry Williams, 'The Tudor State', *Past and Present*, No. 25 (July 1963), 44.

The objectives thus far considered as fitting aims of governmental policy in social and economic affairs conceived of the State as guarantor and protector of a set of standards which were essentially traditional and designed to maintain an equitable balance of welfare between all parts of the body politic. As the oft-used corporeal analogy implies, this in turn would be conducive to the optimum strength of that body as a whole; a happy coincidence existed between the medieval concept of social justice and the healthy condition of the emergent concept of the national economy, for the well-being of the whole was made up of the welfare of its parts. But may one not tentatively ask whether a significant change of emphasis now takes place? The traditional ideal envisaged the bridling of man's selfish acquisitive instincts in accordance with moral and religious criteria, with equitable distribution as the immediate and imperative norm of conduct. To what extent was this gradually replaced, both in thought and in actual policy, by the desire to control and direct those instincts in the interests of national welfare, defined in terms of maximum wealth and economic efficiency?

As yet, the coincidence referred to was accepted. It has been argued that 'security, not prosperity, was the main object of Tudor economic policy', which derived from fear of war, the need to 'stay the fury of the inferior multitude' by provision of cheap food and fuel and maintenance of employment, and an ideal of social conservatism.[1] Indeed, both what Heckscher has described as a 'policy of provision',[2] and the maintenance of social equity, accorded with the political interests of government, while the strength of the State—as well as the security of government—was thought to rest upon the welfare of its subjects. This belief, held by Hales, Forrest and many others, is typified in the inclusion by the author of *Policies* of '*the people being wealthy* [which is underlined in the manuscript], and not oppressed with famine nor penury of victuals' as an essential condition of a powerful realm.[3]

At the same time, the duty of the Crown to take positive steps to increase the national wealth received more attention, often within the context of discussion of the relationship between English manufacture and foreign trade. Industrial activities were

[1] L. Stone, 'State Control in Sixteenth-Century England', 111, 115, and 118.
[2] *Mercantilism*, ii, 80–95. [3] *T.E.D.*, iii, 313.

commended as furnishing employment and money within the realm, whereas export of raw materials and import of foreign wares would drain it of both. The genesis of this mercantilist interpretation of the interrelationship between English raw materials, foreign trade, domestic employment and national wealth has been traced at least as far back as two anonymous works of the fifteenth century,[1] but there now evolved quite a body of thought on the duty of the State to nurture industry.[2]

Starkey argued that 'the carriage out of wool to the staple is a great hurt to the people of England; though it be profitable both to the prince and to the merchant also'. For it injured our own cloth-making industry, which we should encourage so as to generate employment and pay for necessary imports. Again, our merchants exported tin and lead and brought them back as manufactured articles. The remedy was to prohibit the import of anything which might be made within this country.[3] Cholmeley sought royal support for his scheme for dyeing cloth in England, being 'persuaded ... that God hath not enriched us with commodities which we can not through the weakness of our wits make perfect', and suggested that skilled Flanders craftsmen be procured 'to teach our countrymen'.[4] We have noted his over-sanguine estimate of resultant employment.[5] William Lane was another to condemn the import of 'superfluous commodities' and to make it the object of policy that 'our commonwealth be yearly gainers of them and not they of us', and our realm thus enriched in money.[6]

One of the most acute analyses of the place of industry in the economy appears in the *Discourse*. The Doctor, in reply to the Knight's allusion to the danger of unemployed clothworkers, advocates the encouragement of crafts, especially new ones, so as to set people on work and avoid reliance on wool alone. He proceeds to categorize artificers: the first type, including 'mercers, grocers, vintners, haberdashers, milliners', and other importers, lose

---

[1] *The Libel of English Policy*, and *On England's Commercial Policy* printed in T. Wright, ii, 157–205 and 282–7.

[2] J. U. Nef, *Industry and Government in France and England, 1540–1640*, 12.

[3] *Dialogue*, 173.

[4] *The Request and Suite of a True-Hearted Englishman*, 2 and 19.

[5] Above, 182.   [6] In *T.E.D.*, ii, 184–6.

our treasure; the second, 'shoemakers, tailors, carpenters, masons, tilers, butchers, brewers, bakers, victuallers of all sorts', get and spend within our country; the third, 'clothiers, tanners, cappers, and worsted makers', bring in treasure—these we must cherish. For 'our wool, fells, tin, lead, butter and cheese' are but 'the commodities that the ground bears, requiring the Industry of a few persons' and will not in themselves suffice, whereas 'Mysteries do enrich countries that been else barren ... [as] flanders and Germany do well declare'.[1]

The decay of certain towns and crafts—such as Coventry's 'blue thread' trade and Bristol's 'points' trade—is explained by the fact that 'while men were contented with such things as were made within the market towns next unto them, then were they of our towns and Cities well set awork' and the money spent remained in the country, whereas now the poorest young man must have 'gear' from London and overseas. The cure is to restrict the import of trifles, of any article that we could make ourselves, and especially of re-imports of our own materials made up. Manufactures of cloth, apparel, leather, glass, and iron goods are particularly mentioned.[2]

Newcomers to a town who are skilled in any craft should be welcomed, not kept out, the Capper's defence of local privileges being answered by the Doctor with the contention that where 'a singular good workman in any mystery comes ... I would, in that case, have private liberties and privileges give place to a public wealth', and admit him without 'any charge for his first entry or setting up'. Indeed, new crafts should be 'allured' by such inducements as freedom from rent and loaned stock. Within the towns, enforcement of standards is essential.[3] To sum up, industry may be nurtured in three ways: by control of imports, restriction of export of raw materials, and encouragement of manufactures under town control.[4] Here, clearly, is the wish for a policy for industry which would set national before particular interests, and which would face the fact that 'we may not set the price of things at our pleasure but follow the price of the universal market of all the world'.[5]

The warning that our treasure would drain abroad if import of

---

[1] 87–93.   [2] Ibid., 125–8.   [3] Ibid., 77–8; above, 176.
[4] Ibid., 128–31.   [5] Ibid., 87.

trifles and re-import of our own raw materials made up were not checked[1] had been sounded by Armstrong, who pictured England as 'always stuffed, stored and pestered' with 'strange merchandise and artificial fantasies. ... All nations sitting in the countries deviseth fantasies to make English men fools to get the riches out of the realm ... and daily carrieth out of England old shoes, horns and bones, and bringeth it into the realm again made into fantasies.' Thus 'all strangers in other realms hath work, and English men hath none, which in a right order might make all kind of artificiality needful to suffice the whole realm'. In fact 'the whole wealth of the realm is for all our rich commodities to get out of all other realms therefor ready money. ... And after it is in the realm, better it were to pay 6d. for any thing made in the realm than to pay but 4d. for a thing made out of the realm. ...' Also 'it shall be the great wealth to the king and all his lords to set as much people as can be to artificiality, for as much as they labour and work all for money, that their money may always run out of their hands in to the hands of such as occupieth husbandry' and thence 'into the hands of the king and of his lords of the earth'. The two chief types of productive activity are therefore 'works of husbandry to increase plenty of victuals, and the works of artificiality to increase plenty of money'.[2]

The ideas considered in these last few pages sometimes found statutory expression. An act forbidding the export of 'Broad White Woollen Cloths' referred, in Armstrong-like phraseology, to 'Merchant Strangers studying and imagining the policies, ways and means to set awork the people inhabited in foreign Countries ... by the commodities of this Realm', depriving Englishmen of the dyeing and finishing processes.[3] A later enactment deplored the drain of treasure, and domestic unemployment, caused by imports 'ready wrought by manual occupation', and attempted to foster the making of 'Linen Cloth' by ordering the 'sowing of Flax and Hemp'.[4] Again, 'An Act for the making of Russells Satins Sattens Reverses and Fustian of Naples in the City of Norwich', after declaring that imports of such cloths, made of Norfolk wools, have decayed the native worsted industries, takes

[1] Ibid., 87–8, and 126.   [2] *Treatise*, *T.E.D.*, iii, 105, 109–10, and 116.
[3] 14 & 15 Hen. VIII, c.1; see also 3 Hen. VIII, c.7.
[4] 24 Hen. VIII, c.4.

the logical step of sanctioning and regulating their manufacture in Norwich itself.[1]

A clear recognition of both the ethical and the practical case for international trade[2] is outweighed by the paramount need to check any loss of treasure abroad. The author of *Policies* declares that 'the only means to cause much Bullion to be brought out of other realms unto the king's mints is to provide that a great quantity of our wares may be carried yearly into beyond the Seas and less quantity of their wares be brought hither again'. This may be done by imposing a levy of 4s. or 5s. in the pound upon imported wares 'whereof the like may be made and wrought or had within this Realm, or whereof we stand in no very great need'. Such a regulation—from which iron, steel, copper, pitch and tar were to be exempt—would do more to moderate excess of apparel than any statute, and would be of incalculable benefit to a long list of crafts.[3]

It is suggested that by mid-century such motives as the achievement of a favourable balance of trade, the accumulation of 'treasure', and the support of native manufactures and employment exercised considerable weight in the formulation of policy, and that 'the merchants were laying the foundations of economic nationalism'.[4] In a recent examination of the 'making of the Statute of Artificers' Professor Bindoff traces the influence brought to bear by businessmen in the Commons' amendment of the original bill so as to shift the emphasis from agriculture to industry and trade, and to assert 'the claims of these growing branches of the country's economy to share in the assumed benefits of national regulation'.[5]

Meanwhile, economic nationalism might lead not only to the 'ousting of the merchant-stranger'[6] but to the direct encouragement of the immigrant foreign craftsman as suggested by Cholmeley. During the reign of Edward VI there are signs 'that immigrants were being encouraged on a large scale, not only as persecuted Christians, but also as economic groups'.[7] They were

---

[1] I & 2 P. and M., c.14. [2] Above, 170.
[3] *T.E.D.*, iii, 326 and 331–2; also 318.
[4] M. Beer, *Early British Economics*, 72–3.
[5] In *Elizabethan Government and Society*, 92–3. [6] M. Beer, loc. cit.
[7] L. H. Williams, *The Alien Contribution to the Social and Economic Development of England and Wales in the Sixteenth Century*, p. v.

associated mainly with attempts to diversify the textile industry. Indeed, the apparent contradiction between Cecil's support of these projects and his wariness as to the overall expansion of textiles may be resolved by crediting him with a realization that it was the broadcloth trade that was menaced by the satiation of the foreign market and the slump after 1551, and that one remedy was to encourage the weaving of lighter types of cloth. The best-known project of Edward's reign was Somerset's short-lived Glastonbury settlement of Walloons which consisted of 46 families, about 230 people;[1] it was patronized by Cecil after Somerset's fall, but the death of the king presaged its failure.

Here, surely, we see the emergence of a mercantilist aim: the conscious promotion of the aggregate wealth of the economy. Indeed, to look ahead, it may be suggested that the State—or at least those interests within the State which determine the direction of policy—may tend to adopt the practical criteria of wealth and power, rather than that of consonance with a customary ethical and moral code. R. de Roover stresses the essential continuity of economic doctrine, and the fact that traditional 'scholastic economics' did not vanish in the sixteenth century but continued as a current of thought alongside mercantilism into the eighteenth. He nevertheless points to some fundamental contrasts: 'mercantilism was never more than a conglomerate of uncoordinated prescriptions by which the authors of the mercantilist tracts sought to influence economic policy, usually in a sense favourable to their private interests', whereas scholastic economics formed 'an integral part of a coherent philosophical system ... a coherent body of doctrine according to which economic relations ought to be ruled by the laws of distributive and commutative justice'.[2] As yet, the latter tradition remained the essential core of mid-Tudor thinking on the economic and social aspects of the commonwealth, and provided the framework in relation to which the State was expected to play its part; but future trends may be clearly discerned.

Did a more aggressive concept of the economic role of the

[1] L. H. Williams, *The Alien Contribution*, Chap. I; see E. Lipson, *Economic History of England*, ii, 492–4.
[2] 'Scholastic economics: survival and lasting influence from the sixteenth century to Adam Smith', 177–8 and 187–90.

State imply a more realistic assessment of the extent to which the selfish economic interests of its members could be controlled, and a shift to the adoption of measures which might more fruitfully attempt to direct and exploit rather than to stifle them? With respect to the nature and type of law or action requested of government, it has been contended that many of the commentators were in effect asking it to check the course of economic and social evolution, even to reverse it. Despairing of the enforcement or even the clear enunciation of Christian principles in this shifting society, they sought refuge in a return to the conditions and values of a previous age. It is suggested that the plans of social reformers were usually nostalgic rather than constructive and the writings of idealists, while sincere in their protest, often ill-informed and economically naïve.[1] J. W. Allen describes Crowley as 'asking men to be other than they are. His ideal was conservative in that it involved a stereotyping of the social structure. It was, even, reactionary in the sense that it aimed at restoring a state of things vaguely supposed to have existed in a happy past.'[2]

With much of this it is impossible to disagree. The vast majority of the social and economic criticisms reviewed here—from Protestant and Catholic sources alike—derived directly from the moral code laid down by the medieval Church, and hankered after an idealized set of conditions which were held to be the functional expression of that code in the field of economic and social relations. The changing expressions of opinion regarding monastic landlords typify the way in which nostalgia for the past became heightened by revulsion against present evils. But the picture must be qualified. Thus the statement that 'Crowley's appeal was not to government [but] to the moral and religious consciousness',[3] cannot be applied too rigidly, for his *Informacion and Peticion* was addressed specifically to 'them that have to do in the Parliament', exhorted them to repeal their predecessors' enactment which had sanctioned usury up to 10 per cent, and expressed the hope that the Spirit which dwelt in the primitive Church would guide their actions.[4]

---

[1] L. Einstein, *Tudor Ideals*, 237; J. W. Allen, *Political Thought in the Sixteenth Century*, 134–5, and W. Cunningham, *Growth of English Industry and Commerce*, 558–9.
[2] Op. cit., 142.   [3] Ibid.,   [4] R. Crowley, *Works*, title-page and 170–5.

In fact, 'appeal . . . to government' was often quite literally what would-be reformers did—vague and impractical though they may sometimes have been as to the steps which they expected it to take. For we have seen the civil power envisaged as legatee or guardian of the traditional communal conscience, equipped moreover with a power of enforcement which it was sometimes urged to use even against the Church where that body was itself at fault. The pleas of the idealists as well as the schemes of practical men were addressed to Crown, ministers or parliament. The former, it is true, expected example as well as precept from their rulers, but they also besought action, legislative and administrative; the idealist Latimer could cry 'for God's sake make some promoters'.[1] For their idealism was not always impracticable; of this fact the work of Ridley in helping to organize the relief of poverty in London is an outstanding instance.[2]

But even more striking is the fact that some commentators do not rest content with the coupling of protests against current economic and social trends with appeals to government to stem the tide, but seem prepared to come to terms with, control and channel acquisitive instincts for the good of the commonwealth. It may be argued that certain of the proposals made, in effect and by implication, anticipate the philosophy of Mandeville 'that Private Vices by the dextrous Management of a skilful Politician may be turned into Publick Benefits'.[3] Morison's ideal prescription for a 'common wealth ... wealthy and worthy his name' might indeed include subjects of such a disposition that each one, while 'glad to do that, that he may lawfully do', is 'gladder to do that, which he seeth shall be for the quietness of the realm, all be it his private profit biddeth him do the contrary',[4] but we have already seen evidence of a realization that legislative enactment, if it ran counter to the harsh logic of economic reality, might not succeed in its intention.[5] The logical deduction was to advocate the framing of measures which would harness the working of economic forces for the common good rather than oppose them in indiscriminate and futile fashion.

[1] *Sermons*, 279.   [2] As is that of Strassburg, in a European context.
[3] B. Mandeville, *The Fable of the Bees: or, Private Vices, Publick Benefits*, i, 369.
[4] *Remedy*, p. A.iiii.   [5] Above, 150–1.

The unknown author of *Policies to Reduce this Realme of Englande vnto a Prosperus Wealthe and Estate*, which he addressed to Somerset in 1549, showed on occasion a particularly clear understanding of such factors, remarking shrewdly that 'surely there cannot be a more pernicious thing to bring the people from a due obedience than to make such laws as shall not be kept'.[1] This work is a puzzling mixture of naïve misconceptions and exaggerations, particularly in regard to coinage debasement and the foreign exchanges,[2] of perceptive and hard-headed judgements of marketing and pricing realities within the country, and of strikingly and sometimes quite impractically original suggestions for substituting fiscal controls in place of a fruitless combination of prohibition and exhortation. We have already met with its proposals for a subsidy on sheep[3] and for the imposition of discriminatory import duties.[4]

The writer is critical of attempts to hold prices at an artificially low level by means of proclamations and the intervention of local officials: 'for every man will sell his wares at the highest price he may'. What was the effect, he asks, of an occasional compulsory sale of a poor woman's pig at half the market price? 'Do this anything help the general price of victual?' No, for the victim must needs sell the dearer again or lack her rent-money. Again, how can those dwelling near London, paying high rent for their ground, price their butter as cheaply as others living seven or eight score miles away, paying only one-quarter of the rent for the like ground? 'And some ground because it yieldeth far better Cheese, and far sweeter and better coloured butter than many other grounds doth, hath always upon that Consideration been set upon a higher rent.' Therefore proclamations and penal statutes will accomplish nothing: 'it is not the setting of low prices that will any thing amend the matter. But it must be the taking away of the occasion of the high prices.' Apart from the inexpediency of such controls the writer maintains that when those empowered to set prices are themselves engaged in trade they sometimes 'under the Colour of a common wealth ... abuse their authority unto their own proper lucre', deliberately underpricing and driving away potential competition so as to leave the

---

[1] *T.E.D.*, iii, 335.
[2] Ibid., iii, 315–17, 324 and 343–4.
[3] Above, 166.
[4] Above, 190.

field clear for their own wares 'to sell at such high and unreasonable price' as they will.[1]

He suggests positive encouragement of tillage and of the fishing trade, by fiscal methods. To prevent decay of tillage when a good harvest lowers prices of grain, the Crown should pay a fixed price at certain ports and, in effect, subsidize exports.[2] Consumption of fish will not be encouraged merely by the present laws on meatless days; for 'as straight a law [is] made for the excess of Apparel and yet could not the king nor all his council find the means to have that Statute kept'. Now apparel is worn openly, while flesh is eaten at home: 'and if he were accepted for a busy Promoter which would sue a man for manifest contempt of the Statute of apparel, shall he now be accounted for an honest neighbour which shall trouble a man for eating of his meat in his own house?' Rather should licences be sold openly granting permission to eat flesh on fish-days, the proceeds payable to 'Fraternities' of fishermen set up in each 'circuit' of sea-coast shires. This will encourage fishermen and mean a larger supply, and cheaper prices, of fish for the poor to eat on fish-days! It will injure no one, 'for only the wanton money coming out of the rich man's purse, shall cause the poor man to buy his victual cheaper'.[3] Granted the elements of exaggeration and impracticability, it is quite startling to find this commendation of the redistributive effects of a method of fiscal control. Clearly the author of *Policies* wished the government to use the pricing mechanism for its purposes.

He was not alone in advocating discriminatory controls. Starkey's *Dialogue*, conceding 'that man by instruction and gentle exhortation, can not be brought to his perfection', and that fear of punishment, which custom in time will reinforce, must be used to induce correct conduct, for 'this is the end and virtue of all law', makes definite economic and social proposals. To eliminate fear of depopulation marriage must be encouraged, by privilege and by penalty. Secular priests should be allowed to marry, and all men with five or more children declared exempt from war service and from certain taxation; but bachelors should be subjected to income tax of 1s. in the pound and a tax of 1d. in the pound on all moveable goods in excess of £5, while half of what they bequeath must

---

[1] *Policies*, T.E.D., iii, 317 and 339–41.
[2] Ibid., iii, 329–31.   [3] Ibid., iii, 334–7.

go to charity. Unemployment and idleness may be banished partly by judicious import- and export-control and partly by the appointment of officers like the Censors of ancient Rome who shall oversee the education of youth and the exercise by all of profitable and beneficial crafts.[1]

To prevent ill-proportion in the body politic—too few tillers and artisans, too many idlers—which would result from the tendency to rush to the easiest and most lucrative occupations, there must be 'a chief means in every craft, art, and science, some to appoint, expert in the same, to admit youth to the exercise thereof; not suffering every man without respect to apply themself to every craft and faculty'.[2] Village and town courts should be empowered to impose fines for proven negligence of ploughmen and of artisans; in particular Starkey would 'constrain the ploughmen and farmers to be more diligent in rearing of all manner of beasts and cattle'. Rents should be restored to their former level and the laws against enclosure enforced.[3] We noted earlier[4] his advocacy of measures to control trade in the interest of our own manufactures.

Despite the smack of novelty of some of his proposals Starkey's persistent use of the corporeal analogy of society is symbolic of the essentially medieval basis of his thought. Heckscher observes that at a later date, after the discovery of fixed rules governing natural phenomena, the device might be invoked for a different reason, to point the folly of attempting to direct nature.[5] But Starkey employs it for its traditional purpose: to stress the mutual interdependence and duty of all members of the body politic. His account of the purpose of laws would have won ready agreement from his contemporaries, as would also his qualification that the law alone cannot make men perfect. Many of his suggestions listed above are completely conservative, as are his definition of the duty of government 'chiefly to see that all such things may be distributed with a certain equality' and to constrain 'every man in his craft and faculty to meddle with such thing as pertaineth thereto, and intermeddle not with other', and his belief that genuine poverty is ordained of God to awaken charity.[6]

---

[1] Op. cit., 146–56.   [2] Ibid., 159.   [3] Ibid., 171–6.   [4] Above, 187.
[5] E. F. Heckscher, *Mercantilism*, ii, 308–10.
[6] *Dialogue*, 51–4, 157–9, 176 and 206.

A similar blend of concern for traditional values and the communal welfare with a willingness to devise practical expedients to control or harness men's individual self-interest, together with perhaps the clearest contemporary grasp of current economic issues, is found in the *Discourse*. The Doctor voices the usual arguments against enclosures—the fear of 'a mere solitude and utter desolation to the whole Realm, furnished only with sheep and shepherds [and] a prey to our enemies'—and reiterates the principle that 'no man may abuse his own things to the prejudice of the common weal'. But he follows with a realistic analysis of the economic issues, including the shrewd observation that enclosure is not the sole cause of dearth, for it should increase the supply of those things which are dearest, mutton and beef; and he makes practical proposals designed to appeal to the pocket rather than to the conscience. Thus corn-growing might be encouraged if it were possible 'to make the profit of the plough to be as good, rate for rate, as the profit of the grasiers and sheep-masters'. To do this, export of wool should be restricted, above a certain price, and 'the custom of wool that passeth over unwrought' increased; this would lower the price the breeders obtained for their wool. Meanwhile, permission for free export of corn would raise its price and increase production—an argument that was to become familiar. For if merchants and graziers are allowed to raise their prices, why should not the husbandman's wares be freely sold?[1]

The Husbandman himself explains that 'many of us saw, 12 year ago, that our profits was but small by the plows'; therefore 'every day some of us encloseth a (plot) of his ground to pasture; and were it not that our ground lieth in the common fields, intermingled one with another, I think also our fields had been enclosed, of a common agreement of all the township, long ere this time'. The Capper argues that the price of corn ought to be low, 'since every man hath need of corn'; the more necessary, retorts the Doctor, to cherish the men who raise it! We must encourage what is needed, not penalize it, 'for every man will the gladder follow that wherein they see the more profit and gains'. His suggestions would secure more corn and import of treasure, while 'the more husbandry is occupied, the more universal breed should

[1] *Discourse*, 52–6.

be of all victuals, as of neate, sheep, swine, geese, eggs, butter, and cheese, for all these are reared much of corn'.[1]

The question of enclosures is returned to in a most significant passage: 'To tell you plainly, it is Avarice that I take for the principal cause thereof; but can we devise that all covetousness may be taken from men?' No. But what we can do is to take away 'the exceeding lucre that they see grow by these inclosures, more than by husbandry'; we must either diminish the profit of the one or increase that of the other. Grazing is now made lucrative by its low labour costs and the free pricing of its product. This freedom must be given to the corn-grower while pasture should be penalized: 'charge one acre of pasture as much as 2 acres of arable land', or burden wool and fells with heavier customs duties.[2] Here again,[3] the author displays a very sure grasp of the real economic issues. Heckscher ascribes to him the belief that 'people should be taken as they are and should be guided by wise measures in that direction which will enhance the well-being of the state'.[4] Certainly he recognized the futility of laws that would either be evaded in wholesale fashion or would defeat their own object; output of what was needful must be encouraged, and that of the converse checked, by measures designed to control economic processes by appealing to economic motives.

As we have seen,[5] the claim of John Hales to authorship of the *Discourse* is very doubtful—the emphasis upon debasement as 'the original cause' of other problems[6] is missing from those writings which are certainly his. But we may fairly turn to these and to his activities in general as further evidence that sympathy with traditional ideals, and with an inherited concept of social obligation, was not necessarily incompatible with a grasp of present economic realities. For attempts at objective economic analysis and suggestions for practical expedients go side by side with statements and appeals that are wholly traditional. The former included bills for maintenance of tillage, prevention of regrating of cattle,[7] and enforcement of a ratio in the rearing of sheep, cattle and calves.[8] He was also, apparently, in charge of a

---

[1] Ibid., 56–60.   [2] *Discourse*, 121–4.
[3] Above, 141–2, for his monetary analysis.   [4] *Mercantilism*, ii, 293.
[5] Above, 35–7.   [6] Above, 141.   [7] Cf. 3 & 4 Edw. VI, c.19.
[8] Cf. 2 & 3 P. and M., c.3; for these bills see his 'Causes of Dearth' in *Discourse*, pp. lxii–lxiii, also below, 203–4.

measure[1] to implement his proposal for diverting a royal tax on towns 'toward a stock to be occupied ... in setting the poor people of the same on work'.[2] His proposed sheep and cloth tax became law as 2 & 3 Edw. VI, c.36.

The sheep and cloth subsidy which Hales introduced in 1549 is of the very greatest interest as 'an early essay in the use of taxation as an instrument of economic planning',[3] despite its being 'probably the shortest lived tax in English fiscal history'.[4] It was foreshadowed by a set of computations in 1547,[5] and by Hales's paper 'Causes of Dearth' in 1548. Hales's overt purpose was fiscal, to dispense with the unpopular system of purveyance and yet satisfy 'the king's charges [which] daily increase more and more', but the real motive was certainly to check enclosure for sheep-grazing. He proposed that 'the king might have of every sheep kept in the common fields one penny, of every Ewe and Lamb kept in several [that is, enclosed] pasture two pence, and of every other sheep kept in pasture, three half pence'.[6] It is true that the yield of wool from sheep on enclosed pasture was higher, but the other purpose of this differential also seems clear. He suggested an imposition on cloths 'after this rate, that is of the Clothier for a broad cloth 5 s., and a kersey 20 d., and of the [exporting] merchant double custom'.[7]

The measure enacted in 1549 ordered a census of and a poll tax on sheep, together with a levy on home-produced cloth. Ewes on enclosed pasture were to be charged at three halfpence, other sheep on such ground at twopence, and all sheep on commons or enclosed tillage ground at three halfpence. The differential in favour of the 'commoner' is less than in the figures Hales first suggested, but men with less than ten sheep were to pay one halfpenny, and those with ten to twenty one penny, per head. The tax on cloth was to be assessed at 3·5 per cent of its price. Despite its enactment for three years it was in fact repealed in January 1550 by a measure which described it as 'cumbrous to all Cloth makers, and also tedious to the same for making of their

---

[1] 2 & 3 Edw. VI, c.5; see E. Lamond in *Discourse*, 152.
[2] 'Causes of Dearth', in *Discourse*, p. xlv.
[3] S. T. Bindoff, *Tudor England*, 133.
[4] M. W. Beresford, 'The Poll Tax and the Census of Sheep, 1549', 9.
[5] Printed in *T.E.D.*, i, 178–84.   [6] In *Discourse*, pp. xlii–xliii.
[7] Ibid., p. xliv.

books and the accounts thereof', alleged that it could cause unemployment by checking cloth manufacture, and pleaded the
difficulty of collecting the tax.[1] It is of interest that while the
author of *Policies* commended a subsidy on sheep,[2] he criticized
'the relief which was granted upon cloths.... For doubtless it shall
be the cause that the fewer cloths shall be made in England', that
exports shall diminish and unemployment increase.[3] These fears
were expressed also by the Doctor in the *Discourse*.[4] At all events,
the disgrace of Somerset marked the collapse of what has been
described as the most serious attempt in the sixteenth century to
check enclosure for pasture by legislative and administrative action.[5] Ironically, the working of impersonal economic forces—the
result of the calling down of the coinage by Northumberland and
of the slump in the European market—were soon to have the
effect for which Hales and the Commonwealth's Men had striven
in vain.

Above all, Hales was concerned with the urgent need of
'medicines ... to resist, remove, and heal this most hurtful disease
of the commonwealth, private profit ... to take away the inordinate desire of riches ... and to plant brotherly love among
us ... members of one body mystical of our Saviour Christ, and
of the body of the realm',[6] and with the enunciation of the principle of stewardship in the use of earthly possessions.[7] But while
condemning avarice, he also understood clearly that moral exhortation alone, as a means of control, would not suffice. At the
same time, recognition that laws might be obstructed or evaded
if they conflicted with individual economic interests did not mean
that the interests of the commonwealth should be abandoned;
what Hales sought were more effective means of realizing his
ideal.

When he returned from exile a note of disillusioned realism is
clear. A paper 'on the Unwisdom of a New Imposition on Cloth',
addressed to Cecil in 1559, reiterates his belief that 'in making of
Laws and government men ought to have respect to the whole,
more than to any one part', but concedes that at present merchants

---

[1] 3 & 4 Edw. VI, c.23.   [2] Anon., 327.   [3] Ibid., 324–5.   [4] 91.
[5] M. W. Beresford, 'The Poll Tax and the Census of Sheep, 1549' (continued),
27.
[6] 'Charges', in Strype, ii (Part II), 352–6.   [7] 'Defence', in *Discourse*, p. xliii.

are essential to the commonwealth, 'considering the whole riches and wealth of this Realm consisteth at this present in making and uttering of the Cloth. For merchants travail for gain and when gain ceaseth they travail no more.' He reflects ruefully that 'ye remember how once it was attempted, and had no such success as was hoped', and questions the political expediency of such a measure when 'the queen's majesty is not yet so well settled as I wish she were'.[1] His 'Oration' to Elizabeth I appeals for the body politic 'to be cleansed, made whole, and then kept in good order', which 'may not be done with piecing and patching, cobbling and botching, as was used in time past', but insists that unless that body 'be clean purged from corruption, all the particular laws and statutes that can be devised, shall not profit it. .... For this body, which is the people, is universally, naturally, disposed to evil, and without compulsion will hardly do that is its duty.'[2]

On this note we may not inappropriately conclude our study of Commonwealth thought on the scope, objectives and nature of social and economic legislation. For Hales is perhaps most representative of its hopes and its frustrations. He exemplifies not only its uneasy mixture of the medieval and the modern, its sense of moral outrage at many tendencies of contemporary society and its attempts at devising practical expedients to check or control those tendencies, but also the willingness of some of its leaders to put their careers at risk in order to further their ideals. The traditional belief that social and economic regulation must be seen as part of a moral code persists, but it is modified, first by an ever-clearer realization that only the State has the power to enforce such regulation, and secondly, at least in some commentators and most notably perhaps in the *Discourse*, by a realistic recognition of the futility of mere exhortation, of the power of economic motives in individuals and in society, and of the fact that those forces might be more effectively channelled than dammed.

[1] Printed in *T.E.D.*, ii, 223–6.
[2] 'An Oration of John Hales', printed in *The Acts and Monuments of John Foxe*, ed. J. Pratt, viii, 673–9.

CHAPTER ELEVEN

The Implementation of Policy

IN considering the nature and purpose of the laws and the
policy established by the government of the commonwealth
we must not take for granted the processes either of enactment
or of enforcement. Contemporaries recognized that it was not
always easy to secure the passage through Parliament of measures
designed to reform economic and social abuses. Brinklow indeed
addressed his *Complaynt of Roderyck Mors* 'unto the parliament
house of England'—suggesting, incidentally, that the two houses
should be combined so as to remove the absurdity of one house
annulling a bill passed by the other—but he felt the Members to
be in need of a sermon at least three times a week. Such sermons,
to last between an hour and an hour and a half, were to remind
members of their duty and of the abuses needing reform, and
attendance should be obligatory, under pain of expulsion. For all
too often private interests defeated the common good. In respect
of the 'enhancing of rents' he complained that 'it is hard to have it
redressed by Parliament, because it pricketh them chiefly which
be chosen to be burgesses', and a burgess, unfortunately, was not
one who cared for honesty or 'such as would his neighbour
should live as himself' but rather 'a jolly cracker and bragger . . .
how can any such study or give any godly counsel for the commonwealth?'[1]

Armstrong, while conceding the urgent need for restrictive
legislation to deal with people displaying 'no dread of God,
but only dreading the actual pains and punishment of the law',
warned those who hoped for the passing of remedial acts in
'the common house, thinking that such as are in the common
house should specially intend the wealth of all common people,
the king's bodily members', that they would find there, if they

[1] Title-page and 8 and 12–13.

searched, farmers with up to fourteen farms, enclosers for sheep-pasture, graziers and regraters of corn and cattle, merchants, 'buyers and sellers, which getteth their riches out of the common weal, always studying by their policy of plenty of all things to make scarcity'. 'These sorts in the common house' will frustrate all efforts of 'the king and his lords in the head house', for they 'cannot suffer no act pass for the common weal, but they must needs destroy their own singular weal'.[1]

William Turner, chaplain and physician to Somerset, had been a Member of Parliament, and the opening pages of *The Huntyng of the Romyshe Wolfe* (c. 1554/5) contain an analysis of recent developments in that body which is the more striking in view of his strong support of Edwardian religious policy. He regrets that

for the common wealth, for these many years, there have been few that were very earnest to help it, although indeed, there were some. . . . I was 5 years together, a burgess of the parliament, in the lower house, but in all my time . . . there was always some, that either sought their own private lucre, as the noble lordly and knightly sheepmasters did, in defending against all honest lovers of the common wealth, the intolerable number of sheep: or else sought very earnestly the King's profit, wherein they intended always to have not all the smallest part. And such were certain of the council, or privy chamber, which contrary unto the order and liberty of the house, would twice or thrice or ofter, speak in one matter, for the King's profit or else for their own. And if we spake any thing freely there, we were taken up like butchers' curs, or else were privily met with all, afterward.[2]

'The defence of John Hales against certain slanders and false reports made of him' (1549) includes a bitter account of the fate of his own legislative projects: 'The one for re-edifying houses decayed, and for the maintenance of tillage and husbandry' was introduced in the Lords and 'being read was not liked'. A second, 'for regrating of victual and other things, wherein I remember one principal point, that Graziers nor no man should buy any cattle and sell the same again within a certain time', the Lords 'allowed and augmented, and sent down to the lower house, which if ye had there heard debated, and had seen how it was tossed, and to whose hands at length it was committed, and how it was deferred, if ye should have seen men's affections wonderfully,

[1] *Reforme*, T.E.D., iii, 121-2 and 126.   [2] Pp. A.iiii–A.iiii.b.

perchance ye would have said that the lamb had been committed to the wolf to custody'.

A third proposal, to establish a compulsory ratio between sheep and cows in order to furnish the markets 'with milk butter and cheese, which is the common and principal sustenance of the poverty', was first read in the lower house and received like treatment, for 'demetrius and his fellows soon spied whereunto this thing tended. There was then, hold with me, and I will hold with thee.' The objection that a sufficient remedy already existed for any threatened scarcity of cattle by the issue of an order that 'no calves should be killed for a time'—an expedient which had indeed twice been adopted by statute under Henry VIII[1]—Hales ridiculed, since the effect would be 'to make scarcity and dearth and to undo, yea, rather starve the poverty'. Finally, his charge that the feature of the bill which aroused most alarm was its proposal of effective machinery of enforcement is very telling.[2] For

the matter of this bill did not so much grieve them, as for that there was a way found thereby to have it always truly executed. For I had thus devised that the parson or Curate of every parish to whom belongeth the tithes, and two honest men should yearly survey every man's pastures and should not only present who did transgress this law, but also who did observe it. This was it that bit the mare by the thumb. Men pass not much how many laws be made, for they see very few put in execution.

Indeed, he asked bluntly, 'who passeth on offending and breaking the laws when he hath plenty of money to stop the execution of them?'[3]

Hales and his contemporaries were only too well aware that legislation was not administration. Starkey alleged that 'there be few laws and statutes, in parliaments ordained, but, by placards and licence obtained of the prince, they are broken and abrogate, and so the common weal do little profit'.[4] But negligence, corruption, and selfish partiality, rather than royal dispensations, were more often advanced in explanation of why well-intentioned edicts were not enforced. In 1550 Crowley, writing 'of the Exchecker', described a flimsily hypothetical case of a monarch, defrauded by

---

[1] 21 Hen. VIII, c.8; and 24 Hen. VIII, c.7.   [2] In *Discourse*, pp. lxii–lxv.
[3] 'Defence', in *Discourse*, pp. lxiv–lxv.   [4] *Dialogue*, 102.

bribe-taking ministers of his 'court for receipt of money', who rebuked them that

> No statute could cause
> The offenders to amend,
> Because you bare with them,
> When they did offend.[1]

A proclamation of 1533(?) complained of failure to enforce certain laws,

the very default whereof resteth in the King's justices of the peace, mayors, sheriffs ... and other ministers of justice ... which for the most part so negligently, dulcetly, favourably, and unwillingly use their offices that justice is decayed. ... For lack of due execution of which good statutes ... the offenders, being shameless, stand without dread of the laws, and so daily increase ... to the high displeasure of Almighty God, ... and the whole subversion of the commonwealth of this realm.

This order[2] referred directly to legislation concerning false rumours, idle vagabonds, excess in apparel, unlawful games and maintenance of archery, and sewers, but several other proclamations deplored evasion or non-enforcement of anti-enclosure legislation.[3] One of these, significantly, had invited 'relaters and furtherers of the commonwealth ... that they, by writing and bills, secretly disclose unto the Lord Legate, his Chancellor of England, the names of all such person and persons of what estate, degree, or condition he or they be', guilty of enclosing or of holding more farms than one.[4]

Hales himself remarked to the Enclosure Commissioners that 'as there be many good men that take great pains to study to devise good laws for the commonwealth; so there be a great many, that do with as great pains and study, labour to defeat them; and as the common saying is, to find gaps and starting holes'. In order to evade the law 'some about one hundred acres of ground ... make a furrow, and sow that; and the rest they till not, but pasture with their sheep. ... Some, to colour the multitude of

---

[1] *Works*, 29.   [2] *Proclamations*, No. 138 (after 1532), 206–8.
[3] Ibid., Nos. 309 (June 1548); and 327 (Apr. 1549).
[4] Ibid., No. 119 (15 May 1528), 174–5.

their sheep, father them on their children, kinsfolks and servants.'[1]
His experience on the Commission gave him first-hand knowledge
of other reasons for failure. For when it started its inquiries 'some
found the means to have their servants sworn in the Juries, to the
intent to have them hazard their souls to save their greediness';
indeed the number of their 'Retainers and hangers on' often made
it impossible to obtain a jury without them and any attempt at
true execution of the law was hopeless. Some poor men, with no
security of tenure, dare not say anything that would offend their
landlords: 'As it pleaseth my landlord so shall it be. A godly
hearing in the common wealth.' In fact, 'some also were Indicted
because they presented the truth, and some were persuaded that
the end of the Commission should [be] but a money matter, as it
had been in time past'.[2]

Latimer, preaching on evasion of anti-enclosure legislation,
alluded to 'a certain giant, a great man, who sat in commission
about such matters; and when the townsmen should bring in what
had been enclosed, he frowned and chafed, and so near looked,
and threatened the poor men, that they durst not ask their right'.[3]
The 'Petition' of the leaders of Ket's Rebellion, in asking that
commissioners should be appointed from among them, stated explicitly that this was to enable them 'to redress and reform all such
good laws, statutes, proclamations, and all other your proceedings,
which hath been hidden by your Justices of your peace . . . and
other your officers from your poor commons, since the first year
of the reign of . . . King henry the seventh'.[4]

Understandably, the question has been raised whether the
intervention of statesmen in this field was not 'simply the expression of a pious opinion', as witnessed in the recurring pattern
of fresh proposals and failure of implementation.[5] First, policy
might be hamstrung by the opposition of vested interests: of the
31 persons who got grants of £200 a year or more from church
estates between 1548 and 1552, 14 were members of the Privy
Council; Somerset could hardly have hoped for wholehearted
support in his agrarian policy from such colleagues![6] When lack

[1] 'Charges', in Strype, ii (Part II), 361–2.
[2] 'Defence', in *Discourse*, p. lix.   [3] *Sermons*, 248.
[4] Printed in F. W. Russell, *Kett's Rebellion in Norfolk*, 55–6.
[5] R. H. Tawney, *The Agrarian Problem in the Sixteenth Century*, 377.
[6] Ibid., 380.

of support at the centre for a formally adopted policy was matched by equal reluctance to implement it at the periphery then an administrative machine run largely on cooperation and consent could hardly accomplish much.

This in turn points to a second major difficulty, the fact that in some respects Tudor social and economic policy 'demanded feats of administrative efficiency that a rudimentary bureaucratic structure based on the voluntary work of local gentry was quite unable to provide', as was amply shown by the failure of laws forbidding usury and controlling food prices.[1] Yet on balance it would be rash to equate partial failure with complete inefficacy. The course of economic change might not be diverted or reversed, but it might be slowed down; all individual hardships and injustices might not be prevented, but some might be mitigated. There is a fair measure of agreement[2] that governmental intervention had a greater degree of restrictive and protective effect than is sometimes conceded.

We may look briefly at one or two special expedients proposed or adopted for the enforcement of economic and social regulation. For the question arises not only of the formulation of a law, and of its honest application by the courts, but also of the searching out of a breach of the law and the bringing to trial of an offender. A significant part in the performance of this function was sometimes played by the 'promoter' or common informer. Latimer alluded approvingly to this method of checking offences, and expressed his regret that 'there lack men to promote the king's officers when they do amiss, and to promote all offenders. I think there is great need of such men of godly discretion, wisdom and conscience, to promote transgressors, as rent-raisers, oppressors of the poor, extortioners, bribers, usurers.'[3] But public approval of the principle of reporting offenders was often qualified by hearty dislike of the type of person who performed this duty, and of the 'marriage of justice with malice or avarice'[4] which might characterize his motive and action. Even an act 'for penal Statutes &

[1] L. Stone, 'State Control in Sixteenth-Century England', 103.

[2] R. H. Tawney, op. cit., 390–1; L. Stone, loc. cit.; and M. W. Beresford, *Lost Villages*, 212.   [3] *Sermons*, 279.

[4] M. W. Beresford, 'The Common Informer, the Penal Statutes and Economic Regulation', 221; see also G. R. Elton, 'Informing for Profit', in *Star Chamber Stories*, 79–80.

Action popular' referred to prosecutions undertaken 'more for malice than for Justice'.[1]

We have noted[2] the scepticism expressed by the author of *Policies* as to the value of this device. For 'what quiet person will take upon him the slanderous name of a promoter, or what honest man will in that cause procure the utter undoing of his neighbour, therefore if ever you will have any penal Statute well kept, there must be set at the first but a small and a reasonable penalty, and certain bailiffs and officers appointed in every shire truly to receive and gather them'.[3] The dismal career of one George Whelplay, who incurred much opprobrium (with little profit!) as a professional informer during the later 'thirties and early 'forties, exemplifies not only the unfortunate nature of governmental reliance upon such promoters but also the difficulty of securing a conviction owing to complicity of local officials, partiality or often brazen dishonesty of local juries, and lack of zeal in such central bodies as Exchequer or Privy Council, and finally the degree of contempt with which the informer was so often regarded.[4]

Economic offences were, apparently, those most eagerly sought by the common informer, whose activities expanded during the last ten years of Henry VIII's reign and reached their maximum during the period after 1550. Before this mid-century boom customs and foreign trade offences were the mainstay of the informer, then marketing offences assumed an overwhelming primacy of place, with allegations of illegal methods and standards of manufacture becoming quantitatively important only during the years 1557 to 1562. A correlation existed between profitability of informing and time of dearth, since many penalties were in proportion to the value of the illegal transaction.[5]

Tardiness in enforcement of social and economic regulation by the ordinary courts might sometimes call for special action by central authority. This could take the form of the despatch of *ad hoc* commissions for particular problems or areas (the Enclosure Commissions or the commission appointed to investigate the West Riding cloth industry) or of the activity of the special or

[1] 7 Hen. VII, c.3.   [2] Above, 195.   [3] *T.E.D.*, iii, 332.
[4] For a full account of Whelplay see G. R. Elton, *Star Chamber Stories*, 78–113.
[5] M. W. Beresford, 'The Common Informer', 222–30.

prerogative courts.[1] In this context we must consider contemporary discussion of projected law reforms. The belief that in the second quarter of the sixteenth century English Common Law was in danger of being swamped by the 'reception' of Roman Civil Law is no longer widely held.[2] But at the same time it is clear that the scope of equity jurisdiction and the amount of work done by Chancery, Star Chamber and Court of Requests increased.

From the point of view of the Commonwealth theme the crucial consideration is that equity jurisdiction was often appealed to in order to protect traditional rights of individuals (such as rights of common or in the open fields), within a context of social justice, against the abuses they might suffer from the legal niceties or technicalities, the loopholes, expense, delay, or outright chicanery, of the Common Law and its exponents. Common lawyers might resent the incursion of equity jurisdiction and practice; but their resentment was matched by that of many poorer members of society at the inroads made upon those traditional but legally unenforceable rights which they felt to be morally theirs. C. M. Gray finds clear evidence of the expanding, and most significant, role of equity jurisdiction in protecting copyhold rights during the first half of the century, and concludes that this led to the gradual recognition of such rights by the Common Law shortly after the mid-century.[3]

The defects of existing Common Law procedure were only too well known. Pole, in Starkey's *Dialogue*, remarks of the administration of justice that 'lucre and affection ruleth all therein'.[4] Aylmer deplores the influence of the great man in any judicial procedure in his own area, so that 'the case shall weigh as he will', with 'juries and quests corrupted'.[5] In Heywood's dispute between the Spider and Fly the former's request for 'the trial to be had in his own lordship' encounters the Fly's objection that

> ... some say, sometime, that the law is ended
> In some case in some place, as folk are friended,

while the Spider, for his part, is horrified by the proposal to take

[1] For instances see G. D. Ramsay, *Wiltshire Woollen Industry*, 9, and *Overseas Trade*, 23; and P. J. Bowden, *The Wool Trade*, 127–8.
[2] Sir C. Ogilvie, *The King's Government and the Common Law. 1471–1641*, 77.
[3] *Copyhold, Equity, and the Common Law*, especially 13, 34–6, 51–3, and 59–68.
[4] 86.   [5] *An Harborowe For Faithfull and Trewe Subiectes*, p. L.2.

the case to Westminster Hall.[1] Pole and Lupset, in the *Dialogue*, argue over the removal of cases to Westminster, 'from the judges of the common law to the chancery', the former urging that the abuse of this appeal by a litigant who could bear the expense 'causeth many poor men to be wrongfully oppressed', while Lupset stresses the essential need for appeals against wrongful judgements. But they are agreed that 'these hungry advocates and cormorants of the court study much to delay causes for their lucre and profit'.[2]

Perhaps even more fundamental are the attacks on the weaknesses in the structure of the law itself—its origins and mode of expression, its inconsistency and uncertainty. John Rastell, in his legal writings, points to the need for 'a good, reasonable, common law',[3] which should be written in English.[4] Starkey makes Pole agree that the fact 'that our common law is written in the French tongue . . . is again the commonweal'.[5] He also has 'no doubt, but that our law and order thereof is over confuse. It is infinite, and without order or end. . . . There is no stable ground in our common law to lean unto. The judgements of years be infinite and full of much controversy, and beside that, of small authority' because of the judges' freedom of interpretation.

He goes on to commend Roman procedure and in particular the works of Justinian, and 'would wish that all these laws should be brought into some small number', indeed that we might 'have the civil law of the Romans to be the common law here of England with us'. It has been urged that his wish 'to receive the civil law of the Romans'[6] 'summed up the views of the English humanists on the Common Law'.[7] There is no doubt that the influence of humanist scholarship led some to look elsewhere for what might appear a more logical model, while the spectacle of the Crown setting aside the canon law of the Church of Rome might invite the suggestion of a parallel ousting of the legal relics of the 'barbarous' past in favour of a new comprehensive set of civil and criminal laws in which equity would rule.

Wolsey had greatly increased the availability of equity juris-

---

[1] *Spider and Flie*, 111–21.   [2] 117–18.

[3] J. Rastell, *Expositions of the Terms of English Laws* (1525?), extract printed in E. M. Nugent, *Thought and Culture of the English Renaissance*, 176.

[4] *An Abridgement of the Statutes* (1527), extract in E. M. Nugent, op. cit., 173–5.

[5] *Dialogue*, 122; also 134.   [6] *Dialogue*, 192–5.   [7] Sir C. Ogilvie, op. cit., 75.

diction to the poorer members of society—this was not least of the reasons for the hatred which he aroused in its upper ranks.[1] Reform of the legal system as a whole was certainly much discussed at this time. It is suggested that 'by 1536 the Lawyers had been brought to a more tractable frame of mind by fear of projects of far-reaching reform'.[2] But the 'Tudor Revolution in Government' was carried through largely in Parliament, with the cooperation of the common lawyers. Some authorities suggest an implied bargain between them (and their clientele) on the one hand, and the Crown on the other.[3] Radical reform of Common Law was no longer envisaged; but equity jurisdiction, particularly on social and economic issues, continued.[4]

The prerogative courts are seen at their best in 'protecting the poorer classes against economic tyranny', for the ordinary courts were subject to intimidation or partiality, ignored customary rights or enforced only the letter of the law, while courts backed more immediately by the Crown could enforce equity. Somerset, in particular, used the Court of Requests as an instrument for protecting tenants against landlords. Such actions infuriated those whose wishes were frustrated, and were denounced as tyrannical. But it is urged that the prerogative courts, despite the jealousy of common law lawyers and landowners, dealt with problems with which the ordinary courts could or would not cope in this time of economic and social change.[5] In so doing they helped preserve liberty and justice in a meaningful sense for the poorer classes.

In the sphere of industrial regulation, aimed primarily at enforcement of standards of manufacture and protection of craftsman and consumer, we have noted that government was attemping to coordinate on a national scale the functions traditionally performed by the gilds.[6] Thus the gilds appeared to be the natural instruments for enforcement of such regulation, with which they were often charged, though awareness of the occasional incompatibility between the interests of a particular group of tradesmen and those of the community is also clear. Continued faith in

[1] Ibid., 68–72.　　　[2] Ibid., 76.
[3] Ibid., 77; W. S. Holdsworth, *A History of English Law*, v, 222–3.
[4] W. S. Holdsworth, op. cit., 213–15; Sir C. Ogilvie, loc. cit.
[5] R. H. Tawney, *The Agrarian Problem in the Sixteenth Century*, 355–8 and 367; F. le V. Baumer, *The Tudor Theory of Kingship*, 175–7; Strype, ii (Part I), 285; and C. M. Gray, loc. cit.　　　[6] Above, 175.

town regulation of manufacture is expressed both in recourse by statutory enactment to the enforcement potential of gilds or of municipal authorities and in the writings of Armstrong, Starkey and Smith.[1]

Occasionally, both in literary discussion and official contemplation, projects were formulated for the establishment of officers specially charged with enforcement of economic and social regulations or even with more general powers to take action conducive to the welfare of the body politic. Despite the general dislike and suspicion of the freelance informer, and the notorious abuses of dishonest promoters, such as blackmailing a prospective victim into compounding privately for his offence, the wish to encourage 'promotion' for sincerely public-spirited motives led the Privy Council in 1552 to set up a Committee of Ten in order to encourage informers genuinely concerned for the commonwealth.[2] Nothing more is known of this scheme or of a more fundamental proposal in a draft bill of *c.* 1534 which would have eliminated reliance upon haphazard action by private prosecutors.

This sought to establish a court of six 'justices or Conservators of the Common weal of this Realm', to sit at Whitehall, with full power to determine all matters concerning the common weal and to summon all those guilty of infringing any acts and ordinances enacted since 1485. A further clause empowered this court 'to Constitute ordain and make in every County and liberty of this Realm officer or officers to search and to enquire' for violations of any enactment 'made for the establishment and increase of the Common weal of this Realm. . . . These officers . . . shall be called Sergeants or servants of the Common weal.' A system of public prosecutors would thus have been created.[3] The seal of the proposed court is of symbolic interest: on one side, a ship with the royal arms; on the other, a plough, two hand cards, a hammer and a spade, 'signifying that by the good industry of draping of cloths and of merchants fishers mariners miners and handy crafts the great burden of the Common Weal of this Realm . . . hath been always sustained'.[4] The term Conservators of the Common

[1] As above, 176, 188 and 196.
[2] M. W. Beresford, 'The Common Informer', 222–31.
[3] T. F. Plucknett, 'Some Proposed Legislation of Henry VIII', 128 and 136–7.
[4] Ibid., 138.

Weal is identical with that used by Starkey in the context of his proposal that there should be officers in every town to supervise crafts and occupations and the education of youth. While he likens these officials to the Roman Censors, certain other officials who 'should be appointed . . . to see that all other officers diligently did execute their office and duty', and who had powers of dismissal upon lawful proofs of negligence, he calls Conservators of the Common Weal.[1] 'Correctors of manners, called Censors', and 'Conservators of the weal public', in ancient Rome are also described in Elyot's *The Image of Governance*.[2]

[1] *Dialogue*, 155–6 and 204–5. [2] 19.b–21.b; 34.b; 37–8; and 45.b.

CHAPTER TWELVE

Conclusion

How may we conclude our study of the effects of mid-Tudor developments upon contemporary ideas of the economic and social responsibilities of government in the commonwealth? In the last analysis discussion of the concept of the commonwealth was concerned with the perennial problems of the nature and purposes of society, the degree of obedience it may exact from its members, the measure of its responsibility towards those members, the reconciliation of individual social and economic liberties with communal interests and well-being, and the protection of the weak and unfortunate. It is well to remember that what is *not* in the material studied is also of implicit significance; for we will find there no conception of political rights in the modern sense—no idea of the right of the mass of the people to participate in any way in government. For these belonged to 'the fourth sort of men which do not rule. . . . These have no voice nor authority in our common wealth, and no account is made of them but only to be ruled, not to rule other.'[1] But there is a very definite expression of the right to be governed well—and good government is conceived of very much in economic and social terms. Liberty, in a meaningful sense, is the right to enjoy one's own within the protection and the restriction of a customary moral code. Liberty is not, where property is concerned, the right to use one's possessions unreservedly and selfishly, regardless of the welfare of others.

For while the concept of society derived from religious origins and assumptions, discussion of its functions was concerned very largely with economic issues. J. W. Allen suggests that in More, Starkey and Crowley 'society is regarded mainly as an association for economic purposes', and that because Tudor England was

[1] Sir T. Smith, *De Republica Anglorum*, 46.

214

passing through an economic as well as a religious revolution 'the idealists of the mid-century therefore tended to see in cooperation for economic purposes the immediate object of the social and political structure'.[1] The persistent belief that economic relationships and transactions should be judged according to a moral standard, in regard to their effects upon individuals and upon society as a whole, explains the close concern of the clergy with such matters as land tenure, prices, or poverty. Hence also the conviction that it was the duty of government to enforce an accepted socio-economic code.

Any attempt to put into perspective mid-sixteenth-century ideas of the purposes and methods of governmental action in this sphere must begin by stressing the evidence both for the continuity and for the metamorphosis of the medieval tradition. Contemporary discussion of these problems is of particular interest because it took place during such a crucially important era of transition, and because it looks both backward to the religion-dominated philosophy and economic values of the Middle Ages and forward to the divergent possibilities of laissez-faire and the Welfare State.

We have seen in mid-Tudor England a combination of reasons why responsibility for declaring and enforcing a code of conduct in socio-economic relationships fell more and more upon the shoulders of the developing State. Several of these were strong trends elsewhere in Western Europe: the increasingly lay approach to the problems of political and social organization, the growing complexity of the economic aspect of society, and the ferment of speculation aroused by the doctrinal Reformation. We must therefore beware lest by implication we overstate the originality of the ideas of Englishmen. But at the same time, the 'Tudor Revolution' in government and in relations between Church and State occurred in a nation with a rapidly evolving economy and against a background of religious debate. This conjunction of circumstances makes mid-Tudor England a case of exceptional interest.

It may be argued schematically that in the Middle Ages social and economic duties were owed first to one's local community and secondly to the moral code of a universal church, the practical

[1] J. W. Allen, *Political Thought in the Sixteenth Century*, 134 and 151.

application of whose teachings was in fact made easier by the relative immediacy and simplicity of economic and social relationships. By contrast, in the modern era the emergence of the nation state sees the growth both of an economic entity too big for the former, and of a lay organization strong enough to free itself from the suzerainty of the latter. Now at the very time when the increasing complexity of economic society made both the enunciation and the application of such a moral code more difficult and confronted the Church with problems of readjustment—a situation which had arisen in commercial Italy as early as the thirteenth century—the Church itself became increasingly subject to criticism and was forced to cede power to the State. The scope and functions of the State were meanwhile extended first by the fact that within an expanding national economy local regulation would no longer suffice, and secondly by the weakening of Church unity and the prince's arrogation of greater powers over church property and religion itself.

But in some respects continuity must be stressed as much as innovation. For to the Tudor mind Church and State were in general simply different aspects of a unitary society, rather than the two distinct entities which later theorists would often make them. In his *De Vera Obedientia* (1535) Stephen Gardiner, following Marsiglio, explicitly urged this identity.[1] Thus the governing power in England, as envisaged by Cromwell and by many of the mid-Tudor Commonwealth idealists, while repudiating all suggestion of being a mere localized agent of a supra-national ecclesiastical body, and asserting itself as the supreme authority in all respects within its own territorial boundaries, was still regarded as inheritor and trustee of the moral code of the medieval Church in social and economic affairs, having a duty to reconcile that code with contemporary realities.

In the long run one might discern the rise of a tendency to judge economic and social questions by the test of State expediency, to substitute for the question 'Is it ethical?' the question 'Is it practicable?' But as yet the continued popularity of the corporeal analogy of society is symbolic of the wish to satisfy both. What the most forward-looking commentators did was to combine a

[1] S. Gardiner, *The Oration of True Obedience*, 95 ff.; also P. Hughes, *The Reformation in England*, i, *The King's Proceedings*, 337–41.

continued belief in traditional ethics and medieval standards of commutative justice with a clearer realization of the extent to which the growing power of the State could be used to influence economic and social developments. The belief in a regulated economy appears very clearly at the very end of the period chosen for study, in the programme formerly attributed to Cecil.[1]

In Chapter 1 the concept of the Commonwealth was related to the background of earlier and concurrent European developments; it remains to consider the later fortunes of some of the ideas and ideals expressed. Many of these—for example, belief in State intervention to preserve equity within a hierarchical society, to maintain economic stability, or to protect and further national economic interests—remained as basic objectives of the governmental paternalism of the later Tudor and early Stuart period. The continuity is typified by Sir Francis Bacon's commendation, in 1597, of 'the opening and well balancing of trade; the cherishing of manufactures; the banishing of idlers; the repressing of waste and excess by sumptuary laws; the improving and husbanding of the soil; the regulating of prices of things vendible; the moderating of taxes and tributes, and the like'.[2]

It has indeed been suggested that in many ways the ideals of the Commonwealth were now achieved, 'gradually, carefully and, within human limits, effectively, under the long rule of William Cecil, the practical heir of the Commonwealth Men'.[3] But the more critical expressions of social indignation and the occasional suggestion of revolutionary political implications tended to die away.[4] The assertion that 'the accession of Elizabeth was the signal for the cessation of political thinking'[5] has a certain validity in this particular context, since several of the circumstances conducive to the note of urgency in our material now disappeared. If one may validly distinguish between those periods in which the term 'commonwealth' is a commonplace of political discussion, to which lip-service is paid with varying degrees of sincerity, and others when its use, sometimes by a 'Commonwealth party' or 'Commonwealth men', becomes linked with the vigorous

---

[1] *T.E.D.*, i, 325–30; above, 42.   [2] *Essays*, 38.
[3] H. R. Trevor-Roper, *Historical Essays*, 90.
[4] See F. Caspari, *Humanism and the Social Order in Tudor England*, 199–205.
[5] G. P. Gooch, *English Democratic Ideas in the Seventeenth Century*, 32.

advocacy of specific social and economic reforms, then in this sense the concept now entered an era of comparative quiescence.

Bacon indeed concerns himself with social and economic issues, but his approach is utilitarian and designed 'to the effecting of all things possible', so that impracticable ideas and ideals 'must be sent to Utopia'.[1] The contemporary comment that 'we are not living in Plato's Republic, nor in the Utopia of Sir Thomas More, but in the *Res Publica* of Sir Thomas Smith'[2] points in the same direction. Not only in Smith or Bacon but also in writers as disparate as Hooker and Hobbes the word 'commonwealth' becomes once more a rather platitudinous synoym for 'society' or 'body politic', free of any challenging social implication. When this does obtrude it is in sinister form, as when Raleigh echoes the definition of Elyot: 'A commonwealth . . . is the government by the common and baser sort without respect of the other orders.'[3]

One is tempted to conclude not only that in the reign of Elizabeth I the political and religious uncertainty which had supplied much of the stimulus for the discussion of an earlier age tended to diminish, but also that after the events of 1549 the Commonwealth's men were tarred with the brush of rebellion. Neither in Hooker, concerned to defend the concept of the unity of Church and State as two aspects of society against Puritan attacks,[4] nor in the Erastian *De Republica Anglorum* of Sir Thomas Smith does the note of idealist criticism which had been so characteristic of mid-century Commonwealth thought recur; nor do they evince much interest in the social and economic duties of the State. In the light of the suggestion that the identity of Church and State defended by Hooker had first been specifically formulated by Gardiner,[5] it is interesting to recall that the latter had been expressly concerned to circumscribe the socio-economic responsibilities of the State. The more secular approach of the *De Republica* suggests that if Smith was indeed the author of the *Discourse*, then the questing physiology of that work has now been transmuted into calm anatomy. Not only were Smith's personal circumstances

[1] *Essays*, 107 and 205.
[2] Cited in P. Munz, *The Place of Hooker in the History of Thought*, 89.
[3] Cited in G. P. Gooch, *English Democratic Ideas*, 52.
[4] *Works of Richard Hooker*, ed. I. Walton, ii, 485.
[5] P. Munz, op. cit., 72; above, 216.

now greatly changed from the near-disgrace—after Somerset's rejection of his plea for a cessation of the reckless debasement policy—of the summer months of 1549 during which he probably composed the *Discourse*,[1] but the complex crisis in the nation's affairs which was the subject of that composition was a thing of the past.

The implication that social and political uncertainty may be a stimulus to speculation and discussion obliges us, in seeking the necessary background for radical political thought in the later decades of the century, to shift our gaze from England to France, to the Huguenot *Vindicae Contra Tyrannos*. The parallels which have been drawn between the contents of that work and the ideas of Locke might just as validly and far more immediately be directed to those of Ponet or Goodman. Yet once the Protestantism which these exiles were concerned to defend against the Marian regime had again become reconciled with existing authority under Elizabeth I we find the views of the *Vindiciae Contra Tyrannos* being officially condemned as treasonable by Bancroft at St Paul's Cross.

The fact that the nature of the commonwealth once more became a topic of lively discussion in England during the disturbed middle decades of the seventeenth century is most significant. For the conjunction of social and economic distress with political and religious uncertainty which had characterized the mid-Tudor era had by then returned. Without pressing the parallel too closely, one cannot but remark in particular the similarity between the position after 1647 and that of exactly a century earlier. The economic impact of the Civil War, in terms of dislocation of industry, commercial uncertainty, and unemployment, culminated in the crisis years of 1649 and 1650. Reports in the news sheets of food shortage in many parts of England; the concern of both London authorities and Parliament with speculation in foodstuffs, with the price of bread, and with projects for setting the unemployed on work; the fears of rioting and insurrection by the poor; all combine to produce a striking resemblance to the events of 1549–1551. But the expressions of a strain of idealist optimism, and the eager expectancy of religious, social and economic reforms which would continue a half-accomplished revolution, were once more

[1] M. Dewar, 'The Authorship of the "Discourse of the Commonweal" ', 389.

followed by disillusion and bitterness, and apparently by a 're-markable absence of social criticism' during later decades.[1]

The examination of specific issues in a little more detail may perhaps most conveniently start with political speculation. In the mid-Tudor sources this normally remained within an essentially medieval matrix as far as concerned the relations between ruler and subject, and the crucial issue of obedience. What mattered were not the origins of political power but the terms of obedience; discussion was directed to the quality and purpose of government, not to any right of participation. By and large, complete sub-servience to established political authority was normally coun-selled in mid-sixteenth-century England because that authority stood forth as the custodian of the whole social order, whose re-moval would open the flood-gates of social anarchy. Submission was prescribed by the voice of religion and implicit in the organic and hierarchical concept of society.

Nonetheless, while rebellion against social and economic grievances was always in the last resort condemned, we found the occasional advocacy of a right of resistance in defence of funda-mental religious truth. The genesis of the Civil War may be traced largely to the propagation and elaboration of this principle. But the success of the Parliamentary forces in that struggle gave an enormous fillip to more unrestrained political and social speculation. For now established political authority had been successfully opposed without any consequent collapse of the foun-dations of society. Hence the much freer and more advanced political ideas associated with the Levellers. In their beliefs we may trace the breaking of one link with the medieval hierarchical ideal still almost universally accepted in the mid-Tudor decades, in that demands for political rights for the individual stand side by side with demands for economic and social justice.

In these circumstances there reappeared the spectre enlisted by mid-sixteenth-century conservatives to discredit those who sought radical social and economic reform. A pamphlet of 1648 warned fellow-Levellers to

beware that ye be not frightened by the word *anarchy* . . . 'Tis an old threadbare trick of the profane Court and against the liberties of the

---

[1] W. Schenk, *The Concern for Social Justice in the Puritan Revolution*, 158.

people, who, whensoever they positively insist for their just freedoms, are immediately flapped in the mouths with these malignant reproaches: 'Oh, ye are for anarchy. Ye are against all government. Ye are sectaries, seditious persons, troublers both of church and state, and so not worthy to live in a commonwealth.'[1]

Whatever interpretation of the outbreak of the Civil Wars one may choose to take, it remains clear that after the defeat of the Crown the conflict between the hopes of the radicals and the fears of the moderates became a major issue, as 'a long-buried stream of social discontent'[2] burst forth, and a cynical pamphleteer could ask: 'Is not all the Controversy Whose Slaves the poor shall be?'[3]

For expression of radical opinion was now much freer, not only because of the inroads made upon the principle of reverence for established political authority and upon the hierarchical concept in general, but also because the taint of heresy which had been so effectively attached to unwelcome social criticism in the mid-sixteenth century had now diminished. The anonymous *Tyranipocrit* (1649) was admittedly an expression of extreme views, but a comparison with *Philargyrie*[4] suggests significant pointers not only to the elements of continuity but also to the change in background, in emphasis, and in implicit assumptions between the two mid-century eras. The theme of both is an attack upon the use of religion as a cloak for selfish interests, but whereas the latter is concerned primarily to condemn the medieval sin of greed it is hardly too much to describe *Tyranipocrit* as an analysis of class-exploitation.

The aspirations of the mid-Tudor idealists as to the objectives and priorities of government—the belief that a commonwealth should use 'all friendliness . . . towards the meanest of people especially'[5]—are now revived, against this sharper and more outspoken religious and political background. The Levellers have been described as concentrating primarily upon democratic political rights, and as defending the economic rights and liberties

[1] Anon. (J. Wildman?), *A Call to all the soldiers*, extract printed in A. S. P. Woodhouse, *Puritanism and Liberty*, 440.
[2] M. James, *Social Problems and Policy During the Puritan Revolution, 1640–1660*, 90.
[3] Cited in W. Y. Tindall, *John Bunyan, Mechanick Preacher*, 92.
[4] Above, 21.   [5] W. Schenk, op. cit., 55.

of the small man against privilege and monopolistic oppression. Nonetheless, they fell foul of those such as Ireton who viewed the right to vote as itself a species of property right.[1] Moreover, their writings were often concerned with such issues as enclosure, unjust taxation, the inadequacy of the system of poor relief, and the need for governmental action to eliminate begging and unemployment.[2] Any attempt at a clear-cut distinction between Levellers and Diggers courts some danger of over-simplification, yet it remains true that the latter strove primarily for radical economic and social reform, upon a basis of religious idealism, rather than for the individual's political rights.

In Winstanley we find not only a demand for social justice untrammelled by any hierarchical restrictions, but a changed view of the necessary economic prerequisites. For to Winstanley the continued existence of private property rights was not only an insuperable barrier to truly Christian social justice; it implied interference with personal political liberties by the restoration of a ruling caste. His insistence that political rights alone were not enough explains the eagerness in some quarters to claim him as a Marxist forebear, but a much more valid line of descent may be traced in the opposite direction. Winstanley wanted an idealistic Christian society, characterized in its economic life by the elimination of covetousness. His condemnation of 'buying and selling' is significant of the reactionary element in his thinking. In him the voice of the mid-sixteenth-century idealist may be heard again, freed now of the twin restrictions imposed by belief in the hierarchical principle and in private property. Morison's struggle to preserve the second while admitting the principle of social mobility into the first was resolved by the abandonment of both. By his advocacy of communal ownership Winstanley took one step further Morison's conclusion that jealousy over the possession of private property was the gravest of social dissolvents. These beliefs reflect his Anabaptist and Familist personal background, the continuity of many of his views with those of mid-sixteenth-century radical social reformers, and his readiness to go beyond them to the teachings of the medieval sects. He developed in earnest, and to its logical conclusion, Rainsborough's gibe in

---

[1] A. S. P. Woodhouse, op. cit., 53–72.
[2] Ibid., 320, 322, 338–40, 425 and 434.

answer to Ireton in the Putney Debates: 'Sir, I see that it is impossible to have liberty but all property must be taken away.'[1]

The judgement that the More who spoke in *Utopia* wrote for Winstanley and the Diggers is not wide of the mark.[2] But the framework of governmental regulation which might be considered a *jeu d'esprit* in the former was commended in earnest by the latter. For Winstanley, like his counterparts of the sixteenth century, appealed to governmental intervention and regulation to direct the conduct of the members of the commonwealth.[3] Thus the attainment of Christian social equity is no longer sought within a hierarchical system, through individual exercise of property rights delegated in trust, but is now directly enforced by the coercive power of the secular saviour. Winstanley at once inherited and developed to a conclusion the plea for economic justice of the mid-Tudor Commonwealth's Men and repudiated the political and social framework to which they clung.

Those strands of mid-sixteenth-century thought which were more particularly concerned with individual political and economic liberties also found their inheritors. If certain of the basic assumptions of Hobbes remind us of Morison, then the assertions of Ireton and of Locke follow closely in the footsteps of Ponet.[4] It is tempting to relate the closer preoccupation of this last group with the origins of government to the fact that they were concerned with the individual political, economic and religious rights or properties of citizens. Winstanley rejected the medieval social order but held tenaciously to its emphasis on the duty of society to implement Christian social justice and, despairing of individuals, appealed to government as an enforcing agent. Ponet's successors retained the belief in a hierarchical type of society but were much more concerned to discuss individual property rights as guaranteed by the State.

Thus unity of belief concerning the type of society which it was the duty of government to maintain had broken down. But what of the objectives and methods of its intervention on specific

---

[1] A. S. P. Woodhouse, op. cit., 71.

[2] R. H. Murray, *The Political Consequences of the Reformation*, 242.

[3] Particularly in *The Law of Freedom*, written after the disillusionment of failure on St George's Hill.

[4] It is significant that in 1642 the opposition to the Crown reprinted Ponet before any other pamphlet—see G. P. Gooch, *English Democratic Ideas*, 30.

issues? Many of the schemes in mid-seventeenth-century writings which have excited comment closely resemble those of the mid-Tudor period, and in turn foreshadow later trends of thought. We may glance briefly at proposals for assisting the poor, generating employment and encouraging national output of wealth. Before so doing, it is well to remind ourselves that those who sought the good of the commonwealth in mid-Tudor England had included, within a common framework of concern for social equity and the welfare of the body politic, what were by implication logically divergent courses of action for the realization of their millennia: the one characterized by nostalgia for the organic and non-commercial society of an idealized past; the other by a willingness to come to terms with economic realities and human selfishness, which government might channel and direct towards the common good. No clear dichotomy between these two is implied; nonetheless, they are discernible. By the mid-seventeenth century we may trace the disintegration of the first course, as in Winstanley's rejection of hierarchy and of private property, but also the complication of the second. For alongside development of that line of thought leading through Mandeville to Adam Smith we find the projection of expedients or 'devices' by humanitarian well-wishers to the poor, including Winstanley himself, which point ahead to the producer-cooperative concepts of Robert Owen. Both these trends have clearly identifiable beginnings in mid-Tudor thought.

With regard to poor relief, that mid-sixteenth-century compromise which strove to reconcile acknowledgement of the inevitability, indeed of the blessedness, of poverty with the realization that in fact many of its manifestations were a social evil demanding action, is still to be found in some quarters a century later. But in general there are strong indications that a somewhat harsher attitude towards poverty by then prevailed. It may well be urged that Winstanley's resolve to abolish poverty by the suppression of private property was a natural reaction to the tendency first to divorce property ownership from the medieval obligations of charity, and secondly to condemn poverty as a sign of idleness. But it is significant that several, and indeed the best known, of the writers who sought to help the poor did so by devising schemes of self-help.

This might or might not be done on a national scale; in either case, there emerge striking resemblances to certain mid-Tudor proposals, as in Chamberlen's suggestion that nationalized church and crown lands be used to establish a national stock not only for charitable relief but also for financing construction of roads and canals or for manufactures.[1] The proposals of Peter Cornelius[2] and of John Bellers[3] relate as closely to mid-sixteenth-century projects as to the schemes of Robert Owen, who avowed his debt to Bellers. The idea that true charity consisted in the stimulation of employment and output, which we found in Cholmeley's cloth-finishing project,[4] recurs. G. Plattes, in *Practicall Husbandry Improved* (1649), attributes to the man 'that found out the way of fertilizing of land, with Lime or Marl . . . a more charitable deed in publishing thereof, than if he had built all the Hospitals in England, for the one feedeth and clotheth a few hungry and naked persons, the other enableth an infinite number both to feed and clothe themselves and others'.[5] The State had its part to play in encouraging or even enforcing the full utilization of society's resources. Indeed, Samuel Hartlib urged that the State as an economic institution should direct and supervise every branch of production and exercise the right of confiscation of property from owners who failed to use it aright.[6]

The Macaria which Hartlib took as the title of his book had been mentioned by More as a place not far from Utopia.[7] But significant differences have been suggested between several of the 'Utopias' of the seventeenth century and the idealism of the sixteenth. Thus Bacon's New Atlantis has been described as a scientific and technological rather than a social Utopia, a 'Utopia with emphasis on the aspect of production [which] involves a contracting of the social horizon, as individual utility is the immediate concern'.[8] It is only fair to remark that *New Atlantis* was an unfinished work, and that Bacon's list of objectives of governmental social policy evidences continuity of tradition;

---

[1] P. Chamberlen, *The Poore Mans Advocate* (1649), 3; cf. above, 123, and 130.
[2] P. Cornelius, *A Way Propounded to Make the poor . . . happy* (1659).
[3] J. Bellers, *Proposals for Raising a Colledge of Industry* (1695).
[4] Above, 182.
[5] Cited in M. James, *Social Problems and Policy*, 114.
[6] S. Hartlib, *A Description of the Famous Kingdome of Macaria* (1641), 3–4.
[7] *Utopia*, 40.   [8] E. Bernstein, *Cromwell and Communism*, 32–3.

but it is broadly true that a shift of emphasis takes place. General governmental supervision was still desired, but maximum production tended to replace optimum distribution as the primary objective. The 'welfare economist' might find the atmosphere of opinion becoming less and less congenial as we move from the sixteenth century to the eighteenth.

The Middle Ages put little emphasis upon the achievement of maximum output of wealth, and accepted its distribution within the existing social framework; the eager acquisition of wealth was deprecated but attention was concentrated upon the correct application and consumption of goods as the field for exercise of Christian charity and of *liberalitas*. By the mid- and late seventeenth century one finds much more stress on the need to increase production; the acquisition of property was applauded but, as we have noted, the partial rejection of any social obligation attaching thereto had led some to attack the whole concept of private property. The organic and hierarchical interpretation of society was fading. Margaret James has suggested the analogy of the machine consisting of thousands of individual wheels all turned in the same direction by the motive force of self-interest as more appropriate to English thought at this time.[1] It is significant that Mandeville's famous (or notorious) use of the analogy of the beehive had already occurred to Hobbes.[2] The former's own use of the musical analogy for society showed a telling change from its traditional medieval form:

> This was the State's Craft that maintain'd
> The Whole of which each Part complain'd:
> This as in Musick Harmony,
> Made Jarrings in the main agree.[3]

Now it is true that a clear-headed appreciation of individual economic motives, and a recognition both of the potentialities and of the limitations of governmental control of their exercise, are clearly present in the literature of the mid-sixteenth century.[4] The socio-economic ideas and projects discussed at that time sometimes foreshadowed the egalitarian-idealist socialism of

[1] M. James, op. cit., 34. [2] *Leviathan*, 130–1.
[3] B. Mandeville, *The Fable of the Bees*, i, 24.
[4] Above, 150–1, 153–4, and 193–201.

Winstanley, the producer-cooperative solutions of Chamberlen, Cornelius, Bellers and Owen, and both enlightened mercantilism and laissez-faire impatience of restrictive legislation. But as yet these were embedded within an organic ideal of society which still upheld differentiation of status and of function, equity of distribution as well as efficiency of production, delegation of power and of property in trust: an ideal not yet adrift from its medieval moorings.

It may be suggested that in the long run the changing circumstances which led the Commonwealth idealists to appeal to the State to enforce a traditional social and economic code were also conducive to a metamorphosis in the concept of the State itself, and to its emergence as an entity which rejected any supra-national authority. In its approach to economic and social problems this State came to adopt as its criterion not so much an inherited moral and ethical code as the relation of such problems to its own wealth and power. In effect, the mid-Tudor idealist was still, in the medieval tradition, appealing to the temporal power within an essentially unified society. As such, he expected that power to enforce the economic and social aspects of a moral code of universal validity, to which *all* individual or sectional rights or liberties were subordinate. But once the idea of the State as an agent of some superior authority, subject to judgement by non-material standards of equity and morality, starts to lose its force, once the unity of society and the universality of the ethical code commence to break down, then lines of development diverge. The State may be envisaged either as an entity supreme in itself or as an agent for the preservation of the individual rights of its members. It may, in either case, be appealed to on grounds of power and wealth, criteria whose validity would not have been accepted within a medieval religious context, rather than on those of equity and morality. Diversity of national and sectional interests—the latter sometimes masquerading as the former—leads to variant interpretations of mercantilism and laissez-faire. But these, in turn, are succeeded by the revival of many Commonwealth ideals, reshaped by a very different political, social and religious background, in the philosophies of collectivism and the Welfare State in the nineteenth and twentieth centuries.

BIBLIOGRAPHY

PRIMARY SOURCES

ANONYMOUS, *A Newe Interlude of Impacyente pouerte* (1560). Printed in '*Lost*' *Tudor Plays*, ed. J. S. Farmer, E.E.D.S. (London, 1907).

—, *A pretty interlude called Nice Wanton* (1560). Printed in R. Dodsley, *A Select Collection of Old English Plays*, 4th edition, ed. W. C. Hazlitt, ii (London, 1874).

—, *A proper dyaloge betwene a Gentillman and a husbandman* . . . (*c.* 1529–30), ed. E. Arber, in *English Reprints* (London, 1895).

—, *An enterlude of welth, and helth,* . . . (1558). Printed in '*Lost*' *Tudor Plays*, ed. J. S. Farmer, E.E.D.S. (London, 1907).

—, *Interlude of Youth* (*c.* 1554). Printed in R. Dodsley, *A Select Collection of Old English Plays*, 4th edition, ed. W. C. Hazlitt, ii (London, 1874).

—, *On England's Commercial Policy. Temp.* Edward IV. Printed in *Political Poems and Songs*, ed. T. Wright, ii (London, 1861).

—, *Policies to reduce this realme of England vnto a prosperus wealthe and estate* (1549). Printed in *T.E.D.*, iii.

—, *Respublica* (1553), ed. L. A. Magnus, E.E.T.S. (London, 1905).

—, *Spare your good* (*c.* 1555), ed. E. G. Duff (Cambridge, 1919).

—, *The boke of Marchauntes* . . . (1547). (Printed, Richard Iugge.)

—, *The decaye of England only by the great multitude of shepe* (1550–53). Printed in *T.E.D.*, iii.

—, *The Institucion of a gentleman* (1555). (Printed, T. Marshe.)

—, *The Libel of English Policy* (1436–37). Printed in *Political Poems and Songs*, ed. T. Wright, ii (London, 1861).

—, *The prayse and commendacion of suche as sought comenwelthes:* . . . (*c.* 1548). (Printed, A. Skolokre.)

—, *Vox Populi Vox Dei* (1547–48). Printed in *Ballads from Manuscripts*, ed. F. J. Furnivall, i, Ballad Society (London, 1868–72). Also in *T.E.D.*, iii.

—, *A Defence of Liberty against Tyrants*. A translation of the *Vindiciae Contra Tyrannos*, by Junius Brutus, ed. H. J. Laski (London, 1924).

—, ('I.D.') *A Cleare and Evident Way* (London, 1650).

—, *Stanleyes Remedy* . . . (London, 1646).

—, *Tyranipocrit* (Rotterdam, 1649).

ARMSTRONG, Clement, *A treatise concerninge the Staple and the commodities of this realme* (*c.* 1519–35). Printed in *T.E.D.*, iii.

—, *Howe to reforme the Realme in settyng them to werke and to restore Tillage* (*c.* 1535–36). Printed in *T.E.D.*, iii.

228

BIBLIOGRAPHY

AYLMER, John. *An Harborowe For Faithfull and Trewe Subiectes* (1559).

BACON, Sir Francis, *Essays, or Counsels Civil and Moral, with other Writings* (London, 1892).

BALDWIN, William, *A Myrroure For Magistrates* (1559). Also a modern edition: *A Mirror for Magistrates*, ed. L. B. Campbell (Cambridge, 1938).

BALE, John, *A Comedy Concerning Three Laws* (1538). Printed in *Dramatic Writings of John Bale*, ed. J. S. Farmer, E.E.D.S. (London, 1907). This edition also contains:
John King of England (c. 1539).

BARLOW, Jerome, *Burial of the Mass* (1528). Printed as *Rede me and be nott wrothe*, by William Roy and Jerome Barlow, ed. E. Arber, in *English Reprints* (London, 1895).

BARLOW, William (Jerome?), *Bishop Barlowe's Dialogue on the Lutheran Factions* (1531), ed. J. R. Lunn (London, 1897).

BATESON, Mary, *The Pilgrimage of Grace. Aske's Narrative. E.H.R.*, v (1890).

BECON, Thomas, *Early Works* (c. 1542-43), ed. J. Ayre, Parker Society (Cambridge, 1843).

—, *The Catechism of Thomas Becon, ... with other pieces ...* (*Temp.* Edward VI), ed. J. Ayre, Parker Society (Cambridge, 1844). This edition also contains:
The Jewel of Joy (1550).
The Fortress of the Faithful (1550).

BELLERS, John, *Proposals for Raising a Colledge of Industry* (London, 1695).

BLAND, A. E., BROWN, P. A. and TAWNEY, R. H. (eds.), *English Economic History, Select Documents* (London, 1914).

BODIN, Jean, *The Six Bookes of a Commonweale*, ed. K. D. Macrae (Cambridge, Mass., 1962).

BRADFORD, John, *The Writings of John Bradford* (*Temp.* Edward VI and Mary), ed. A. Townsend, Parker Society (Cambridge, 1848).

BRINKLOW, Henry, *The Complaynt of Roderyck Mors ...* (c. 1542), ed. J. M. Cowper, E.E.T.S. (London, 1874). This edition also contains:
A Supplycacion to ... Kynge Henry the Eyght (1544).
The Lamentacyon of a Christen Agaynst the Cytye of London ... (1545).
A Supplication of the Poore Commons (1546).

BUCER, Martin, *A Treatise How By The Worde of God, Christian mens Almose ought to Be distributed* (c. 1557).

BULLINGER, Henry, *A Treatise or Sermon ... concernynge magistrates and obedience of subiectes* (1549).

—, *A most necessary & frutefull Dialogue, betwene ye seditious Libertin or rebel Anabaptist, & the true obedient christian ...*, trans. and introd. John Veron (Worcester, 1551).

Calendar of State Papers, Domestic Series, of the Reigns of Edward VI, Mary, Elizabeth. 1547-1580, ed. R. Lemon (London, 1856).

CHAMBERLEN, Peter, *The Poore Mans Advocate* (London, 1649).

CHEKE, Sir John, *The hurt of sedition ... The true subiect to the rebell* (1549). Printed in Raphael Holinshed's *Chronicles*, iii (London, 1808 edition).

CHOLMELEY, William, *The Request and Suite of a True-Hearted Englishman* (1553), ed. W. J. Thoms, *Camden Miscellany*, ii (1853).

229

CHRISTOPHERSON, John, *An exhortation to all menne to take hede and beware of rebellion* (1554).

COKE, John. *The Debate Betwene the Heraldes of Englande and Fraunce* (1550).

COOKE, John, *Unum Necessarium* (London, 1647/8).

COPLAND, Robert, *The Highway to the Spital-House* (1535/6). Printed in *The Elizabethan Underworld*, ed. A. V. Judges (London, 1930).

CORNELIUS, Peter, *A Way Propounded to Make the poor . . . happy* (London, 1659).

CRANMER, Thomas, *Miscellaneous Writings and Letters*, ii, ed. J. E. Cox, Parker Society (Cambridge, 1846).

CROMWELL, Thomas, *Life and Letters of Thomas Cromwell*, R. B. Merriman, 2 vols. (Oxford, 1902).

CROWLEY, Robert, *The Fable of Philargyrie The Great Gigant* (1551). Facsimile reprint, ed. W. A. Marsden (London, 1931).

—, *An informacion and Peticion . . . (c.* 1549). Printed in *The Select Works of Robert Crowley*, ed. J. M. Cowper, E.E.T.S. (London, 1872). This edition also contains:
One and thyrtye Epigrammes (1550).
The Voyce of the laste trumpet (1550).
Pleasure and Payne (1551).
The Way to Wealth (1551).

DUDLEY, Edmund, *The Tree of Common Wealth* (1509–10), ed. D. M. Brodie (Cambridge, 1948).

EDWARD VI, *Literary Remains of King Edward the Sixth*, ed. J. G. Nichols, Roxburghe Club (London, 1857).

—, *Writings of Edward the Sixth, &c*, Religious Tract Society (London, 1831).

—, *The Chronicles and Political Papers of King Edward VI*, ed. W. K. Jordan (London, 1966).

ELYOT, Sir Thomas, *The Boke named the Governour* (1531), ed. H. H. S. Croft, 2 vols. (London, 1883).

—, *The Image of Governance* (1541).

FISH, Simon, *A Supplicacyon for the Beggers (c.* 1529). Printed in *Four Supplications. 1529–1553 A.D.*, ed. F. J. Furnivall and J. M. Cowper, E.E.T.S. (London, 1871).

—, *The Summe of the holy scrypture* (1529(?)).

FORREST, William, *Pleasaunt Poesye of Princelie Practise* (1548). Printed in *England in the reign of King Henry the Eighth*, Part I, *Starkey's Life and Letters*, ed. S. J. Herrtage, E.E.T.S. (London, 1878).

FOXE, John, *The Acts and Monuments of John Foxe*, ed. Rev. G. Townsend, v (London, 1846); vii (London, 1847). Another edition, ed. Rev. J. Pratt, viii, Religious Tract Society (London, n.d.).

FRITH, John, *A Mirror, or Glass, to Know Thyself* (1532). Printed, with other works of Frith, in Vol. iii of *The Works of William Tyndale and John Frith*, ed. T. Russell, 3 vols. (London, 1831).

GARDINER, Stephen, *The Oration of True Obedience* (1535). Printed in *Obedience in Church and State. Three Political Tracts by Stephen Gardiner*, translated and edited by P. Janelle (Cambridge, 1930). This edition also contains:

Gardiner's Answer to Bucer (1541).

The Letters of Stephen Gardiner, ed. J. A. Muller (Cambridge, 1933).

GILPIN, Bernard, *Sermon . . . before King Edward VI* (1552). Printed in *Life of Bernard Gilpin*, by William Gilpin (London, 1752).

GOFFE, William, *How to advance the Trade of the Nation, and employ the Poor.* Printed in *Harleian Miscellany*, iv (1745), 366–70.

GOODMAN, Christopher, *How Superior Powers Oght to be Obeyd* (1558), ed. C. H. McIlwain; reproduced from 1558 edition, Facsimile Text Society, (New York, 1931).

GRIFFITHS, J. (ed.), *The Two Books of Homilies Appointed to be Read in Churches* (Oxford, 1859).

GUEVARA, A. DE, *A Dispraise of the life of a Courtier, and a commendacion of the life of the labouryng man* (1548).

HALES, John, 'The charges of Mr. John Hales . . . for the execution of the commission for redress of enclosures', including 'Instructions . . . to . . . commissioners'. Printed in Vol. ii (Part II) of *Ecclesiastical Memorials*, by J. Strype (Oxford, 1822).

—, *A Discourse of the Common Weal of this Relam of England* (1549), ed. E. Lamond (Cambridge, 1893), is no longer confidently attributed to Hales, but this edition contains several papers which are his:
'Causes of Dearth' (1548).
'Bill on Decay of Tillage' (1548).
'The defence of John Hales ayenst certeyn sclaundres and false reaportes made of hym' (1549).

HALL, Edward, *Chronicle* (1548) (1809 edition, London).

HARMAN, Thomas, *A Caveat . . . for Common Cursitors . . .* (1566). Printed in *The Elizabethan Underworld*, ed. A. V. Judges (London, 1930).

HARRINGTON, James, *Oceana* (1656), ed. S. B. Liljegren (Heidelberg, 1924).

HARTLIB, Samuel, *A Description of the Famous Kingdome of Macaria* (1641).

—, *Londons Charitie* (1649).

HENRY VIII, *The Letters of King Henry VIII*, ed. M. St. C. Byrne (London, 1936).

HEYWOOD, John, *The Spider and the Flie* (1556), ed. J. S. Farmer, E.E.D.S. (London, 1908).

HOBBES, Thomas, *Leviathan* (Oxford, 1909 edition).

HOLINSHED, Raphael, *Chronicles* (London, 1808 edition).

HOLME, Wilfrid, *The fall and euill successe of Rebellion* (1537). Printed in 1573.

HOOKER, Richard, *The Works of Richard Hooker*, 2 vols., ed. I. Walton (Oxford, 1850).

HOOPER, John, *Early Writings*, ed. S. Carr, Parker Society (Cambridge, 1843).

—, *Later Writings*, ed. C. Nevinson, Parker Society (Cambridge, 1852).

HUGHE, William, *The Troubled Mans Medicine* (1546).

HUGHES, P. L. and LARKIN, J. F. (eds.), *Tudor Royal Proclamations*, i, *The Early Tudors* (1485–1553) (New Haven, 1964); vols. ii and iii, *The Later Tudors* (1553–1603) (New Haven, 1969), appeared too late for use herein.

HUTH, Henry, *Huth Ballads*. Collection of Printed Broadsides (*c.* 1560). (British Museum).

INGELEND, Thomas, *The Disobedient Child* (*c.* 1560). Printed in R. Dodsley, *A*

Select Collection of Old English Plays, 4th edition, ed. W. C. Hazlitt, ii (London, 1874).

LANGLAND, William, *Piers the Ploughman* (1377–1379), translated and edited by J. F. Goodridge, Pelican edition (London, 1959).

LARKE, John, *The boke of wisdome otherwise called the Flower of Vertue* (c. 1565).

LATIMER, Hugh, *Sermons* (1528–1552), ed. G. E. Corrie, Parker Society (Cambridge, 1844).

—, *Sermons and Remains* (Sermons 1552–1555, and Letters), ed. G. E. Corrie, Parker Society (Cambridge, 1845).

—, *Sermons*, ed. Canon Beeching, Everyman edition (London, 1926).

LEE, Leonard, *A Remonstrance* (1644).

Letters and Papers, Foreign and Domestic, of the Reign of Henry VIII, ed. J. S. Brewer, J. Gairdner, and R. H. Brodie (London, 1862–1932).

LEVER, Thomas, *Sermons. 1550*, ed. E. Arber, English Reprints (London, 1870).

LLOYD, C. (ed.), *Formularies of Faith put forth by Authority during the Reign of Henry VIII* (Oxford, 1825). These include:
The Institution of a Christen Man (1537).
A Necessary Doctrine and Erudition for any Christian Man . . . (1543).

LONGLAND, John, *A Sermonde made before the Kynge . . . vpon good Frydaye* (1538). Also same title, dated 1536.

LUPSET, Thomas, *A Compendiovs . . . treatyse, teachynge the way of Dyenge well* (1534).

—, *A Treatise of Charitie* (1533). Printed in *Tho. Lupsets workes* (1546).

—, *The Life and Works of Thomas Lupset*, J. A. Gee (New Haven, 1928), includes *A Treatise of Charitie* and *An Exhortation to Yonge men* (1535).

LUTHER, Martin, *An Appeal to the Ruling Class of German Nationality*. Printed in *Reformation Writings of Martin Luther*, translated and edited by B. L. Woolf, i (London, 1952).

MANDEVILLE, Bernard, *The Fable of the Bees: or, Private Vices, Publick Benefits*, ed. F. B. Kaye, 2 vols. (Oxford, 1924).

MARSHALL, William, *The Ypres Scheme of Poor Relief*, a translation of *Forma Subventionis Pauperum* (1535). Printed in *Some Early Tracts on Poor Relief*, ed. F. R. Salter (London, 1926).

MORE, Sir Thomas, *The supplicacion of soules . . . Agaynst the supplicacion of beggars* (1529). Printed in *The Workes of Sir Thomas More Knyght* (London, 1557).

—, *Utopia*, trans. Raphe Robinson (1551), ed. John O'Hagan, Everyman Edition (London, 1941).

MORISON, Sir Richard, *A Remedy For Sedition* (1536).

—, *A Lamentation in which is shewed what Ruyne and destruction cometh of seditious rebellyon* (1536).

—, *An Invective Ayenste the great and detestable vice, treason* (1539).

NUGENT, E. M. (ed.), *The Thought and Culture of the English Renaissance. An Anthology of Early Tudor Prose* (Cambridge, 1956).

PAYNELL, Thomas, *The preceptes teachyng a prynce or a noble estate his duetie* (1530).

PISAN, Christine de, *The booke whiche is called the body of Polycye* . . . (1521).

POCOCK, N. (ed.), *Troubles connected with the Prayer Book of 1549*, Camden Society (1884).

PONET, John, *A Shorte Treatise of politike power, and of the true Obedience which subiectes owe to kynges and other ciuile Gouernours* . . . (1556).

RASTELL, John, *Gentleness and Nobility* (1529), ed. A. C. Partridge and F. P. Wilson (Malone Society Reprints, 1950).

RHODES, Hugh, *The Boke of Nurture, for Men, Seruauntes, and Chyldren* (c. 1554), ed. F. J. Furnivall, Roxburghe Club (London, 1867).

RIDLEY, Nicholas, *The Works of Nicholas Ridley*, ed. H. Christmas, Parker Society (Cambridge, 1843).

SALTER, F. R. (ed.), *Some Early Tracts on Poor Relief* (London, 1926).

SKELTON, John, *The Complete Poems of John Skelton, Laureate*, ed. P. Henderson (London, 1948).

SMITH, Sir Thomas, *De Republica Anglorum* (1565; published 1583), ed. L. Alston (Cambridge, 1906).

—, *A Discourse of the Common Weal of this Realm of England* (1549), ed. Elizabeth Lamond (Cambridge, 1893), is now thought to have been written by Smith.

STARKEY, Thomas, *An Exhortation to the people, instructynge theym to Unitie and Obedience* (1536).

—, *A Dialogue between Cardinal Pole and Thomas Lupset* (1538). Printed in *England in the Reign of King Henry the Eighth*, Part II, *The Dialogue*, ed. J. M. Cowper, E.E.T.S. (London, 1871).

Statutes of the Realm, iii, 1509–10 to 1545 (London, 1817); iv, Part I, 1547 to 1585 (London, 1819).

STEELE, R. (ed.), *A Bibliography of Royal Proclamations of the Tudor and Stuart Sovereigns*, i (Oxford, 1910).

TAVERNER, Richard, *A Catechisme or institution of the Christen Religion* (1539).

TAWNEY, R. H. and POWER, E. (eds.), *Tudor Economic Documents*, 3 vols. (London, 1953 edn.).

Tudor Treatises, ed. A. G. Dickens, The Yorkshire Archaeological Society, Record Series, cxxv (1959). This prints:
Bigod, Sir F., *A Treatise Concernynge Impropriations of Benefices* (c. 1535).
Sherbrook, M., *The Falle of Religiouse Howses* (c. 1567–c. 1591).

TURNER, William, *A preseruatiue, or triacle, agaynst the poyson of Pelagius* (1551).
—, *The Huntyng of the Romyshe Wolfe* . . . (c. 1554–1555).
—, *A new book of spirituall Physik for dyuerse diseases of the nobilitie and gentlemen of Englande* (Basle (?), 1555).

TYNDALE, William, *The Works of William Tyndale and John Frith*, ed. T. Russell, 3 vols. (London, 1831). Volume i contains *The Obedience of a Christian Man* (1528), and also:
The Parable of the Wicked Mammon (1528).
The Practice of Prelates (1530).
Volume ii contains:
An Answer unto Sir Thomas More's Dialogue (1530).
Exposition upon . . . Matthew (n.d.).

TYTLER, P. F. (ed.), *England under the Reigns of Edward VI and Mary*, 2 vols. (London, 1839).

UDALL, Nicholas, *An answer to the articles of the commoners of Devonshire and Cornwall* (1549). Printed in N. Pocock (ed.), *Troubles connected with the Prayer Book of 1549*, Camden Society (1884).

VIVES, Juan Luis, *De Subventione Pauperum* (1526). Translation in *Some Early Tracts on Poor Relief*, ed. F. R. Salter (London, 1926).

—, *Introduction to wisedome*, trans. Sir R. Morison (1540).

WALKER, Gilbert (?), *A Manifest Detection of... Dice-play* (1552). Printed in *The Elizabethan Underworld*, ed. A. V. Judges (London, 1930).

WEVER, R., *Lusty Juventus* (*Temp.* Edward VI). Printed in R. Dodsley, *A Select Collection of Old English Plays*, 4th edition, ed. W. C. Hazlitt, ii (London, 1874).

WILKINS, D., *Concilia Magnae Britanniae et Hiberniae*, iii (London, 1837).

WINSTANLEY, Gerrard, *Works*, ed. G. H. Sabine (Ithaca, 1941).

WOODHOUSE, A. S. P. (ed.), *Puritanism and Liberty* (London, 1938).

WYCLIF, John, *The English Works of Wyclif*, ed. F. D. Matthew, E.E.T.S. (London, 1880).

SECONDARY AUTHORITIES

ADAIR, E. R., 'William Thomas', in *Tudor Studies*, ed. R. W. Seton-Watson (London, 1924).

ALLEN, J. W., *A History of Political Thought in the Sixteenth Century* (London, 1951).

—, 'The Political Conceptions of Luther', in *Tudor Studies*, ed. R. W. Seton-Watson (London, 1924).

ARMYTAGE, W. H. G., *Heavens Below. Utopian Experiments in England 1560–1960* (London, 1961).

ASTON, M. E., 'Lollardy and Sedition. 1381–1431', *Past and Present*, No. 17 (April 1960), 1–44.

—, 'Lollardy and the Reformation: Survival or Revival?' *History*, xlix (1964), 149–70.

AYDELOTTE, F., *Elizabethan Rogues and Vagabonds* (Oxford, 1913).

BAINTON, R. H., *Here I Stand. A Life of Martin Luther* (New York, 1951).

BALDWIN, F. E., *Sumptuary Legislation and Personal Regulation in England* (Baltimore, 1926).

BALDWIN, J. W., *The Medieval Theories of the Just Price*. Transactions of the American Philosophical Society, New Series, 49, Part 4 (Philadelphia, 1959).

BAUMER, F. LE V., *The Tudor Theory of Kingship* (New Haven, 1940).

BEER, M., *Early British Economics* (London, 1938).

BERE, R. DE LA, *John Heywood, Entertainer* (London, 1937).

BERESFORD, M. W., *The Lost Villages of England* (London, 1954).

—, *History on the Ground* (London, 1957).

—, 'The Poll Tax and the Census of Sheep, 1549', *Agricultural History Review*, i (1953), 9–15, and ii (1954), 15–29.

—, 'The Common Informer, the Penal Statutes, and Economic Regulation', *Econ. H.R.*, 2nd Ser., x (1957), 221–38.

BERNSTEIN, E., *Cromwell and Communism*, trans. H. J. Stenning (London, 1930).

BINDOFF, S. T., *Tudor England* (London, 1966).

—, *Ket's Rebellion*, Historical Association Pamphlet No. 12 (1949).

—, 'The Making of the Statute of Artificers', in *Elizabethan Government and Society*, ed. S. T. Bindoff *et al.* (London, 1961).

—, 'Clement Armstrong and His Treatises of the Commonweal', *Econ. H.R.*, xiv (1944), 64–73.

BOWDEN, P. J., *The Wool Trade in Tudor and Stuart England* (London, 1962).

—, 'Wool Supply and the Woollen Industry', *Econ. H.R.*, 2nd Ser., ix (1956), 44–58.

BRENNER, Y. S., 'The Inflation of Prices in Early Sixteenth Century England', *Econ. H.R.*, 2nd Ser., xiv (1961), 225–39

—, 'The Inflation of Prices in England, 1551–1650', *Econ. H.R.*, 2nd Ser., xv (1962), 266–84.

BRIDBURY, A. R., *Economic Growth. England in the Later Middle Ages* (London, 1962).

BRODRICK, J., *The Economic Morals of the Jesuits* (Oxford, 1934).

BROOKE, C. F. T., *The Tudor Drama* (London, 1912).

BROWN, E. H. PHELPS and HOPKINS, S. V., 'Seven Centuries of the Price of Consumables, compared with Builders' Wage-rates', *Economica*, New Ser., xxiii (1956), 296–314.

—, 'Wage-rates and Prices: Evidence for Population Pressure in the Sixteenth Century', *Economica*, New Ser., xxiv (1957), 289–306.

BUSH, M. L., 'The Lisle-Seymour Land Disputes: A Study of Power and Influence in the 1530s', *Historical Journal*, ix (1966), 255–74.

CAMERON, K. W., *Authorship and Sources of 'Gentleness and Nobility'. A Study in Early Tudor Drama* (Raleigh, North Carolina, 1941).

CAMPBELL, M., *The English Yeoman* (New Haven, 1942).

CAMPBELL, W. E., *More's Utopia and his Social Teaching* (London, 1930).

CASPARI, F., *Humanism and the Social Order in Tudor England* (Chicago, 1954).

CHALK, A. F., 'Natural Law and the Rise of Economic Individualism in England', *Journal of Political Economy*, lix (1951), 332–47.

CHALLIS, C. E., 'The Debasement of the Coinage, 1542–1551', *Econ. H.R.*, 2nd Ser., xx (1967), 441–66.

CHANDLER, F. W., *The Literature of Roguery*, i (London, 1907).

CHAPMAN, H. W., *The Last Tudor King* (London, 1958).

CHRIMES, S. B., *English Constitutional Ideas in the Fifteenth Century* (Cambridge, 1936).

CLAPHAM, J. H. and POWER, E. (eds.), *The Cambridge Economic History of Europe*, i, *Agriculture* (Cambridge, 1941).

CLAPHAM, Sir J., *A Concise Economic History of Britain. From the Earliest Times to 1750* (Cambridge, 1949).

COHN, N., *The Pursuit of the Millennium* (London, 1957).

COLEMAN, D. C., 'Labour in the English Economy of the Seventeenth Century', *Econ. H.R.*, 2nd Ser., viii (1956), 280–95.

CONSTANT, G., *The Reformation in England*, i, *The English Schism, Henry VIII*, trans. R. E. Scantlebury (London, 1934).

—, *The Reformation in England*, ii, *Edward VI (1547–1553)*, trans. E. I. Watkin (London, 1941).

CRAIG, Sir J., *The Mint* (Cambridge, 1953).

CRANZ, F. E., *An Essay on the Development of Luther's Thought on Justice, Law, and Society*. Harvard Theological Studies, xix (Cambridge, Mass., 1959).

CROWTHER, J. G., *Francis Bacon* (London, 1960).

CUNNINGHAM, W., *The Growth of English Industry and Commerce during the Early and Middle Ages* (Cambridge, 1922; reprint of 5th edn., 1910).

DANNENFELDT, K. H. (ed.), *The Renaissance, Medieval or Modern?* (Boston, 1959).

DARBY, H. S., *Hugh Latimer* (London, 1953).

DAVIES, C. S. L., 'Slavery and Protector Somerset; the Vagrancy Act of 1547', *Econ. H.R.*, 2nd Ser., xix (1966), 533–49.

D'ENTREVES, A. P., *The Medieval Contribution to Political Thought* (Oxford, 1939).

DEWAR, M., *Sir Thomas Smith* (London, 1964).

—, 'The Memorandum "For the Understanding of the Exchange": its Authorship and Dating', *Econ. H.R.*, 2nd Ser., xvii (1965), 476–87.

—, 'The Authorship of the "Discourse of the Commonweal"', *Econ. H.R.*, 2nd Ser., xix (1966), 388–400.

DICKENS, A. G., *Thomas Cromwell and the English Reformation* (London, 1959).

—, *Lollards and Protestants in the Diocese of York, 1509–1558* (Oxford, 1959).

—, *The English Reformation* (London, 1964).

—, *Reformation and Society in Sixteenth Century Europe* (London, 1966).

—, *Martin Luther and the Reformation* (London, 1967).

—, 'Secular and Religious Motivation in the Pilgrimage of Grace', *Studies in Church History*, iv (1967), pp. 39–64.

DIETZ, F. C., *English Government Finance, 1485–1558* (Urbana, 1921).

EHRENBURG, R., *Capital and Finance in the Age of the Renaissance*, trans. H. M. Lucas (London, 1928).

EINSTEIN, L., *Tudor Ideals* (New York, 1921).

ELTON, G. R., *The Tudor Revolution in Government* (Cambridge, 1953).

—, *England Under the Tudors* (London, 1957).

—, *The Tudor Constitution* (Cambridge, 1960).

—, (ed.), *The New Cambridge Modern History*, ii, *The Reformation* (Cambridge, 1958).

—, 'Parliamentary Drafts, 1529–1540', *Bull. Inst. H.R.*, xxv (1952), 117–32.

—, 'An Early Tudor Poor Law', *Econ. H.R.*, 2nd Ser., vi (1953), 55–67.

—, 'The Political Creed of Thomas Cromwell', *Trans. R.H.S.*, 5th Ser., vi (1956), 69–92.

—, 'Informing for Profit' in *Star Chamber Stories* (London, 1958).

—, 'State Planning in Early Tudor England', *Econ. H.R.*, 2nd Ser., xiii (1961), 433–9.

—, 'The Tudor Revolution: A Reply', *Past and Present*, No. 29 (Dec. 1964), 26–49.

EMMISON, F. G., *Tudor Secretary. Sir William Petre at Court and Home* (London, 1961).

FANFANI, A., *Catholicism, Protestantism and Capitalism* (London, 1939).

FARNHAM, W., *The Medieval Heritage of Elizabethan Tragedy* (Oxford, 1956).

FEAVEARYEAR, A. E., *The Pound Sterling*, ed. E. V. Morgan (Oxford, 1963 edn.).

FERGUSON, A. B., 'Renaissance Realism in the "Commonwealth" Literature of Early Tudor England', *Journal of the History of Ideas*, xvi (1955), 287–305.

—, 'The Tudor Commonweal and the Sense of Change', *Journal of British Studies*, iii (1963), 11–35.

FERGUSON, W. K., 'The Church in a Changing World. A Contribution to the Interpretation of the Renaissance', *American Historical Review*, lix (Oct. 1953), 1–18.

FIGGIS, J. N., 'Political Thought in the Sixteenth Century', in *Cambridge Modern History*, iii, Chap. XXII.

—, 'Respublica Christiana', *Trans. R.H.S.*, 3rd Ser., v (1911), 63–88.

FISHER, F. J., 'Commercial Trends and Policy in Sixteenth Century England', *Econ. H.R.*, x (1940), 95–117.

—, 'The Development of the London Food Market. 1540–1640', in E. M. Carus-Wilson (ed.), *Essays in Economic History*, i (London, 1955).

—, 'The Sixteenth and Seventeenth Centuries: The Dark Ages in English Economic History?', *Economica*, New Ser., xxiv (1957), 1–18.

— (ed.), *Essays in the Economic and Social History of Tudor and Stuart England* (Cambridge, 1961).

FISHER, H. A. L., *The Political History of England*, v, 1485–1547 (London, 1913).

FUZ, J. K., *Welfare Economics in English Utopias* (The Hague, 1952).

GAY, E. F., 'Inclosures in England in the Sixteenth Century', *Quarterly Journal of Economics*, xvii (1903), 576–97.

GEORGE, C. H. and K., *The Protestant Mind of the English Reformation, 1570–1640* (Princeton, New Jersey, 1961).

GOOCH, G. P., *English Democratic Ideas in the Seventeenth Century*, 2nd edn., ed. H. J. Laski (Cambridge, 1927).

—, *Political Thought from Bacon to Halifax* (London, 1933).

GOULD, J. D., 'Mr. Beresford and the lost villages', *Agricultural History Review*, iii (1955), 107–13.

—, 'The Price Revolution Reconsidered', *Econ. H.R.*, 2nd Ser., xvii (1964), 249–266.

—, 'Y. S. Brenner on Prices: A Comment', *Econ. H.R.*, 2nd Ser., xvi (1963), 351–60.

GRAMPP, W. D., 'The Liberal Elements in English Mercantilism', *Quarterly Journal of Economics*, lxvi (1952), 456–501.

GRAS, N. S. B., *The Evolution of the English Corn Market* (Cambridge, Mass., 1915).

GRAY, C. M., *Copyhold, Equity, and the Common Law* (Cambridge, Mass., 1963).

GREEN, R. W. (ed.), *Protestantism and Capitalism. The Weber Thesis and its Critics* (Boston, 1959).

HABBAKUK, H. J., 'The Market for Monastic Propety, 1539–1603', *Econ. H.R.*, 2nd Ser., x (1958), 362–80.

HANCOCK, W. K., *Politics in Pitcairn* (London, 1947 edn.).

HARRIS, J. W., *John Bale, A Study in the Minor Literature of the Reformation* (Urbana, 1940).

HAWEIS, J. O. W., *Sketches of the Reformation . . . from the contemporary pulpit* (London, 1844).

HAY, D., *The Italian Renaissance in its Historical Background* (Cambridge, 1961).

—, 'Late Medieval-Early Modern', *Bull. Inst. H.R.*, xxv (1952), 26–7.

HEATON, H., *The Yorkshire Woollen and Worsted Industries* (Oxford, 1920).

—, *Economic History of Europe* (New York, 1948).

HECKSCHER, E. F., *Mercantilism*, 2 vols., trans. M. Shapiro. Revised edn., ed. E. F. Söderbund (London, 1955).

HEXTER, J. H., *Reappraisals in History* (Aberdeen, 1961).

—, *More's Utopia. The Biography of an Idea* (Princeton, N.J., 1952).

HILL, C., *Puritanism and Revolution* (London, 1958).

HOGREFE, P., *The Sir Thomas More Circle* (Urbana, 1959).

HOLDSWORTH, W. S., *A History of English Law*, v (London, 1924 edn.).

HOLMES, G., *The Later Middle Ages, 1272–1485* (Edinburgh, 1962).

HOOPER, W., 'The Tudor Sumptuary Laws', *E.H.R.*, xxx (1915), 433–49.

HOPF, C., *Martin Bucer and the English Reformation* (Oxford, 1946).

HORST, J. B., 'Anabaptism in England', in *The Mennonite Encyclopedia*, ed. H. S. Bender and C. H. Smith, ii (Scottdale, Penn., 1956), pp. 215–21.

HOSKINS, W. G., *Essays in Leicestershire History* (Liverpool, 1950).

—, *The Midland Peasant* (London, 1957).

HUDSON, W. S., *John Ponet (1516?–1556), Advocate of Limited Monarchy* (Chicago, 1942).

HUGHES, E., 'The Authorship of "The Discourse of the Commonweal" ', *Bulletin of the John Rylands Library*, 21, No. 1 (Manchester, 1937).

HUGHES, P., *The Reformation in England*, i, *The King's Proceedings* (London, 1950).

—, *The Reformation in England*, ii, *Religio Depopulata* (London, 1953).

HURSTFIELD, J., 'Corruption and Reform under Edward VI and Mary: The Example of Wardship', *E.H.R.*, lxviii (1953), 22–36.

JACOB, E. F., *The Fifteenth Century, 1399–1485* (Oxford, 1961).

JAMES, M., *Social Problems and Policy During the Puritan Revolution, 1640–1660* (London, 1930).

JARRETT, B., *Social Theories of the Middle Ages* (London, 1926).

—, *Medieval Socialism* (London, 1935).

JORDAN, W. K., *The Development of Religious Toleration in England*, i (London, 1932).

—, *Philanthropy in England, 1480–1660* (London, 1959).

KEIR, Sir D. L., *The Constitutional History of Modern Britain, 1485–1937* (London, 1938).

KELSO, R., *The Doctrine of the English Gentleman in the Sixteenth Century* (Urbana, 1929).

KERRIDGE, E., *The Agricultural Revolution* (London, 1967).

—, 'The Movement of Rent, 1540–1640', *Econ. H.R.*, 2nd Ser., vi (1953), 16–34.

—, 'The Returns of the Inquisitions of Depopulation', *E.H.R.*, lxx (1955), 212–228.

KEYNES, J. M., *A Treatise on Money*, ii (London, 1930).

KIERNAN, V. G., 'State and Nation in Western Europe', *Past and Present*, No. 31 (July 1965), 20–38.

KNAPPEN, M. M., *Tudor Puritanism* (Chicago, 1939).

KOSMINSKY, E. A., *Studies in the Agrarian History of England in the Thirteenth Century*, ed. R. H. Hilton (Oxford, 1956).

KRAMER, S., *The English Craft Gilds* (New York, 1927).

LECLER, J., *Toleration and the Reformation*, i, trans. T. L. Westow (London, 1960).

LEONARD, E. M., *The Early History of English Poor Relief* (Cambridge, 1900).

LIPSON, E., *The Economic History of England*, i, *The Middle Ages* (London, 9th edn., 1947).

—, *The Economic History of England*, ii and iii, *The Age of Mercantilism* (London, 5th edn., 1948).

LUBASZ, H. (ed.), *The Development of the Modern State* (New York, 1964).

LÜTGE, F., Chap. 2 in *New Cambridge Modern History*, ii, ed. G. R. Elton (Cambridge, 1958).

MACKIE, J. D., *The Earlier Tudors, 1485–1558* (Oxford, 1957).

MACLURE, M., *The Paul's Cross Sermons, 1534–1642* (Toronto, 1958).

MAITLAND, F. W., *Selected Historical Essays of F. W. Maitland*, ed. H. Cam (Cambridge, 1957).

MASON, J. E., *Gentlefolk in the Making* (Philadelphia, 1935).

MCCONICA, J. K., *English Humanists and Reformation Politics* (Oxford, 1965).

MCKISACK, M., *The Fourteenth Century 1307–1399* (Oxford, 1959).

MORGAN, E. V., *The Study of Prices and the Value of Money* (Historical Association, 1950).

MORRIS, C., *Political Thought in England. Tyndale to Hooker* (Oxford, 1953).

MORRIS, W. D., *The Christian Origins of Social Revolt* (London, 1949).

MUNZ, P., *The Place of Hooker in the History of Thought* (London, 1952).

MURRAY, R. H., *The Political Consequences of the Reformation* (London, 1926).

MYERS, A. R., *England in the Late Middle Ages (1307–1536)* (London, 1961).

NEF, J. U., *Industry and Government in France and England, 1540–1640* (Philadelphia, 1940).

—, 'Prices and Industrial Capitalism in France and England, 1540–1640', *Econ. H.R.*, viii (1937), 155–85.

—, 'Progress of Technology and the Growth of Large-Scale Industry in Great Britain, 1540–1640', in E. M. Carus-Wilson (ed.), *Essays in Economic History*, i (London, 1955).

NOONAN, J. T., *The Scholastic Analysis of Usury* (Cambridge, Mass., 1957).

O'BRIEN, G., *An Essay on Medieval Economic Teaching* (London, 1920).

—, *An Essay on the Economic Consequences of the Reformation* (London, 1923).

OGILVIE, Sir C., *The King's Government and the Common Law, 1471–1641* (Oxford, 1958).

ORWIN, C. S. and C. S. L., *The Open Fields* (Oxford, 1938).

OWST, G. H., *Literature and Pulpit in Medieval England* (Cambridge, 1933).

PALMER, R. L., *English Social History in the Making. The Tudor Revolution* (London, 1934).

PARKER, L. A., 'The Agrarian Revolution at Cotesbach, 1501–1612', in W. G. Hoskins (ed.), *Studies in Leicestershire Agrarian History* (Leicester, 1949).

PARKER, T. M., *The English Reformation to 1558* (Oxford, 1952).

PIRENNE, H., *Economic and Social History of Medieval Europe*, trans. I. E. Clegg (London, 1947).

PLUCKNETT, T. F., 'Some Proposed Legislation of Henry VIII', *Trans. R.H.S.*, 4th Ser., xix (1936), 119–44.

POLLARD, A. F., *England under Protector Somerset* (London, 1900).

—, *The Political History of England*, vi, *1547–1603* (London, 1910).

POLLARD, A. W. and REDGRAVE, G. R., *Short Title Catalogue of Works printed in England, 1475–1640* (London, 1923).

PORTER, H. C., *Reformation and Reaction in Tudor Cambridge* (Cambridge, 1958).

POSTAN, M. and RICH, E. E. (eds.), *The Cambridge Economic History of Europe*, ii, *Trade and Industry* (Cambridge, 1952).

POSTAN, M., RICH, E. E., and MILLER, E. (eds.), *The Cambridge Economic History of Europe*, iii (Cambridge, 1963).

POTTER, G. R., 'The Beginnings of the Modern State', *History*, xxxi (1946), 73–84.

— (ed.), *The New Cambridge Modern History*, i, *The Renaissance. 1493–1520* (Cambridge, 1957).

PRESCOTT, H. F. M., *Mary Tudor* (London, 1952).

PRICE, F. D., 'Gloucester Diocese under Bishop Hooper 1551–3', *Transactions of the Bristol and Gloucester Archaeological Society for 1938*, 60 (Gloucester, 1939), pp. 51–151.

RAAB, F., *The English Face of Machiavelli* (London, 1964).

RAMSAY, G. D., *The Wiltshire Woollen Industry in the Sixteenth and Seventeenth Centuries* (Oxford, 1943).

—, *English Overseas Trade During the Centuries of Emergence* (London, 1957).

RAMSEY, P., *Tudor Economic Problems* (London, 1963).

READ, C., *Mr. Secretary Cecil and Queen Elizabeth* (London, 1955).

— (ed.), *Bibliography of British History: Tudor Period, 1485–1603* (Oxford, 2nd edn., 1959).

REDDAWAY, T. F., 'The King's Mint and Exchange in London 1343–1543', *E.H.R.*, lxxxii (1967), 1–23.

REED, A. W., *Early Tudor Drama* (London, 1926).

REID, R. R., *The King's Council in the North* (London, 1921).

RICH, E. E. and WILSON, C. H. (eds.), *The Cambridge Economic History of Europe*, iv, *The Economy of Expanding Europe in the Sixteenth and Seventeenth Centuries* (Cambridge, 1967).

RIDLEY, J. G., *Thomas Cranmer* (Oxford, 1962).

—, *Nicholas Ridley* (London, 1957).

ROBERTSON, H. M., *The Rise of Economic Individualism* (Cambridge, 1933).

ROGERS, J. E. T., *Six Centuries of Work and Wages* (London, 1891).

ROOVER, R. DE, 'Scholastic economics: survival and lasting influence from the sixteenth century to Adam Smith', *Quarterly Journal of Economics*, lxix (1955), 161–90.

—, 'Dry Exchange', *Journal of Political Economy*, lii (1944), 250–66.

ROSE-TROUP, F., *The Western Rebellion of 1549* (London, 1913).

ROUTH, E. M. G., *Sir Thomas More and His Friends* (Oxford, 1934).

RUPP, E. G., *Studies in the Making of the English Protestant Tradition* (Cambridge, 1947).

RUSSELL, F. W., *Kett's Rebellion in Norfolk* (London, 1859).

SAMUELSSON, K., *Religion and Economic Action*, trans. E. J. French, ed. D. C. Coleman (London, 1961).

SAVINE, A., *English Monasteries on the Eve of the Dissolution*. In Vol. i of Oxford Studies in Social and Legal History, ed. P. Vinogradoff (Oxford, 1909).

SCHENK, W., *The Concern for Social Justice in the Puritan Revolution* (London, 1948).

SCOTT, W. R., *The Constitution and Finance of English, Scottish and Irish Joint Stock Companies to 1720*, i (Cambridge, 1912).

SÉE, H., *Modern Capitalism, Its Origin and Evolution*, trans. Vanderblue and Doriot (London, 1928).

SLAVIN, A. J., *Politics and Profit. A Study of Sir Ralph Sadler 1507–1547* (Cambridge, 1966).

—, 'Sir Ralph Sadler and Master John Hales at the Hanaper: A Sixteenth-Century Struggle for Property and Profit', *Bull. Inst. H.R.*, xxxviii (1965), 31–47.

SMITH, L. B., *Tudor Prelates and Politics, 1536–58* (Princeton, N.J., 1953).

SOUTHGATE, W. M., 'Erasmus: Christian humanism and political theory', *History*, xl (1955), 240–54.

STEPHEN, L. and LEE, S., *Dictionary of National Biography* (London, 1908–9).

STONE, L., 'State Control in Sixteenth-Century England', *Econ. H.R.*, xvii (1947), 103–20.

—, 'The Political Programme of Thomas Cromwell', *Bull. Inst. H.R.*, xxiv (1951), 1–18.

—, *Social Change and Revolution in England, 1540–1640* (London, 1965).

STRYPE, J., *Ecclesiastical Memorials*, 3 vols. (Oxford, 1822).

SUPPLE, B. E., *Commercial Crisis and Change in England, 1600–1642* (Cambridge, 1959).

TALBERT, E. W., *The Problem of Order* (Raleigh, North Carolina, 1962).

TAWNEY, R. H., *The Agrarian Problem in the Sixteenth Century* (London, 1912).

—, *Religion and the Rise of Capitalism*, Pelican edition (London, 1942).

—, Introduction to T. Wilson's *A Discourse upon Usury* (London, 1925).

THIRSK, J., *Tudor Enclosures*, Historical Association Pamphlet No. 41 (1959).

— (ed.), *The Agrarian History of England and Wales*, iv, *1500–1640* (Cambridge, 1967).

THOMAS, K., 'Work and Leisure in Pre-Industrial Society', *Past and Present*, No. 29 (Dec. 1964), 50–64.

THOMSON, J. A. F., *The Later Lollards, 1414–1520* (Oxford, 1965).

TILLYARD, E. M. W., *The Elizabethan World Picture* (London, 1943).

TINDALL, W. Y., *John Bunyan. Mechanick Preacher* (New York, 1934).

TREVOR-ROPER, H. R., *Historical Essays* (London, 1957).

—, 'The General Crisis of the Seventeenth Century', in *Crisis in Europe, 1560–1660*, ed. T. Aston (London, 1965), pp. 59–95.

TROELTSCH, E., *The Social Teaching of the Christian Churches*, trans. O. Wyon, 2 vols. (London, 1931).

ULLMANN, W., *Principles of Government and Politics in the Middle Ages* (London, 1961).

UNWIN, G., *Industrial Organization in the Sixteenth and Seventeenth Centuries* (Oxford, 1904).

—, *The Gilds and Companies of London* (1908).

VAN GELDER, H. A. ENNO, *The Two Reformations in the Sixteenth Century*, trans. J. F. Finlay and A. Hanham (The Hague, 1961).

WALKER, P. C. GORDON-, 'Capitalism and the Reformation', *Econ. H.R.*, viii (1937), 1–19.

WEBB, S. and B., *English Local Government: English Poor Law History*: Part I. *The Old Poor Law* (London, 1927).

WEBER, M., *The Protestant Ethic and the Spirit of Capitalism*, trans. Talcott Parsons (London, 1930).

WHITE, H. C., *Social Criticism in Popular Religious Literature of the Sixteenth Century* (New York, 1944).

WILLIAMS, G. H., *The Radical Reformation* (London, 1962).

WILLIAMS, L. H., *The Alien Contribution to the Social and Economic Development of England and Wales in the Sixteenth Century*, University of Wales M.A. Thesis (1953).

WILLIAMS, P. and HARRISS, G. L., 'A Revolution in Tudor History?', *Past and Present*, No. 25 (July 1963), 3–58.

WILSON, C., *Mercantilism*, Historical Association Pamphlet No. 37 (1958).

WOODWARD, G. W. O., *The Dissolution of the Monasteries* (London, 1966).

WRIGHT, L. B., *Middle-Class Culture in Elizabethan England* (Raleigh, North Carolina, 1935).

ZEEVELD, W. G., *Foundations of Tudor Policy* (Harvard, 1948).

INDEX

Rome, 17, 76, 196, 213; Church of, 21, 39, 44, 65, 78, 112, 210
Roo, John, 14, 66
Rouse, William, 40
Rumours, rumour-mongers, 54–5, 56, 205
Russell, John, earl of Bedford, 34

Sacramentarianism, 70
Sadler, Sir Ralph, 34–5
Sampson, T., 113
Scory, John, bishop of Rochester, 165
Scotland, 135
Scriptures, the, 51, 60, 63, 71, 72 n. 7, 73, 74, 78, 79, 90, 104, 121, 153
Sedition: see Rebellion
'Sergeants of the Commonweal', 212
Sermons: see Preaching
Servants, 71, 90, 94, 100, 101, 112, 141, 206
Seymour, Edward, earl of Hertford, duke of Somerset, 11, 17, 19, 24, 32, 33–5, 36–42, 52, 79, 80, 89, 90–1, 126, 131, 167, 191, 194, 200, 203, 206, 211, 219
Seymour, Sir Thomas, of Sudeley, 33, 36, 79
Sharington, Sir William, 40
Sheep, sheep-farming, 28, 52, 98, 99, 114, 145, 158–68, 178, 197–200, 203, 204, 205–6; -tax, 36, 40, 166, 194, 199–200
Sherbrook, Michael, Fall of Religious Houses, 118 n. 2
Silk, 102, 111, 144, 171
Silver: see Bullion
Skelton, John, 89; Magnificence, 66; Poems, 88–9
Smith, Sir Thomas, 33, 35–6, 36–7, 41, 42, 55, 106, 131, 212, 218–19; De Republica Anglorum, 106, 218
Smithfield, 76
Society:
    hierarchical concept of, 13, 14, 15, 26, 45, 57–8, 60, 63, 64, 70, 81, 86–107, 156, 186, 192, 217, 220–4, 226, 227

concern for stability of, 43–64, 67–75, 80, 86–107
social mobility, 31–2, 82–3, 103–6; see also Upstarts, Vocation
social orders: see Gentry, Nobility, Yeomanry
Somerset, duke of: see Seymour, Edward
Somerset, county of, 172
Spain, Spanish, 120 n. 2, 137
Spare your good, 95
Stage, the, 23, 30, 55, 66
Star Chamber, Court of, 209
Starkey, Thomas, 27, 29, 31, 196, 214; Dialogue, 16, 19–20, 27, 31, 94–5, 107, 115, 121, 124, 125, 161, 163, 164, 167, 170–1, 184, 187, 195–6, 204, 209, 210, 212–13; Exhortation to Unitie and Obedience, 31, 44–5, 49–50, 71, 110
St. Bartholomewes, The Ordre of the Hospital of, 113–14
Staple: see Wool
State, concept of, 4, 25, 106, 201, 226, 227; Church and, 2, 5, 6, 10, 11, 65, 77, 84–5, 128, 215–17, 218; see also Crown, Government
Stephens, John, 146
Stewardship, concept of, 68, 81, 95, 110, 160, 200
Strassburg, 121, 193 n. 2
Stumpe, William, 173–4
Suffolk, 40, 174
Sugar, 148
Sumptuary legislation, 102, 217
Syder, Robert, 40

Taverner, Richard, Catechisme, 49
Taxation, 20, 61, 63, 74, 130, 195, 199–200, 217, 222
Thomas, William, 79; 'Discourse', 50
Tillage and husbandry, 19, 42, 145, 147, 161–8, 181, 189, 195–9, 203
Tithes, 8, 30, 204
Tower of London, the, 36, 40, 41
Towns, 138, 139, 169, 172–3, 176, 177, 180, 182, 188, 212, 213

INDEX